CHRIST OVER ALL

A HISTORY OF JOHN BROWN UNIVERSITY

Printed in the United States of America by
Versa Press, Inc. of East Peoria, Illinois

Cover and interior design by Greg Jackson '95, Thinkpen Design
Interior layout by Julie Gumm '95
Editing by Jeff Reimer '03 and Julie Gumm
Archival support by Marikit Schwartz Fain '05

CHRIST OVER ALL

A HISTORY OF JOHN BROWN UNIVERSITY

BY PAUL T. SEMONES '99

With John E. Brown III, Dr. A LeVon Balzer
& Dr. Charles W. Pollard

"According to the grace of God which was given to me, as a wise master-builder, I have laid the foundation, and another is building upon it. But let each man be careful how he builds upon it, for no man can lay a foundation other than the one which is laid, which is Jesus Christ."
— 1 CORINTHIANS 3: 10, 11 NAS

TABLE OF CONTENTS

FOREWORD

A UNIVERSITY FOUNDED WITH CHRIST OVER ALL

by John E. Brown III

The history of John Brown University is unusual, if not unique, in a number of ways. The original campus was first a vocational college with an associate's degree program that required students to work half a day while attending classes and studying half a day. The founder's hope was to offer a tuition-free education, which included training for the head, heart, and hand. In 1934, the program expanded into a four-year bachelor's degree program with an emphasis on professional degrees in building construction, engineering, agriculture, radio and television broadcasting, the sciences, teacher education, and other fields, along with a core of liberal arts and Bible classes.

After regional accreditation in 1962, both the enrollment and degree-program offerings were expanded. Vocational training units were aligned with the students' career interests as well as with work-study financial-aid positions. In the 1970s the university passed the 750-student mark in enrollment, and added degrees in accounting, journalism, and the visual arts. The university exceeded an enrollment of 1,000 students for the first time in 1991. New undergraduate- and graduate-degree programs were added through off-campus classes for working adults.

Between 2001 and 2018, 21 new building or major renovation projects were completed. By 2018, the endowment program topped $125 million in assets, as the university developed a long list of new endowed scholarships. Thankfully, many faithful alumni and friends continue to give generously each year in support of JBU's historic mission as an evangelical Christian university. By the fall of 2019, in conjunction with the university's one-hundredth anniversary, the university will complete a $125 million Campaign for the Next Century, further increasing the endowment, providing for the renovation of four buildings, and funding four new buildings, including a new health-education facility that

i

supports JBU's newest degree program—nursing.

Throughout this time, John Brown University has been blessed with an unusual continuity in leadership and educational mission. From 1919 to the present day (not including one year when a new president was replaced for a short time by an interim president), there have been only five presidents of the university—a succession of leaders who felt themselves *called* of God to service at JBU. Each one in turn was *committed* to the mission of providing students with a holistic Christian education equipping the Head, Heart, and Hand. Each president and his spouse has *cared* lovingly for the community of faculty, staff, and students, bound together under the founding motto—Christ Over All.

It is an interesting, amazing, and at times miraculous story of how God's hand has been on his people who, as in the days of Nehemiah, "put their hands to the good work" (Nehemiah 2:18 NASB) of building an exceptional learning community and Christian university in Northwest Arkansas.

CHAPTER 1

THE EARLY YEARS OF FOUNDER JOHN ELWARD BROWN SR.

After the American Civil War ended in 1865, a war-weary twenty-five-year-old soldier named John Franklin Brown made his way home to Iowa. His father, Benjamin Franklin Brown, was a Quaker physician from Indiana who had migrated the family to Iowa some years before the war. Even though Quaker tradition is generally opposed to war, a few months after the outbreak of open conflict in 1861 John Franklin enlisted in a Pennsylvania Cavalry regiment of the Union Army, which was drawing volunteers from across Iowa. He mustered out four years later as the first sergeant of his company. Despite the toll that the years of war had taken on his body, he took up farming in Iowa. Within a year of the war's end, John Franklin married Julia Ann Brammer, who was also from an Iowa Quaker family, and they welcomed the first of nine children in 1867.[1]

On April 2, 1879, Elward Brown was born to the family in Oskaloosa, Iowa. He was the fifth child born to the family, and four more siblings would be born after him, though three of the children died at a young age. Not long after Elward's birth, John Franklin Brown took his growing family to Center Point, Iowa, which became the hometown of Elward's youth.

All of the Brown boys were given first and middle names except Elward, who eventually decided that he wanted two names too. Early in his childhood, spurred by the fact that Elward was so often mispronounced, the boy adopted his father's name, John, as his own first name. In line with Quaker tradition, the Brown parents ran a strict home for the children. Farming in the fertile lands of Iowa ought to have provided a comfortable living for such a large family, but the father was not physically able to do the heavy work that a productive farm required. Still, the home was a kind and loving place, if the family was impoverished. Neighbors would often hear, across the open Iowa farm fields, the voice of John Franklin singing as he sat on his porch. The family's meager income—as well as the physical difficulties the war had imposed on the father—meant that young John Elward had to quit school at age eleven and go to work on a neighbor's farm.[2]

In that humble environment, John Elward Brown learned self-discipline and hard work, virtues on which he would eventually build a university.

Young John Elward's life was not all work and no play, however. There was plenty of time for fun and athleticism, so much so that his friends gave him the nickname "Sport." He sang in the church choir, joined a boys' drum corps, played the harmonica while the other children danced, and by age seventeen had earned a reputation as a good square-dance caller.[3]

Young John's activities did not always please his father's Quaker sensibilities. He became something of a wayward youth by the standards of the day. "The boy will never amount to anything," John Franklin once remarked to his wife. "We might as well let him go and forget about him."[4]

As John grew, he found other types of work in those last years of the nineteenth century, including working in a livery stable. Since Center Point was, as its name suggests, something of a hub for the area, traveling salesmen often arrived there on the train in need of a horse to carry them to the surrounding towns. John was fond of horses, and occasionally traded them for fun. He was even known to indulge in horse races at times. On at least one occasion, he earned a little money by helping a carnival crew operate one of the era's popular merry-go-rounds, which in the 1890s were often turned by a horse-drawn apparatus. Throughout many of his early life experiences, he was becoming a keen observer of people, and if he could not learn of literature and mathematics in a classroom, he was learning of human character in the world around him.[5]

Perhaps the most significant and influential employment John found in his Iowa years was in a printing shop in Center Point, where he learned the basics of the trade as a "printer's devil." For much of the rest of his life, he would remain interested in the printing industry, and would spend many years writing, editing, and publishing Christian periodicals on a monthly or even weekly basis from a printing press he owned.[6]

In his late teens, John set out to make a life for himself beyond the eastern Iowa farmlands. His older brother Ben, already married with children, planned to buy a fruit farm in the town of Rogers, Arkansas, an area known around the turn of the century for its productive apple orchards. The brothers had an aunt and uncle already living in Northwest Arkansas, and this couple agreed to put their nephews up while they got their new lives started. Thus, in the fall of 1896, at the age of seventeen, John left Iowa with his older brother Ben and headed south in a covered wagon.[7]

During the next year, John and his brother found various jobs in the area as Ben worked to establish himself before sending for his wife and children. The brothers cut railroad ties and hauled them in a horse-drawn wagon. They worked ten-hour days in a limestone quarry, pushing the blasted and hammered rock fragments in wheelbarrows to a kiln. The young men's typical earnings for such dusty manual labor in turn-of-the-century rural America were sixty cents a day—with half paid in coin and half paid in credit at the company store. In later years, newspapermen and others fascinated by John Brown's successes would credit him as the "boy from the lime kilns."[8]

On one wet, chilly night in downtown Rogers in 1897, John's life was changed forever. After eating dinner in a downtown café with some friends, John stepped outside into the cool night air to smoke a cigarette. In the distance he "heard the beat of a drum and a voice raised in song."[9] It was the call to meeting for the night's Salvation Army service.

John knew some of the Salvation Army members in town, including a Swedish officer of the organization named Ensign J. W. Olson, who often sang and played music on the street corners of Rogers. On that night, some of John's friends came outside to make fun of the uniformed Swede singing and drumming in the rain. But John lingered and did not laugh. He threw down his cigarette and followed Ensign Olson to the meeting. In retelling the story of this night many years later, Brown said his thoughts were, "If this man is willing to sing and beat his drum on a night like this, he has something I want!"[10]

After attending the services for several nights, John went forward to kneel at the altar on May 15, 1897, where he dedicated his life to serving Christ. He was eighteen years old.

Ensign Olson's habit was to call on new converts, a few nights after their decision, to stand and give their testimony. When John's turn came a few meetings later, he simply froze. "I stood up speechless," he recalled years later. "I just couldn't talk." On his way home after that dumbstruck evening, John stopped under a tree and prayed fervently that he could give a testimony in the Sunday morning service.

When Sunday morning came and John was called on to lead the prayer, he said, "I prayed like a house afire, and could not find a place to stop. The next night I did not wait to be called upon. I was the first to testify. I began talking and have been doing it ever since."[11]

John Elward soon wrote a letter to his father, John Franklin, telling him of his conversion. Though the father had once written off the son as a wayward boy who would never amount to anything, now he was overjoyed. With letter in hand, the father eagerly drove his horse team back home from town to tell his wife the good news. "Get ready," he told her. "We are going to Arkansas." Perhaps that night the neighbors across the Iowa fields heard John Franklin Brown singing, one last time, just a bit more sweetly.[12]

The founder (third from right) plays the banjo with the
Siloam Springs Salvation Army in 1898.

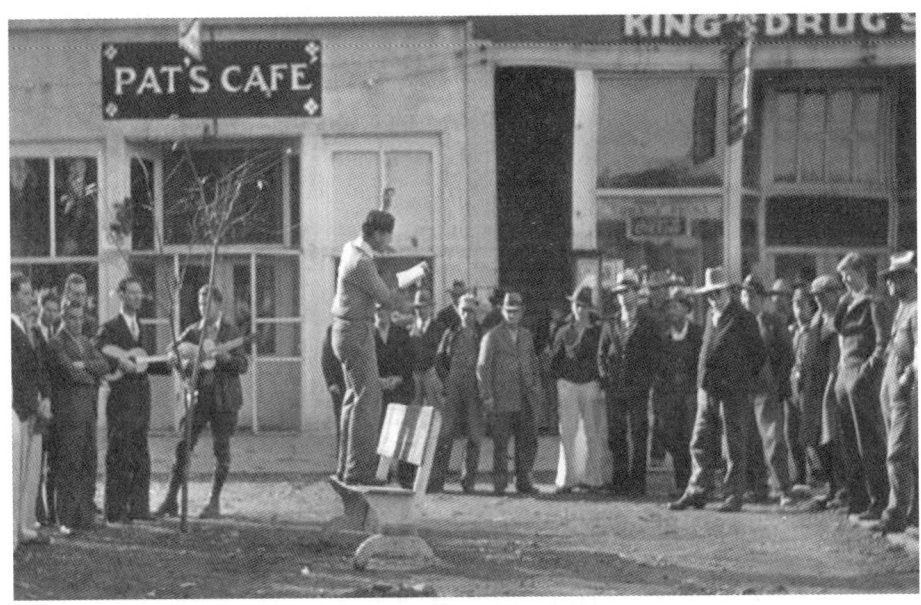

John Brown Sr. (standing on the bench) preaches while
Salvation Army band members stand in the background.

CHAPTER 2

THE FOUNDER AS EVANGELIST

Brown didn't just attend the Salvation Army's meetings in Rogers; he joined the group and made himself available for full-time ministry. John was discipled and mentored by his friend Ensign Olson. But within those first few months of service, John received the assignment to go a few miles southwest to a town on the edge of Indian Territory to help establish a permanent Salvation Army outpost there. That town was Siloam Springs. Using the wagon and team of horses that had brought John's parents from Iowa, John's father carried him and Ensign Olson down to the little town to begin their mission. When John's father returned to Rogers, he told his wife proudly, "The world will hear from that boy someday."[1]

The town of Siloam Springs was less than twenty years old when John Brown arrived in the fall of 1897, but it had recently gained a railroad line, and its many freshwater springs were gradually attracting attention to the town as a summer health resort. Statehood for the adjacent Indian Territory was still a decade away.[2]

John was still just eighteen years old, but he was tasked with essentially directing the Salvation Army's Siloam Springs post—preaching, evangelizing, publicizing the meetings, and maintaining the Army's meeting hall on the hill overlooking Twin Springs Park. Though he had arrived as the partner of Ensign Olson, he was soon left alone when Olson was reassigned to a different Salvation Army outpost. John Brown worked hard to repair the little mission hall, building benches and cutting and hauling the wood necessary to heat the place. For a time, the hall was where he slept. His income from odd jobs around town was so meager that there was once a stretch of two weeks when he had nothing to eat but plain oatmeal, without even sugar or milk to give it flavor. He led meetings five nights a week, with three more each Sunday.[3]

His evangelistic skills and public reputation were growing, but John was very aware of his lack of formal education. He was determined, however, to make up for that deficit with a rigorous personal discipline of reading great books and authors. "Since as a boy I did not have the advantage of the schools, I spent much of my time in my early public life in reading," he once said. He also admitted that he didn't know much about the Bible in those early years, and so "naturally that book took first place in my life."

He made sure his self-education was well-rounded too, buying and reading many books in history and science. He also devoted time to great literature, ranging from Shakespeare (of whom he said "I never became enthusiastic") to Victor Hugo ("I did read everything [he] wrote"), and including American authors Ralph Waldo Emerson, Edgar Allan Poe, Mark Twain, and a couple of popular American humorists of the day who wrote under the pen names of Bill Nye and Artemus Ward. (Ironically, one of the earliest men to join John Brown in the work of his college was a professor of Greek and science who was also named Dr. Artemus Ward.)

Within a few years, his interest in the humanities even led him to purchase several large, multivolume sets published shortly after the turn of the century— *The Historian's History of the World*, a twenty-five-volume collection of more than two thousand classic authors' works on Western civilization; *The Ideas That Have Influenced Civilization*, a ten-volume set of original documents and ancient works, of which it is said only one thousand copies were printed; and *The Complete Works of John Ruskin*, a thirty-nine-volume collection of writings by the prominent nineteenth-century English art critic and social commentator.[4]

In 1898, John briefly entered army service as the outbreak of the Spanish-American War drew many eager young men to enlist. But the romantic ideas of military life that he had held in his childhood were quickly dashed. "I remember when I was a boy, a beautiful three-colored poster, used to secure recruits for the Regular Army, was put up in the post office of our little town," he said years later. "That poster with the beautiful scenery and charging horses and attractive uniforms and many men so inflamed my imagination. . . . Later, in the Spanish-American War, when volunteers were called for, I immediately volunteered, and the first discovery I made was that the man who drew that poster was a liar."[5]

While his soldierly experience provided for a humorous quip in later years, John's short stint as an enlisted bugler in the Third Texas Infantry only lasted a few months and involved no actual deployment to any of the war's far-flung combat zones. When he was discharged, he decided to return to his Salvation Army work in Siloam Springs. After a couple of months, the Salvation Army transferred him to an office position in Kansas City, but Brown yearned to preach. Dissatisfied with the assignment, he decided his time with the Salvation Army was through, and he resigned to enter independent evangelism.[6]

In the towns surrounding Siloam Springs, John had developed a good reputation as a speaker and evangelist. When he returned to the area after his unhappy sojourn in Kansas City, a local preacher in Gravette, Arkansas invited him to preach at an upcoming revival, and before long he was devoting most of his time to preaching at churches and revival meetings as a traveling speaker.

One meeting in particular in 1899 had an unexpected impact on the rest of his life. John had committed to opening a series of meetings in Sallisaw, Indian Territory. But in the organizing committee's haste to set up the event, they had failed to secure a pianist. A young lady named Juanita Arrington of Ozark, Arkansas, was visiting friends in town and was willing to play piano for the meetings. Juanita was twenty years old, the same age as John, and her birthday was the day after his. It was love at first sight for young John Brown, but Ms. Arrington made the smooth-talking evangelist wait a year before she agreed to his proposal of marriage.

John's priority of continuing his own self-education extended to the skills of the pulpit. In March 1900, he journeyed to Chicago, where he spent a week attending a series of lectures given by the prominent Christian scholar G. Campbell Morgan of London, England. Much like John Brown himself, Morgan had no formal education for the ministry, and had developed his reputation at an early age. Morgan was still in his thirties when he made his first transatlantic trips to teach and preach in America at the turn of the century. John's aim was to learn from the experience of hearing—in person—some of the greatest preachers and Bible teachers of his era. In the next few years, John made repeated trips to Chicago, where Moody Bible Institute provided a venue for him to hear more great Christian lecturers. Some of John's strongest influences in his early ministry were the evangelists Dwight L. Moody—whom John saw as an ideal role model, though Moody died in 1899, before John had any opportunity meet him in person—and R. A. Torrey, the evangelist who succeeded Moody as president of the Moody Bible Institute.[7]

Perhaps John Elward Brown was inspired by Moody's and Torrey's examples of leading an institution of Christian learning when, in the summer of 1902, he accepted a position as president of a small junior college in Neosho, Missouri, called Scarritt Collegiate Institute. The newly appointed President John E. Brown was just twenty-three years old, at the time the youngest president of any college in the nation.

Scarritt was an institution founded by the Methodist Episcopal Church, South, in 1878, and was thus just one year older than its new president. The small academy and junior college had reached its peak in the late 1800s with a student body numbering only about 125. There was at least one alumnus of the school who could give it a claim to fame: Will Rogers, the American humorist, silent film star, and one of Oklahoma's "favorite sons," attended Scarritt in 1896–1897.

By the time Brown arrived at Scarritt, the college was in failing health and the buildings were in disrepair. For two and a half years under Brown's presidency, the little institute struggled along, but not even Brown's efforts, nor his reputation as a popular regional evangelist, could help it do any better than limp toward an inevitable end. In January 1905, with few students and little hope for any improvement in the school's financial position, Brown resigned his presidency of Scarritt. The school finally closed its campus a few years later.

***

John Brown went right back into full-time evangelism after the Scarritt years. In 1905, while holding revival meetings in east Texas, he was invited to the home of a woman whose nephew, Jesse H. Jones, was to become one of John's lifelong friends, and an influential friend of the John Brown schools. Jones was thirty-one years old, about five years older than John, and already a successful real estate builder and businessman in Houston. In the years ahead, Jones would rise to national prominence as he was appointed to various leadership roles by Presidents Woodrow Wilson, Herbert Hoover, and Franklin D. Roosevelt. Jones's upbringing had some similarities to John's own youth, with an education that did not extend past the ninth grade, and the experience of working hard in agriculture by his early teens in support of the family business. The two men became close friends, riding horses together in the mornings during John's series of meetings in east Texas. At one of the meetings, Jones rose during John's altar call, and he made the decision to walk forward and commit his life to Christ. From this moment, the men's enduring friendship was strengthened by a common dedication to Christian service, and over the next forty years, Jones would play an important role in the establishment of John Brown's educational mission.

In the first two decades of the twentieth century, Brown was able to establish a solid reputation as an interdenominational evangelist with wit, insight, and charm. He traveled across much of the nation holding evangelistic revival meetings in churches and temporary wooden tabernacles, making many visits to California in particular. The relationships he established in California during these tours led to John Brown's essentially living part time in California and part time in Arkansas, for the rest of his life.

Brown was known as a joyful evangelist wherever he went. In his earliest days in Siloam Springs, he was called "Happy Brown,"[8] and years later he would be nicknamed "the Laughing Evangelist" in at least one major city.[9] The following excerpts from newspaper descriptions of his meetings in those early years bear witness to this legacy:

> Brown possesses the magnetism and power to sway an audience that very few speakers ever acquire. However, his messages are not sensational

or highly critical.[10]

He has one tremendous asset in his sincerity. He rings true.[11]

The simple story of the cross was preached in all of its purity; the speaker was scriptural and thoroughly consecrated to the Word; it was not Brown, but Christ, that could be seen, heard, and felt.[12]

The evangelist is genial and humorous, not for effect, but because it is his inner nature finding expression. From his speech we must judge that there is an abundance of life and love and cheer in his inner being.[13]

He is pleasing, persuasive, kindly in rebuke, with a vein of humor in his sarcasm. A regular guy. He is not flamboyant. He makes religion joyful.[14]

It was in early 1911 that John received his first invitation to preach and evangelize in California. When he arrived before the start of a large tabernacle meeting in Fresno, a reporter asked him what he was preaching on that first night. Brown's reply was that he didn't know yet, since he liked to take a good look at his audience first. It was a characteristic reply, and indicative of Brown's free-flowing way of letting his message be dictated by his knowledge of the human heart. In later years folks would fondly recall some of his typical quips when his train of thought went astray—sayings such as, "Now, that doesn't belong in this talk. I just happened to think of it," and, "This is not what I intended to talk about, but I never heard a talk that I more thoroughly endorse!"[15]

In one of Brown's 1914 campaigns in California, a man in his sixties named William Waterhouse, who had been the mayor of Pasadena, was greatly moved by John Brown's messages and offered to support his further evangelistic work. Waterhouse was an experienced and inventive building contractor, and soon became Brown's advance man and tabernacle builder. He would go into a city several weeks before the revival campaign was to begin, and then recruit a couple hundred volunteers to help him build a great temporary wooden structure that could seat as many as two thousand people. Waterhouse's tabernacle design was ingenious: it required almost no wood to be cut, and at the end of a campaign the tabernacle could be deconstructed and the wood sold back to the local lumber yard for reuse. Waterhouse would become another dedicated friend of the John Brown schools in the coming years.

Beginning in 1911, during his earliest trips to California, one of John Brown's regular engagements was to lead the principal services of a Methodist camp meeting every summer in Huntington Beach. Combined with his experience of briefly leading a Methodist college, these activities eventually helped bring about his only ordination credential as a preacher. In 1915 the Methodist Episcopal Church, South, appointed him as one of its "general evangelists." John Brown later called this one of the high points in his life.[16]

The steel Chautauqua Auditorium over Twin Springs Park in Siloam Springs served as a meeting place for many Bible conferences and events.[17]

CHAPTER 3

A COLLEGE IN A CORNFIELD

John Brown's activities in the decade of the teens soon made it appear as if he were traveling in two directions at once. After his first encouraging experience in California in 1911, he returned to Siloam Springs and bought farmland and a home west of the town. The property was atop a steep hillside, about a half mile from the state line and just across the road from the town cemetery. After about two years, during which time he and Juanita welcomed the fourth of their daughters into the world, Brown decided to sell the property and take the family to California, where he could continue with his evangelism.

Yet even as he planned his family's move, he was also arranging a major Bible conference that would convene in Siloam Springs in July of that year, 1913. The event was held in a steel auditorium atop the hill overlooking Twin Springs Park—about the same location where his Salvation Army hall had been some fifteen years before. From this conference would be established the International Federation of Christian Workers, an organization that gained the involvement of many world-renowned evangelists of the day, and that Brown led for some twenty years.[1]

His family did not live in California for long, and John Brown's family ties to Northwest Arkansas remained strong. In the summer of 1914, the elder John Franklin Brown passed away, having lived his last years in Rogers in a home John Elward had bought for his parents. Some of John Elward's siblings continued to live in Arkansas, and by the end of 1914 John and Juanita returned to Siloam Springs in time to welcome their fifth daughter just before Christmas. In 1915, John repurchased the same home and cornfields he had bought two years earlier, all the while continuing his regular evangelistic campaigns in California. In December 1915, he even agreed to travel with Mr. Waterhouse to Hawaii, where Waterhouse had been born, to conduct a series of unannounced revival services. While Waterhouse hoped the trip would be a relaxing one for Brown, the ocean voyage turned out to be quite rough, and the ship was filled with seasick passengers. The seagoing life most definitely did not suit the constitution of the evangelist.

By 1917, Brown was continuing to deepen his ties to Siloam Springs. He was now the owner of the steel auditorium above Twin Springs Park, where he continued to host annual summer Bible conferences, and he had a print shop for his magazine publications established in a building nearby. The printing plant was actually one he had bought in Iowa many years earlier, carried with him to Neosho during his Scarritt years, and finally moved to downtown Siloam Springs. He was also once again involving himself in the endeavors of college education. A small Methodist school called the Arkansas Conference College had been founded in Siloam Springs shortly after Brown's first arrival as a Salvation Army worker, and its campus was a short walk south of downtown. Over its years of operation, the school had rarely had more than a few dozen students, and in 1917 Brown briefly joined its board of directors. Even so, it struggled, as Scarritt had, to remain open. A year later, the school was forced to completely close and its campus was taken over by the Siloam Springs High School. It would not be long before Brown decided to open a new college according to his own ideals.

***

When John Brown explained his resignation as president of Scarritt Collegiate Institute a decade earlier, he had notably called it an "unwise experiment" for him. It had taken time away from his evangelistic mission, and he was not impressed with the results in the students given the costs borne by their families. Brown

The Brown family farm

said, "Most of these young people were from homes of modest means, and in one instance, to my knowledge, the father of the student had mortgaged the farm to get the boy through school." Brown was convinced that the type of education he saw at Scarritt "was working daily injury to most of the students who came to that school. In the midst of what they chose to call a training for life they were actually being trained away from the stark realities, and yet the glorious possibilities of life." Brown had left Scarritt disappointed, but with a budding vision for a type of school "that would turn the minds of youth back from this exaggerated conception of the value of book knowledge, to the realization that all this is valuable only as it becomes the background for, or the foundation under, the real things of life."[2]

The vision that developed in Brown's mind over the years after Scarritt was of a college that integrated book learning—"head"—with training in becoming a faithful servant of God and his people—"heart"—all in the context of a practical, vocational education that exalted the value of work and industry—"hand"—thus preparing young Christian men and women for real life.

It was the year 1919 when John E. Brown took the decisive step that led to the creation of his school in the Ozark hills, which would fulfill his educational vision of head, heart, and hand.

He was in Vancouver, British Columbia, leading a six-week evangelistic meeting during the summer of 1919, when he met a group of young, aspiring Christian workers. "I made a call for young men and women who were ready to dedicate themselves to any and all departments of public service, to present themselves at the platform," he said. "The response was immediate and amazing. Ninety young people, made up of as fine and as high grade material as is found in any audience or in any city, gathered before my platform." Meeting with them afterward, Brown found that hardly any of them had the financial means to get the kind of proper education that would equip them for the services they had chosen. He had seen similar responses of young people in other cities over the years, but now he was overwhelmingly convicted that there was more he needed to do.

"Under God, I was privileged to arouse hundreds of young people to an unselfish dedication of their lives to the public good, and then I had gone away leaving most of them to battle against overwhelming odds and to fail." He asked himself, "What was I to do? What should I do?"[3]

This question burdened him as he left Vancouver and traveled south to California for other engagements. Over the next few weeks, the vision of a school—to be established on his family farm in Siloam Springs—seized his imagination.

"When the hours of dreaming and planning came, and they came often," Brown later recalled, "I could not but feel that such an institution about which I dreamed would be the crowning event of my life and the culminating goal toward which I might, under God, turn all of the fruits of years of friendship and favors."[4]

Finally, on July 23, 1919, after a fitful, sleepless night of struggling with the call of God on his heart, Brown rose from his bed at two o'clock in the morning. "I'll build that school!" he said.[5]

He wasted no time setting the plan in motion and gathering support, as he intended to open his school that fall, less than three months away. Making his way back to Arkansas from California, he first made a stop in Houston, Texas, where John sought the blessing and assistance of an old friend. On the rooftop of one of the man's hotels—one of roughly one hundred buildings he now owned throughout the city—Jesse H. Jones greeted the evangelist. In the fourteen years since Jones had been converted under the preaching of John Brown, he had become a major player in Houston's growth; not only had he been a prolific builder and designer of Houston's first skyscrapers, but he had also become part-owner of the *Houston Chronicle* newspaper and president of a major bank. The Houston Ship Channel, its waters glittering in the distance beyond the rooftop on which Brown and Jones met, had been funded largely through Jones's efforts as chairman of the Houston Harbor board. President Woodrow Wilson came to Houston to dedicate the channel in 1914, and then in 1917 the president tapped Jones to come to Washington, DC, and lead the American Red Cross's military relief efforts during World War I.

With the armistice having drawn that conflict to a close less than a year earlier, Jones had only recently returned home to Houston, where he now greeted his old friend in the city's humid summer haze. John Brown presented his plan for a college of threefold training for underprivileged youth, and Jones offered his hearty approval. Before the school's first year was over, Jones would personally give the school tens of thousands of dollars in support.[6]

Soon after his meeting with Jones, Brown sent a telegram to William Waterhouse in California, asking him to come out of retirement and join him in Siloam Springs. Waterhouse's construction ingenuity would be needed to erect the college's first structure, and to do it swiftly.

On Saturday, August 23, 1919, Waterhouse met with a few family friends on the lawn west of the Brown family home in Siloam Springs, about where the Cathedral of the Ozarks stands today. They bowed their heads for a dedicatory prayer, and then they went to work. Construction, at a cost of $15,000, began two days later with many volunteers. A man named A. E. Leonard was recorded as hammering in the first nail.

A few hundred yards away from the construction site was an old log cabin that had been built in the 1830s by one of the area's earliest homesteaders, Simon Sager. In 1919, Brown's younger brother, J. Alvin Brown, lived there with his family. They also had a boarder—a young man named Ford Maggard from Harrison, Arkansas, who had served in the Navy during World War I. Maggard was among the volunteers helping to build the new college building, and when he began taking classes a few weeks later, he earned the distinction of being the school's first student to have lived "on campus."

Brown selected as the school's first dean of students another war veteran—the "fighting parson," Captain Charles A. Rexroad, who had been a chaplain in the Army's 91st Division on the Western Front during World War I. He had been decorated for valor, receiving the Belgian Croix de Guerre, and had been back home from Europe for less than six months when the school year began. Rexroad was forty, the same age as Brown, and originally from West Virginia, but had moved to Missouri with his wife before the war. Interestingly enough, Rexroad had earned his divinity degree in 1914 from Scarritt-Morrisville College, a school that formed out of the merger of two Missouri Methodist schools, including John Brown's first presidential posting: the defunct Scarritt Collegiate Institute.[7]

Brown's plan for his new school was for it to be distinctly Christian as well as tuition-free. Students would perform the work of the school's various industries both to keep it functioning and to gain vocational training as a part of their curriculum. This approach fulfilled Brown's mission for his school, training the head, heart, and hand. The attraction of this sort of educational opportunity, as well as Brown's evangelistic reputation and many relationships with Christian leaders around the country, ensured that the school would be able to open its doors immediately with an adequately sized student body from diverse parts of the country.

On the night of Monday, September 29, 1919, just a month and four days after Waterhouse's construction crew started their work on the school's first building, the school was dedicated with a program held in Brown's steel auditorium in downtown Siloam Springs. The new institution was dubbed "Southwestern Collegiate Institute," and at the start of its first academic year, ten instructors taught a group of some seventy students in both a high school academy and a junior (two-year) college housed in the new building. About sixty students were residents on the campus, while several others attended as day students from the local area. They came from twelve different states, along with ten students who came all the way from British Columbia, where Brown had been so burdened by the educational challenge facing the youths he had met there just a few months before. Brown told an assembled crowd that evening, "This is not my work. God has achieved this."[8]

The physical environment of the school was centered on Waterhouse's building, which was sturdy enough despite its rapid design and construction that it stood for the school's first dozen years. It was officially dubbed "Southwestern Hall," but as time went on it simply came to be known as "the white building."

Tuesday morning, September 30, 1919, began the scholastic history of the future John Brown University. The morning opened with a chapel service for the gathered student body. Then half the students went to work and half went to class. Those seventy students of the fall of 1919 lived, studied, and worshiped in Southwestern Hall, which was two stories tall and initially had just under five thousand square feet on each floor. Its overall dimensions—45 feet wide by 110 feet long—gave it a footprint slightly less than half the size of the tabernacles Waterhouse had erected for John Brown's evangelism campaigns. One man who was involved with the school in the first few years, Dr. Franklin W. Collins, recalled that as classes began that fall, "the building was in a sorry state of completion so far as finishing and plumbing were concerned, and the hammers were hammering and the plumbers were plumbing and confusion reigned, yea, poured for weeks and weeks and weeks."[9]

In the building's original layout—though this would change frequently during the coming years—a long hallway on the first floor divided classrooms along the east side of the building from the chapel, office, dining room, and kitchen on the west. The chapel originally had no raised area for speakers to stand on, and so

The student body of the 1920-21 school year stands in front of Southwestern Hall, also known as "Old White."

the seating was soon elevated on a series of risers toward the back of the room. It was said that a successful jump sometimes let one get onto the rearmost row from the floor.[10]

Stairwells at each end of the building's main hall led up to the living area, which was a large open space split by a dividing wall into a boys' dormitory at the rear and a girls' dormitory toward the front. The girls' side, at least, had a bath, but neither side had electric lights. There weren't even windows installed in the frames on the school's first day of existence. During the winters of those early years, the few radiators on the dormitory level were known for providing very little heat to the assembled students sleeping in their cots.[11]

Behind "Old White," as the students later called it, was a cottage for the first dean, Captain Rexroad, to live in. And not far away was the home of the Brown family themselves, which in 1919 included John and Juanita's five daughters, ages five to seventeen. The two oldest daughters, Jean Elizabeth and Helen, were students in the high school program of the college.[12]

The campus was situated in the midst of three hundred acres of farm land that Brown had owned previously or purchased as additions around the time of the school's founding. The farm already had a home for a farm manager, several barns and silos, and scores of animals, including more than twenty Jersey cattle, seventeen horses and mules, and nearly fifty hogs and sheep.[13]

The curriculum of the school included Bible study and Christian training for all, even though the school's earliest historian—longtime librarian for the John Brown Schools and confidant of the founder, Miss May F. Boudinot—estimated that many of those enrolled were not yet dedicated to the faith when they arrived. "Although perhaps not more than half of the student body had definitely accepted Christ when they entered school," she wrote, "by the middle of the first year, practically all were happy Christians and active in Christian service."[14] In fact, since many of those earliest students came to the school as a result of Brown's evangelistic endeavors around the country, they had a strong desire to follow in his footsteps, spreading the gospel as he did. A group of these young ministers regularly rode on horseback to their fields of work in the surrounding area whenever the creek and streams near campus were swollen with rain.[15]

The curriculum's vocational aspect involved students working for about four hours each day in order both to support the farm, the industries, and the daily operations of the tuition-free school, and to learn a particular trade. College students worked in the morning while the academy students attended classes, then after lunch the divisions swapped roles.[16]

The students' vocational opportunities included the basic functional needs of the school, such as working in the office, kitchen, or laundry; tending the farm;

and working in the print shop that Brown maintained to produce his many books and periodicals. In actuality, these were all Brown family resources that had been deeded over to the school itself, and for the rest of their lives John and Juanita Brown would devote the majority of their financial holdings and outside income to the continuance of the institution, keeping very little for themselves.

Less than a month after classes began, the student body published its first school newspaper, a monthly periodical called *The Southwestern*. Before the close of that first semester, the school's printing shop—still located during that first school year at the edge of Twin Springs Park in downtown Siloam Springs—also absorbed the publishing company of the organization Brown had helped to form a few years earlier, the International Federation of Christian Workers. During the summer after that first year, an annex was built between the white building and the dean's cottage to house the printing press and bindery operations on campus.[17] The school's press stayed active, and within a few years Brown's students were doing the work of publishing multiple weekly periodicals.

Before the end of that first school year, friends of the founder, who were trying to help him raise funds to operate the institution, urged him to rename the school. In the spring of 1920, the name "Southwestern Collegiate Institute" was retired and "John E. Brown College" (JEBC) was officially incorporated under the laws of the state of Arkansas.

Closing exercises for that first school year were held during the first week of June 1920. Though no diplomas had been earned yet, the week saw a great celebratory gathering on Tuesday morning, with hundreds of people visiting from the surrounding area. Special guests who had been invited from considerably farther distances were welcomed onto a temporary speakers' platform erected in the field, west of the college's white building. With a collection of famous flags fluttering in the breeze—they were donated by a local friend of the college and had previously flown from Admiral Dewey's flagship during the Spanish-American War—John Brown wielded a commemorative silver trowel to lay the cornerstone for JEBC's first permanent brick building, which still stands, a century later, in the center of JBU's campus. It was to be a new dormitory, and in time the students living there would christen it with the name of the founder's younger brother, a man who played a vital role for many years in the establishment of the school—J. Alvin Brown.

After this celebration, students led a parade to the park downtown. The college pep squad rode in a float decorated with flowers, boughs of evergreen, and the school colors—already established as blue and gold. The float was pulled by a team of six horses led by two sorrels known as Jack and Jill. At the park, a fundraiser was set up to sell bricks for the new dormitory construction, and one friend of the school who was visiting from California bought twenty-six hundred of them. Later that evening, as the celebration continued with more addresses at the auditorium overlooking Twin Springs Park, an emissary from Jesse H. Jones closed the day by presenting John Brown with a check for $50,000 in honor of Jones's parents.

Three weeks later, Siloam Springs hosted a carnival in the park to celebrate forty years since the town's founding. The school set up an elaborate booth consisting of a pagoda with flanking bungalows, and staff members entertained the crowds with costumes, piano playing, and songs. John Brown and J. Alvin took turns with a megaphone, helping out as "barkers" for the brick sales fundraiser, and overall the school raised $61,000 in pledges for the future J. Alvin Brown Hall.

Still, as the summer wore on and crews hastened to finish the new brick dormitory before fall, it became clear that construction would not be finished by the opening of the school's second year. Thus it was decided to expand the white building, an effort that doubled its overall length.

***

The school's second year of operation began in the fall of 1920, with a student body that had more than doubled in size to around 150. All of the residential students still lived in the white building, since the brick dormitory would still take another full year to complete. The college dress code now included the requirement that students going off campus wear a uniform. For the boys, this was a suit influenced by the military style of the day, and for the girls a "middy" blouse

Cornerstone Ceremony for J. Alvin Brown Hall in June 1920

resembling a sailor's uniform was required in addition to a uniform skirt.

There were fourteen returning staff and faculty members, as well as several new faces. One of the new faculty was the septuagenarian Dr. Isaac Lowe, professor of philosophy and languages. He had been on the faculty of the earlier Methodist-affiliated junior college that existed in Siloam Springs, the Arkansas Conference College, which closed a year or so before John Brown opened his school. Dr. Lowe would be an important part of the first decade of John E. Brown College until he passed away, in his mid-eighties, in 1929.

Another new member of the faculty was Joshua Williams, a music teacher from California who moved with his wife into a cottage on campus in the summer of 1920. He started the college's first band, with instruments provided as donations from the community. The school also received an Edison phonograph from a local friend of the institution, undoubtedly an important addition to the early music program. By the end of the school year, Mr. Williams's band had six members ready to provide musical accompaniment for the commencement ceremonies.

One critical moment in the history of the fledgling school—and the integrity of its mission—came during this second year of operation. Brown was offered a substantial pledge of money for developing an endowment fund, and so, in coordination with this, plans for a million-dollar fundraising campaign were started. Debts had accumulated fast for the young college, and at the time, the school was again tens of thousands of dollars in debt. But it turned out that this promise of endowment money came with a catch: some of the Christian ideals of the school's charter would have to be modified before the funds came through. Learning this, Brown rejected the entire offer. Brown's tireless efforts, personal donation of his income, and steadfast faith in God's provision would have to be enough to guide the young college into financial stability—though this would prove to take many years.[18]

While the college hummed along as a somewhat self-sustaining enterprise, Brown continued his traveling evangelistic work. Over the winter of 1920–1921 he conducted some of the largest revival meetings of his ministry up to that point, working for several weeks in the San Francisco Bay Area. The largest event of that campaign was held in Oakland, with forty-one churches and other Christian organizations cooperating to publicize the event. The first Sunday afternoon service saw twenty-five hundred people attend, and on one weekend of the campaign there was even a parade put on by the churches that reportedly included some eight thousand children.[19]

One humorous moment came during this evangelistic period when, in the last weeks of 1920, Jesse Jones asked Brown to come to Houston on an urgent matter. Success in business and on the national stage had not interrupted Jones's

The founder's family in 1923. From left: Julia Helen, Jean Elizabeth, John Sr., John Jr., Frances Juanita, Juanita, Jessie Virginia and Mary Jane

friendship with Brown, and he had always offered John free lodging at any of his hotels whenever John was in Texas for his preaching and speaking engagements. On this occasion, it seems Jones may have relied on their friendship to justify being playfully vague on the nature of his urgent request. John promised to come when he had a few days free from his speaking engagements in California, and when he arrived in Houston in December, John found that Jones, age forty-six, was finally getting married. Jones's playfully urgent request was a sincere one—he wanted John to perform the wedding. The unfortunate joke was on Jones and his bride, however, because, to their surprise, Brown told them he wasn't actually licensed to officiate their wedding. Nonetheless, Jesse and Mary Gibbs Jones did get married in that December of 1920, and in their next thirty-five years together they would establish a charitable endowment out of their wealth to help John Brown's schools, in addition to many other colleges and educational institutions.

The throngs of thousands at John Brown's evangelistic meetings in the metropolitan Bay Area that winter must have contrasted starkly with relative handful of students and faculty toiling away at his little college in small-town Arkansas. But Brown's heart was with his school. The promise it offered for untold thousands of future youth to gain a Christian education was always his highest priority. His heart was with his family too, and over the winter months he had taken his wife and youngest daughters with him to California. The two oldest girls, Jean Elizabeth and Helen, remained at school in Siloam Springs, and at the end of the school year Jean Elizabeth was among the first six students to receive their diplomas—for completing their high school work—from John E. Brown College.

By the summer of 1921, after the college's second year had come to a close, Juanita Brown was pregnant with a sixth child and had returned to Siloam Springs. John Brown was once again in California when she gave birth, after which the local Siloam Springs newspaper printed the banner headline, "IT'S A BOY!" John Elward Brown Jr. would grow up on the campus, becoming a beloved fixture in his childhood, then a student leader during his high school years. He would one day follow in his father's footsteps not only as the president of JBU but also as the youngest college president in America at the time of his inauguration.

***

The fall of 1921 opened the third year of JEBC, and the new brick dormitory was nearing completion. It would not receive the name "J. Alvin" by vote of the boys who lived there until 1929, and in fact, according to the original plans, it was very nearly a women's dormitory. But in the summer of 1921, the school acquired a building and several acres of property across the street. This area, known as "South Hill" in the early decades of the school, would later be the site for the Blood Memorial Building (used today as the admissions office), the home of the college president (used as such until 2006), and the small neighborhood of Holly Place. On this acreage was a two-story wood-frame building that was suitable for use as a women's dormitory, once it had been given a bit of remodeling. It was an opportune acquisition, since other interests were considering turning the property into a sanitarium—a use that raised concerns, being in such immediate proximity to the campus—and since the new brick dormitory was still going to be rough living for the first months of the fall semester.

A few days before Halloween—which was a time celebrated with much spooky festivity in the early years of the school (Mrs. Juanita Brown dressed as a forest princess the first year)—the first group of boys were finally given the order to start moving into the still-unnamed J. Alvin dormitory. It had 52 rooms on the residential floors in varying states of readiness, with an intended capacity of 104 students. The building was not yet connected to electricity on that first night, and candlelight flickered in each of the windows of the present-day north wing, whose brick walls stand today as the oldest remaining construction on the JBU campus. It took a few weeks before all of the male students had moved out of the white building and into the new dorm, but after this the white building's interior was significantly rearranged for classrooms and an expanded library. Soon the printing shop would be moved into the bottom floor of J. Alvin, where it would remain for more than a decade.

May Boudinot

In this fall of 1921, the male students were still involved with interscholastic football games. Even though an athletic program had not been particularly emphasized during the first two years of the college's existence, at the start of the third year enthusiasm for the football team ran high. JEBC's first game was scheduled against Siloam Springs High School, and in the cross-town, season-opening battle, John Brown's boys—simply put—got shellacked. Several players were hurt, with two boys named William King and William Libby enduring the most serious injuries. Notably, neither boy was recorded as ever graduating from the John Brown schools. After this disastrous game, the school officially ended all participation in organized athletics outside the intramural realm, a policy that would last until the late 1950s.

It was in this third year that Miss May Boudinot arrived to be the school's librarian and history teacher. Like John Brown, she was originally from Iowa, born about the same time as the founder, and she had lived for several years in California, where she earned an advanced degree and became a school teacher. Once she arrived to join in the effort at Siloam Springs, Miss Boudinot began keeping meticulous records of all manner of events happening about the campus. Over the course of her thirty-plus years of association with the John Brown schools, she would become the first historian of the school's own progress, leaving to posterity two lengthy, unpublished manuscripts covering the detailed history of John Brown University, as well as John Brown's own life story, which she compiled through her own original research and visits to Brown's childhood home.

Boudinot became well-acquainted with life in the white building, where her library occupied various spaces over the years, and she was understandably quite attuned to the daily risk of catastrophic fire in the wooden structure. "In fact it was a common saying," Miss Boudinot wrote, "that if the building should ever catch fire, nothing could save it. Fire drills were frequent." Writing of the years when women lived in the dormitory spaces of the building, she said, "The girls were required at night to lay things out, ready for a hasty escape at any time, if necessary."

Several minor fires did indeed break out in the white building over the years, though none proved disastrous. "One day," she wrote, "when returning from

The Log Cabin Band

town, [I] wondered why a group of boys were playing on the roof, only to learn upon arrival on the Hill that they were extinguishing a fire." Other fires broke out in the laundry, toward the rear of the building, and in the ceiling of the dean's office over the heating stove. Fortunately, all these were extinguished in short order.

Another time, she described her distinct memory "of one night while boys were working in the print shop in the rear of the building that a cry of 'fire' rang through the halls." But it turned out to be just a prank, fortunately—or rather unfortunately for the boys involved. "Those in the dormitory above, looking through an open register in the floor saw a boy with a bucket containing fire coals in an attempt to frighten those above by the smell of fire and smoke."[20]

It was, perhaps, the campus pranksters, such as this boy with the bucket of coals, who drew what must surely have been the saddest vocational assignment of them all—sitting up alone through an entire winter's night, stoking a fire in the food storehouse to keep the campus supply of sweet potatoes from freezing.

Such a lonely duty was actually quite important for life on campus. Sweet potatoes were one of the staples on the dinner table at John E. Brown College in those early years, along with corn bread, peanut butter, and syrup made in the campus sorghum mill. By 1923 a cannery would be established under the trees near J. Alvin for preserving foodstuffs, and at times the various classes and student clubs would hold contests to see which group could fill the most cans in a certain amount of time. With the school aiming to be as self-sufficient as possible, in the fall of 1924 the cannery achieved the remarkable quantity of 3,600 gallons of food stored away for the winter.

The industriousness of the students extended into their free time as well. Professor Joshua Williams's music band had grown in members and popularity, and in the fall of 1921 the boys of the band decided they needed their own practice facility. So they built a log cabin on their own time, and in December they dedicated it by hosting a campus party there. For years thereafter, the "Log Cabin Band" would be a well-known feature of the John Brown schools, going on tours throughout the region and sometimes accompanying John Brown in his nearby speaking engagements.

It was during this holiday season at the end of 1921 that John Brown Sr. came home to Siloam Springs utterly exhausted with the pace of activity he had maintained for so long. He took a six-week break, virtually the only such period of rest recorded by his biographers across his long and productive life.

Over the school's Christmas recess, a number of students had little option but to remain on campus. This was true throughout the early years of the school. On this Christmas Eve of 1921, the remaining students gathered in the Brown family home, doting on the infant Buddy and bringing the weary college founder a dose of cheer. Afterward, Professor Williams rounded up a car and an old bus, and the party rumbled off for a night of caroling through the town.

Venturing out into neighboring communities was a familiar practice for the ministry-minded students of the college. During this third school year, students now walked, bicycled, or rode horses to as many as ten villages around Siloam Springs, bringing gospel preaching and Sunday-school classes on a regular basis to the people of the region.

Not only did students go out into the surrounding world with the gospel, but they also had glimpses frequently brought to them of the work God was doing in the wider world. In this third school year, one visiting chapel speaker delivered a message on the World War's effect on Christianity in Europe, and a missionary to northern China, Miss Ruth Nowlin, spoke of conditions in that part of the world. In the years to come, annual missionary conferences would host many furloughed foreign workers who brought their news of progress from distant mission fields, and in time, many of these visiting missionaries were alumni of John Brown's school itself.

***

After the conclusion of the third school year, John Brown's annual summer Bible conference convened in Siloam Springs during the first week in July; one of the luminaries in attendance was the British scholar and evangelist Dr. G. Campbell Morgan. It was in the middle of this conference that Brown led another celebration on campus of the school's progress, where it was announced that a new brick building—named in honor of the state of California, where so many friends and supporters of the school resided—would be built. Again a throng of hundreds of people came to campus, with Model T's and other varieties of early cars parked by the dozen in the campus fields. Morgan and other notable guests were given seats on the temporary speakers' platform erected for the occasion, and then the groundbreaking for the building took place. A minister from California took up the ceremonial spade and turned the first piece of ground. Morgan and several other friends in attendance each pledged $500 toward the finishing and furnishing of a room of the future dormitory.

The projected cost of the California building was, at the time, $60,000, and it was hoped that the funds could be raised primarily from California donors. Before the end of the summer, friends from that state provided the building plans and came to help lead the student workers in its construction. One of these was Mr. R. N. Allen, who, in addition to directing the building effort and serving as the superintendent of labor on campus, became a member of the school's Bible faculty through the 1930s. Material support from area industries was secured, with a brick company in Fort Smith, Arkansas agreeing to provide bricks at a discount rate, and the Kansas City Southern Railroad offering half-rate on all shipments. A friend in Louisiana even offered to provide and deliver construction materials at cost, without shipping charges. However, it would not be long before momentum was lost for the construction project. An economic decline on the West Coast resulted in lagging donations, and the California building would be a slow-moving work in progress for the next five years.

***

The fourth year of JEBC started in the fall of 1922 with a student body that had grown to about 230, and the new men's dormitory was already essentially at capacity, with about 100 students living there. The white building had been remodeled once again (this would become practically an annual tradition) to devote the majority of the upper floor to women's dormitory space, with Miss Boudinot's library in the rear. The South Hill dwelling that had been acquired a year before was given over to faculty members and married students who lived on campus, and the Browns' home became a teacherage during the fall as well. John took his wife and the smaller children to California, while the three oldest daughters lived on campus as students.

The curriculum now provided a much-expanded array of vocational options, including a broom and furniture factory and a blacksmith shop. But with only two major buildings on campus, and the California project still just a set of drawings to go with a patch of turned-over earth, the school's third major building was started that fall. It was to be known simply as the Mechanical Building, and by February its first wing would be finished, becoming the center of the school's growing vocational activities. Later generations of students would know this building—which was expanded with additional wings later during the same school year and again in 1933—as Mechanical Building 1 after a second such building was added to the campus in 1935, and in its final decades as the "Arkansas Building" after it received a major facelift in the 1950s. It stood for over fifty years, finally being demolished in the 1970s to make way for the Chapman Administration Building and Kresge Dining Hall.

***

From the beginning, John E. Brown College was intended to provide a robust number of practical learning opportunities to equip youth for a productive future. May Boudinot wrote of the founder's ideals for vocational education, "In it all, the Founder was emphasizing 'the dignity and aristocracy of constructive toil' and the necessity of working right, thinking straight, and living straight. He insisted that 'students were not working their way to an education, but were educating their way to work.'"[21]

The 1920 Articles of Incorporation—adopted at the time the school first changed its name—defined the school's mission as "an Industrial College offering courses of instruction in the Arts and Sciences, Industrial Arts, Home Economics, Agriculture, and Mechanical Arts." The articles were amended the following year to include "Civil Engineering, Mining Engineering, Electrical Engineering, and Chemical Engineering."[22]

With the start of the fourth school year came a clear statement of the founder's intentions for the social and spiritual character of the college. In June 1922, John and Juanita Brown had signed a warranty deed giving their family farm to the college corporation. The Browns' wishes in conveying the property to JEBC were "for the specific purpose of founding an institution of learning where worthy and ambitious young men and women may be helped to help themselves."

The Browns did not wish the college to be highly exclusive in its admissions requirements, and kept the vision of providing an education for those same kinds of youths Brown had met in Vancouver, who were limited in their financial means. As the warranty deed put it, "for entrance into this college no requirements shall be made of the student other than those having to do with the clean life and worthy ideals. It [is the founder's] wish and hope that the school shall ever stand with wide open doors to boys and girls who unless educated here will probably never have an opportunity to get an education."

The Browns also enjoined the future leadership of the college that it should never be beholden to any particular denomination of Christian teaching, urging in the deed "that no sectarian religion be taught in this school, but that all students shall be free to choose their denominational affiliations, if they desire to make any, without any persuasion or coercion on the part of the officers, trustees, or faculty or any member thereof."[23]

As the fall of this fourth year got underway, students toiled away at the new buildings and spent time improving the water and sewer system in the white building under the auspices of a new vocational plumbing department. Life in the white building could be adventurous at times, and one memorable moment came on Halloween night as the students were marching down the long central hallway to the dining room for a party. Suddenly, a section of the floor sank underneath the tramping feet. Commotion ensued. A section of the floor's underpinnings had slipped, chalking up one more repair task on the to-do list for the vocational carpentry department.

John Brown's evangelistic travels brought him and his entire California ministry team to campus that January, and the first annual "Revival Week" was held. Brown held services every day for the student body in the mold of his evangelistic campaigns. Two weeks later, he and his team were off again, this time to Chattanooga, Tennessee. It would be his second campaign in that city, the first having been about a year earlier, and as a result of his ministry there, a large influx of Tennessean students would join the college the next fall.

When the Mechanical Building's first unit was ready for use in February, it provided space for an expanded on-campus general store. One had previously been situated in a small room behind the white building's kitchen, but now there was ample room for a well-developed mercantile operation in which students could gain the vocational training of running a business. The building also offered space for another commercial enterprise—auto sales. The "College Motor Company" occupied garage space in the new building and became the local area's dealership for the Durant Star brand of automobiles. Mr. J. Alvin Brown was the manager of the business, and by the summer the dealership had expanded its license to include International Harvester trucks. With auto sales and mechanic services now added to the campus industries, students gained still more opportunities for hands-on, profitable vocational training.

As the fourth year drew to a close in May 1923, Dr. Isaac Lowe treated the college students to an off-campus dinner at an establishment called Statler's, where they honored the first student to complete all of the requirements of the school's two-year junior college curriculum. Miss Geneva Cossel, a twenty-two-year-old young woman who had grown up in Siloam Springs, was John E. Brown College's first graduate. Her upbringing was perhaps representative of her generation at the turn of the century, and of the town of Siloam Springs, which was famed during her childhood for its healing climate and waters. Geneva was born in 1900 as the youngest of a dozen children; her father had moved the family from Kansas to Siloam Springs in 1905, hoping his health might improve after suffering a stroke and a case of smallpox. Mr. Cossel died two years after the move, when Geneva was seven years old, leaving her mother and several children to survive on Mr. Cossel's Civil War pension. As Geneva was honored as JEBC's first college graduate, fifteen more high school students also received their diplomas, including John Brown's second-oldest daughter, Helen.

During the summer of 1923, JEBC was able to essentially clear all of its debt again. Fundraising had, at times, taken on some unusual forms. One donor had offered, a year earlier, to give five dollars for every student, teacher, or staff member who could memorize and recite the entire Sermon on the Mount, from Matthew 5–7. Miss Boudinot, watching with fascination, wrote, "Every place on the campus, in the halls between classes, and while waiting for the dining room bell, students could be seen with Testament in hand." More than one hundred succeeded at memorizing the lengthy passage, earning a total donation of $540. The spry mind of Isaac Lowe was not only up to the task—Dr. Lowe was the first member of the campus family to recite the Sermon in full.

Still, financial worries were frequent in those early years. Two months after John Brown had announced that the school was essentially debt free that summer of 1923, a significant financial emergency arose. For the past several months, Brown had been saving up the proceeds of his book sales for a new family home, since their campus home was so often needed as a teacherage. But now, with this sudden crisis in the school's budget, the Browns sacrificed their personal savings, as they had done so many times before, to set the school's accounts right. It would be another few years before John and Juanita had a more permanent home in which to raise their youngest children.

***

The fall of 1923 was the beginning of the school's fifth year, and it brought the large number of young Tennesseans who were drawn to JEBC after Brown's successful evangelistic campaigns in Chattanooga over the two previous winters.

Some 10 percent of the student body now hailed from the Volunteer State, and they soon formed a student Tennessee Club, the first of its kind in the school's early history. Not to be outdone, the Texans soon formed a Texas Club, and in the next few years other associations would be formed around state and regional allegiances, such as the Hill Billy Club for Arkansans and the Eskimo Club for students from some of the northern states.

Catalina

With the Tennessean students also came a boon of support from their friends and family back home—an organized fundraising campaign to support construction of a dedicated heating and electric plant for the campus. That fall, excavation began on the hillside between the men's dorm and the California construction site. Lodged into this hillside would be a large basement to house the boilers and generators of the campus utility plant, all covered with a roof that could serve as the floor of a future multistory building above. When that upper structure was built a few years later, it would be christened the Alumni Building, and in 1959 it was renovated for the Engineering Department's use as the Hyde Building.

During this 1923–1924 school year, the hilltop overlooking the east valley was a veritable hive of activity for the vocational students of the construction crews. Construction would, for the next several years, be a nearly constant part of campus life, both to provide space for the ever-expanding needs of the college and to provide students the experiential job training the college was established to provide. Almost all of the campus buildings erected during the early decades were built primarily by student hands.

The California building site had seen progress over the last few months, with excavation finished and a concrete foundation poured. Soon after the start of the college's fifth fall semester, the California cornerstone was laid on September 27, more than a year after the building's groundbreaking. By the end of the school year, student labor had given the building its basic shape, with walls erected to a height of two stories. Still, three more years of gradual construction and finishing would be required before the first residents could inaugurate the building's legendary seventy-seven-year run as a beloved dormitory and community space.

Another much smaller building took shape during the 1923–1924 school year after William Waterhouse, now in his early seventies, made a return visit to the campus. Two years earlier he had gone to Japan to work with a Christian evangelist there, and now the energetic builder and father of campus construction—known admiringly by the students as "Pep" Waterhouse—was back with a donation for the college. His gift funded the construction of a small brick bungalow in front of the California site, which was dedicated as the school's hospital in February. Over the years it served several functions, including as the campus general offices, radio studios, and music house. When it was finally converted into a miniature dormitory seven decades later, it gained the affectionate name Catalina—after the "small island off the coast of California," as students liked to put it.

During this school year the campus community began to participate in society's early fascination with radio. America's commercial broadcasting stations and earliest radio news broadcasts had begun less than four years earlier. Some of the earliest documented transmissions covered the election results of the 1920 presidential race. Now on Monday, January 21, 1924, students gathered around a radio receiver set up in the dining room to listen with hushed anticipation for any discernible speech they could make out amid the static. Someone adjusted the tuner ever so carefully, trying to find the broadcast frequency of a station called WDAF out of Kansas City. All listened intently, for at that same moment, JEBC's journalism professor, Robert Leflar, was on the air, providing the first ever broadcast publicity for John Brown's school and speaking about its unique mission. "How eagerly everyone listened, waiting for some familiar words," Miss Boudinot recalled. But sadly, "keen disappointment prevailed when there was very little success in the reception of the broadcast."[24]

The following Saturday, shaking off their disappointment, the students gathered for what must have seemed a hilarious program of entertainment. With cardboard boxes set up to serve as imaginary radio set and loudspeakers, a boy named Fred Goode took to the stage to manage the receiver, struggling to control pretend static, while another boy named Hugh Engels stood before an imaginary microphone, announcing a musical program with fictitious names. Then the Log Cabin Band, now nearly thirty members strong, entertained with an array of musical selections. Little could they know that a decade later, John Brown's students would be enacting this same tableau—only with real radio equipment— and putting on live musical performances to be broadcast for hundreds of miles in every direction around Siloam Springs, all originating out of brightly lit studios in a red brick bungalow known, for now, only as the campus infirmary.

California groundbreaking ceremony

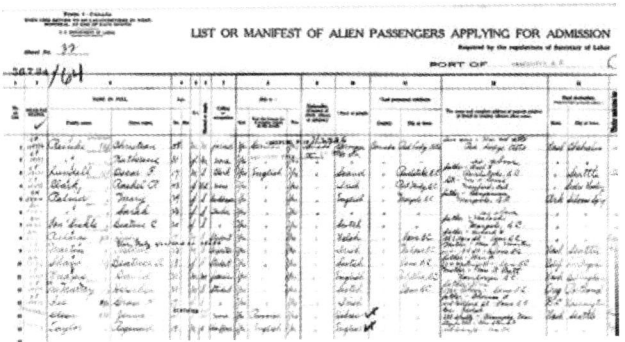

A September 1919 ship manifest from Vancouver, British Columbia lists four passengers (lines 5-8) traveling to Siloam Springs, Arkansas. Among them was Beatrice C. Van Sickle, one of the first college staff members.[25]

CHAPTER 4

THE ERA OF TWO SCHOOLS

The next four years of the John Brown schools would see a dramatic, though short-lived, transformation in how the college at Siloam Springs operated, since it was about to be joined by a sister campus some twenty-five miles north along the Missouri border. During this period, the name "John Brown University" would first be used, although only briefly, for the sister institution established in the small resort town of Sulphur Springs, Arkansas.

In the spring of 1924, John Brown Sr. made the rather astonishing move of buying essentially the entire Sulphur Springs community. A banker in the town named Storm O. Whaley facilitated Brown's acquisition of a wide array of properties, including three hotels, two storefront buildings, and dozens of business and residential lots, as well as a large park that featured natural springs and a small lake nearby. The resort village had been owned and operated by a Kansas landholder named J. G. Edwards. Mr. Whaley helped John Brown acquire the properties at a price far below the quarter-million-dollar appraised value.

The acquisition seemed ideal for setting up a four-year, degree-granting institution in a picturesque location with facilities that were ready-made for housing and teaching a residential student body. The properties had the added benefit of generating income during the summer months, when the hotels used as dormitory space during the school year could be quickly returned to use as paid resort lodging.

In fact, part of the appeal of the acquisition was its promise of relieving the constant financial strain facing John E. Brown College in Siloam Springs. The vision of having a self-sustaining, tuition-free college—funded by donations and by the product of the students' work in campus industries—was difficult to achieve. More steady income was desperately needed for the vocational, pay-by-work institution, and John Brown saw the Sulphur Springs property as an opportunity to set up a separate, tuition-based college that could achieve his goal of providing a complete college curriculum under his educational ideals. Indeed, the previous fall, JEBC had taken steps toward expanding the curriculum to four years at Siloam Springs, and several students spent this year doing college junior-level

IN THE OZARKS — LAND OF A MILLION SMILES.

JOHN E. BROWN UNIVERSITY. SULPHUR SPRINGS. ARK.

A postcard depicting the Sulphur Springs campus of John E. Brown University

work. With the four-year college plan now shifted to the tuition-based Sulphur Springs school, revenue from the second campus could help sustain the vocational, tuition-free ideal of the first.

Work rapidly began over the summer of 1924 to bring the two-college model to fruition, and to immediately put the Sulphur Springs properties to good use. One hotel continued to be open for resort vacationers. The annual summer Bible conference, which John Brown had organized in Siloam Springs for many years, now moved to Sulphur. A Summer Institute of Music followed, and a new periodical newspaper was begun called the *Sulphur Springs American*. Staff from Siloam were shifted over to the new campus, and additional workers were brought in to manage the expanded effort.

It was perhaps a sign of how daunting the two-campus venture would prove to be when the Reverend Fred Hamilton was installed as the new superintendent of all the John Brown industries. Falling under his supervision were now two publishing houses, two stores, two auto garages, a car dealership, a five-hundred-acre farm, the ongoing construction and renovation projects of two college campuses, and the newly acquired summer resort. By November, Hamilton had resigned from his sprawling duties and returned to the pastorate.

While John E. Brown College in Siloam entered its sixth year, the "John Brown University" of Sulphur Springs successfully opened its first year in the fall of 1924, with one hundred students from sixteen different states and two foreign countries. Each student was expected to pay a $450 annual tuition. Over the course of two academic years, the Sulphur Springs university saw six of its students graduate after each had successfully completed a full four-year college curriculum between his or her time at the two campuses.

In early 1926, as the Sulphur campus was in the midst of its second year of operation, John Brown sought accreditation of his four-year university program there. An inspector representing the North Central Association of Colleges and Secondary Schools paid the campus a visit, and reported on a number of advancements that "John Brown University" would need to achieve in order to receive his recommendation for accreditation. As John Brown Sr. considered the costs required to implement these changes, he was also reflecting on the disappointing reception this second college had so far received. Many families who had applauded the creation of this second institution had not, as he had hoped, actually sent their children (and their tuition funds) there. It also seemed that the faculty of the Sulphur Springs campus was not as committed to his head, heart, and hand ideals as he desired, with the result that the school was becoming an "ordinary" college. After just two years of operation, John Brown decided that the name and concept of "John Brown University" would not reopen for a third year.[1]

Still, the John Brown schools boasted two attractive campuses, and so a new plan was experimented with. In the fall of 1926—which began the eighth year of operation at Siloam Springs and the third year at Sulphur Springs—there would be two junior colleges, with the original campus intended for men, and the Sulphur Springs campus intended for women. The two campuses were, somewhat confusingly, given the names of "John E. Brown College" and "John Brown College." Even this plan was not strictly maintained, however, for there were vocational activities at Sulphur that needed male students to maintain, and there were local women from the Siloam Springs community who wished to remain as day students at the original campus. For two school years this experiment continued, but finally in the summer of 1928, after four years of operation at Sulphur Springs, President Brown announced the total closure of the campus as a college, and the consolidation of all educational endeavors in Siloam Springs.

Other than summer activities, the Sulphur Springs properties lay mostly idle for the next two years, until the fall of 1930, when a high school was opened there. Named after the founder's mother, the Julia A. Brown School would be operated in Sulphur for several years, providing the teacher-education students and graduates from Siloam Springs an opportunity to put their training into practice. The campus continued in operation throughout most of the 1930s and 1940s, expanding to include grade-school education, and eventually evolving into the Brown Military Academy of the Ozarks.

Finally, in late 1951, the Sulphur Springs properties were sold to another evangelical ministry whose founder had established a relationship with the John Brown endeavors many years before. In 1934, a young missionary named William Cameron Townsend, who had been frustrated trying to use a Spanish Bible to teach the Cakchiquel Indians in Guatemala, came to Sulphur Springs to begin his first "Summer Institute of Linguistics" with two students. The following year, he taught five students. As this training program for translation of the Bible into other languages grew, so did Cam Townsend's vision. He became the founder of the great Wycliffe Bible Translators ministry in 1942. Seeing the opportunity to assist in a great Christian ministry, Brown sold the Sulphur Springs property to Wycliffe in 1951 for $75,000—a substantial discount from his original asking price of $250,000.

When Brown sold the property to Townsend, he said, "It seems to me that this monumental work started at Sulphur Springs in a school of two students seventeen years ago, may actually circle the globe, if Christ delays His coming. That old bass drum of the Salvation Army is still beating!"[2]

***

During the four years of dual-campus operations, the John E. Brown College in Siloam Springs saw some significant events occur, and the students of the two campuses enjoyed continued camaraderie.

While intercollegiate athletics was still not allowed, the Siloam and Sulphur campuses met for several friendly—if not necessarily highly skilled—athletic competitions. In December 1925, the Sulphur Springs men were the visitors in Siloam for a football game between the two John Brown schools, ending the game in a zero-zero tie. A couple months later, the Sulphur students visited again to continue their rivalry in basketball games, after which they joined together for the first George Washington's birthday banquet, which became an annual campus event for decades to come.

Other events maintained the fellowship between the two campuses, which was especially welcome for those students of Sulphur Springs who had spent their early educational years in Siloam. A few days before commencement 1925—concluding the first year of the Sulphur Springs institution—the John Brown schools hosted their first ever alumni banquet. About fifty former students returned to the Siloam Springs campus, and a student named Wendell Campbell—who would earn his four-year degree from Sulphur the next year—was elected the first president of the John Brown Alumni Association. The first yearbook was printed in 1926—named the "Jebroco"—and by the 1928 edition, it was assembled as a joint endeavor of students from the two campuses.

An important achievement was reached in the spring of 1925 when the Arkansas State Board of Education offered their approval of John E. Brown College's teacher-education program. The college quickly announced that a twelve-week summer course would now be offered in teacher training, and fifty students immediately enrolled. The course was offered again the following summer, but there was a bittersweet ending to the summer 1926 term: President Brown had only recently announced that "John Brown University" would be discontinued, and the female junior college students would be leaving the Siloam Springs campus to be relocated to Sulphur. Miss Boudinot said wryly of the day when the girls withdrew that they were "leaving College Hill to the boys in their loneliness." She added, "However, these boys bravely gave a farewell party for the co-eds before their departure."[3]

The ladies of the John Brown student body made return visits to Siloam Springs on a number of occasions after this. They were hosted by the boys in Siloam on Thanksgiving Day, and in return the ladies came to Siloam to take over Sunday meals for the boys one day in the spring. On those occasions when the Sulphur students came to Siloam, there was often an exuberant greeting, seemingly lifted out of a painting of 1920s small-town America. Arriving in Siloam Springs "in a special car on the regular morning train," Miss Boudinot recalled, "they were met at the depot by JEBC students and all marched four abreast through the town to College Hill, where sports and a good time were enjoyed."[4]

By the end of this dual-campus period in 1928, May Boudinot was now the second-longest-serving member of the faculty. Only the elderly Dr. Isaac Lowe, who joined the college a year before her, had a longer tenure as the school approached a decade of operation. Dr. Lowe passed away just after New Year's Day 1929.

Miss Boudinot had other duties in addition to her history teaching, maintaining the library, and serving as the school's unofficial diarist. In the spring semester of 1925, she coached the academy students' debating team, leading them to the northwestern Arkansas regional trophy on the proposition, "Resolved, That the United States should join the League of Nations." The team lost in the statewide semifinals held in Fayetteville.

As construction on the California building neared completion, Boudinot was also one of the first group of seven people to live in the unfinished dormitory in the fall of 1926. Since this was the year that the women of the college were transferred to Sulphur Springs, she shared space in the building's north wing with four young ladies of the staff, while Mr. Allen—head of construction on the building—and his wife lived in the south wing.

***

In the summer of 1927, after several years of slow progress interrupted by many delays, the California building was finally dedicated. The vocational students of the furniture factory had been busily constructing the furnishings to be used throughout the building over the last several months, and on July 1 another grand event was held on campus to celebrate the building's completion. A giant tent was erected east of the white building, capable of sheltering several thousand guests from the heat of the summer sun, and more than three thousand people came from all corners of the nation. A special train car carried a delegation of thirty-two friends of the college from California, and in nearby Sulphur Springs, the mayor declared a city holiday so townspeople could travel to Siloam for the ceremony.

The governor of Oklahoma, a United States senator representing Arkansas, and more than a dozen other prominent men of local and national fame spoke during the day. The basement of California, which would now become the campus dining room and future cafeteria for the next forty-five years, served the first meal in its history to the distinguished guests, while outside under the tent, more than eight hundred plates were sold—at the then-extraordinary rate of $10—for a great fundraising banquet. Music was provided by the JEBC orchestra and band, and a girls' drum corps that had formed at the Sulphur Springs campus joined in providing the sounds of the day. President Brown delivered a culminating address titled "Watchman, What of the Day?" He spoke of the history of the school and his ideals for education, and asked the audience to consider the urgent question of whether the current system of American education was leading to a society where graduates had any hope of putting their classroom learning into action.

In the evening, as the crowds dispersed, a number of guests were offered the chance to spend the night in specially prepared rooms of the new dormitory. The next day, the building became the home of the summer-session students. California served continuously as a student residence until its final semester of use in the spring of 2001. For much of its history, California served solely as a women's dormitory, but in its final years, it became the only full-time coed dormitory on campus, providing a uniquely egalitarian environment. Its grand meeting hall between the north and south wings on the main floor provided ample space for graduation ceremonies, conferences, and weddings in its early years. Its musty basement would be replaced as a cafeteria by the Kresge Dining Hall in 1972. After more than seventy years of occupancy and numerous updates, renovations, and repairs, the venerable California dorm's age and structural deficiency finally left the school no choice but to tear it down to rubble. Many of its famous red ceramic roof tiles were spirited away as commemorative relics by students and alumni during its demolition.

***

Throughout the 1920s, John Brown's reputation as an evangelist continued to open many opportunities for him to conduct large, citywide campaigns in cooperation with local churches.[5] During these years of evangelism, much of his personal income from that ministry was poured directly into the college in Siloam Springs. Brown's efforts in Tennessee, which had drawn so many students to the college in 1923, began in February 1922 with a thirty-day meeting series in Chattanooga that involved fifty churches and saw overflowing audiences in the six-thousand-seat tabernacle that evangelist Billy Sunday had used a few years earlier.[6] He returned to several parts of Tennessee in the following years.

Another of his largest campaigns was a meeting series in Birmingham, Alabama, in early 1925 that had the support of 125 churches and drew audiences to fill a five-thousand-seat auditorium night after night. In the winter of 1926–1927, he led major campaigns in California, and in 1928 he made some of his only appearances in the eastern United States with campaigns in Virginia and Boston.[7] After this Boston series—where he was invited to gain his first experience speaking over the radio—he took about two years away from the citywide campaign style of evangelism.

During the school's first decade, many students emulated the founder and became deeply involved with evangelism and preaching, carrying forth the Christ Over All motto of the school. During the fall semester of 1926, a dozen boys who were all studying at JEBC for the ministry formed the Young Ministers' Club, which they renamed a year later to the Ministerial Club. The club was founded so these young preachers could share their struggles and build a closer fellowship with one another. Indeed, the responsibilities these young men took upon themselves were significant, with one serving as the assistant pastor of First Methodist Church in Siloam Springs, and many others traveling—often on foot—to surrounding communities to work in churches that had no full-time pastors. The group experienced the pain of loss early in their history after one of their founding members, Paul Loescher, died at home in New York shortly after graduating from the academy in the summer of 1927. Loescher had worked every Sunday in a church near the Lone Elm schoolhouse, a few miles east of town, and just north of the land where the city airfield would one day be constructed. There was a large stone near the school, and Loescher would stop and pray there every Sunday morning before beginning his ministry. A few years after his death, this stone was brought to campus as a memorial to him.[8]

Other members of the Ministerial Club had poignant life stories after their time at JEBC. The club's founding vice president was Thomas McKnight, who arrived at the college a couple months shy of his seventeenth birthday. He was from Yellville, Arkansas, the sixth of eleven children, and the son of a Methodist preacher. During World War II, he became a chaplain with the Army's 7th Cavalry Regiment, and died on a battlefield in the Philippines when he left his foxhole to attend to a wounded man during a mortar attack.

Another member who joined the club in 1929 was Harold Palmer from Oklahoma City. In 1941, after several years pastoring and preparing for the mission field, Palmer took his wife and young daughter to the Philippines, where he became pastor of First Baptist Church of Manila. The family was imprisoned by the Japanese during World War II, and Harold died of an infection after surgery in the POW camp.

Another student who joined the Ministerial Club at the same time as Palmer was a Japanese American named Richard Toshio Funai, who had heard of the John Brown schools while a high school student in Hawaii. He was a recent convert to Christianity, and after learning of the school, he saved enough money to buy passage on an ocean liner to the West Coast, then made his way to Arkansas by the adventurous method of hopping trains across the country. Funai spent the years of World War II in a Japanese relocation camp in Idaho, and after the war returned to Hawaii where he spent many years teaching and working with juvenile delinquents.

The JEBC orchestra plays in the foreground.

Girls' drum corps at Sulphur Springs

Students at the Sulphur Springs campus

Staff and students gather for the dedication of the California building in 1927. The founder is in the center front of the photo, holding his hat.

CHAPTER 5

A UNIVERSITY AND A RADIO TOWER

After enjoying the opportunity in 1928 to try a new kind of speaking engagement during his evangelistic campaign in Boston, John Brown increasingly shifted his attention and his passion to this new method for spreading the gospel—radio.

The John E. Brown College's first foray into radio came in the form of a one-hundred-watt station operating out of Missouri, called KFPW. In the fall of 1928, Brown bought the station and moved its operation first to the resort hotel in Sulphur Springs, then finally to the campus in Siloam. Brown had been impressed with his experience speaking on the radio in Boston earlier that year, and now he had the opportunity to continue that form of ministry from the campus, while also adding a valuable new technology for vocational learning. The station was so underpowered, however, that the KFPW call letters were turned into the acronym "Kind Friends Please Write," in hopes of finding out how many people were actually listening to the broadcasts. The station was eventually sold off less than two years later.

Still, despite that first experience with just a small listenership, Brown had become committed to the power of radio to spread the gospel to people from all walks of life. In 1930, thanks to his relationships in California, he began a daily radio broadcast on station KGER in Long Beach, California, which he called *God's Half Hour*. He would continue a daily radio broadcast on multiple stations up until his death in 1957.

***

The early 1930s saw growth and change continue on the Siloam Springs campus. The boys' dormitory had finally gained an official name by popular vote of the boys living there. During the summer session of 1929, the building was officially christened as J. Alvin Brown Hall in honor of "Uncle Alvin," who had played such an important role in managing the school and its industries over the first ten years, and who would soon leave Siloam Springs to manage the school's affairs in California for many years.

The brick building that was eventually known as the Hyde Building was dedicated as the Alumni Building during the commencement and homecoming celebrations in May 1930—seven years after its basement had been built as the campus utility plant. This building provided expanded facilities for the school's vocational industries, and included a dress factory, laundry, bakery, and cannery. It continued in use as classrooms and science labs for many years, then housed the machine shop and an engineering laboratory into the 2000s. It stood for more than eight decades, and in 2011 it became the last structure of the early years to be demolished, leaving the north wing of J. Alvin Hall as the last remaining physical remnant of the university's founding era.

J. Alvin Brown

Another step in campus facilities expansion was taken during the spring and summer of 1930, when the foundation was poured for the "Oklahoma Building." This proposed administrative facility had been originally envisioned as the "Five States Building." Representatives of Arkansas, Oklahoma, Texas, Missouri, and Tennessee had performed the ceremonial groundbreaking three years before, on the same afternoon that the California dormitory was dedicated. In June 1930, another grand campus celebration was organized, and four thousand people attended the placing of the Oklahoma Building's cornerstone. The school's radio station, KFPW, as well as a station from Tulsa, broadcast the celebration live, including an address by the governor of Oklahoma. It had been hoped that the occasion would be Jesse Jones's first visit to the campus he had given so much to help establish, but illness prevented him from attending.

Unfortunately, the onset of the Great Depression put a halt to the Oklahoma Building project before it could progress any further than a concrete foundation. Indeed, the foundation would sit forlornly at the center of campus for the next twenty-two years, awaiting the time when it would be repurposed as the footprint of a completely different building—the Library of the Cathedral Group.

During the summer of 1930, as the Great Depression began weighing on the economy across the United States, JEBC organized its own College Bank and Savings Corporation. Its offices were initially located in the rear of the upper floor of the old white building, and were moved a number of times over the years. While the bank was only intended to handle internal accounts for the school industries and student funds, as the banking crisis swept the nation it would find a role serving the Siloam Springs community. Two years after the college bank

J. Alvin Brown Hall - 1930s

was founded, the only bank in Siloam Springs failed. President Brown recognized the immediate need in the town, and within hours of the bank's failure, he had set up a branch of the college bank downtown to serve the community as a clearing house for checks and deposits. A year later, newly inaugurated President Franklin D. Roosevelt mandated a four-day bank "holiday" across the nation to provide a cooling-off period from the bank runs, and again the John Brown college bank—which was organized in such a way that it did not fall under the mandate—was the only financial institution still open in Siloam Springs.

In the fall of 1930, after eleven years of attempting to sustain the tuition-free model, John E. Brown College began its twelfth academic year with some three hundred students and dorms filled to overflowing, but now it was a tuition-based school. A typical student application from 1931 would ask simply, "Under which financial plan do you wish to enroll?" and students were admitted under a three-tiered, needs-based pay structure. In another sign of change for the school's financial underpinnings, a "John E. Brown College Corporation" was set up in California in 1931, through which the school would buy revenue-generating businesses such as gas stations and delivery services, whose profits could go toward the sustenance of the school in Siloam Springs.

***

In March 1929, "Mother Brown," the founder's mother, died at a ripe old age after an extended period of declining health. She had lived on campus with one of John Brown's sisters, Mrs. Elsie Miller, for several years, and the founder had spent much time throughout her last months visiting with her and tending to her on a nearly daily basis. He was away in California at the time of her death, and was unable to return in time to attend her funeral, yet he gave many loving tributes to her legacy in the following weeks. He proclaimed, "As you look over College Hill and witness what is here, don't say John Brown did this, but say all of this is here because John Brown had a mother!"[1]

Two years later, sorrow cut the Brown family and the campus community more deeply than ever before. John Brown's second-oldest daughter, Helen Brown Hodges, died suddenly on April 13, 1931. She was only twenty-six years old.

Helen Brown

***

Helen was born in Missouri while her father was president of Scarritt Collegiate Institute, and had come of age as a student at her father's school in Siloam Springs. As a high school senior in the spring of 1923, she had been a popular choice to play the role of the queen in a stage production of the cantata *Daniel*, and by 1926 she was on staff as the director of the dress factory. Her designs were marketed and sold in twenty-five area clothing shops as "Helen Brown Dresses."

On November 23, 1929, Helen Brown married her former classmate Richard Hodges. He had graduated from the junior college at Siloam in 1925, and went immediately to work for his future father-in-law as manager of the Sulphur Springs summer resort hotel. He then enrolled at the short-lived "John Brown University" at Sulphur Springs, but also worked as that school's bookkeeper. After completing a degree in business administration at the University of Arkansas in Fayetteville, during which time he was elected president of a new John Brown alumni organization, Hodges rejoined the John Brown schools in 1929. He would continue to be on the staff for many years thereafter, rising to vice president of JBU by the late 1930s. Helen and Richard were married in the east room of President Brown's home before a large number of faculty and friends.

On their wedding day, shortly after the vows were exchanged, a group of college boys crashed the celebration and took Richard and Helen for a joyride in an old car. The couple started their married lives together living in an apartment behind the college offices, until in early 1931 they moved into a little house built by some previous staff members across the street, on South Hill.

John Brown had a close relationship with his second daughter. "Probably not even his closest friends knew how much Mr. Brown missed his 'Wonderful Helen' as a companion and councilor," Miss Boudinot reflected. "He had learned to consult her for her viewpoint on so many matters."

One month before Helen's death, President and Mrs. Brown had returned from their latest sojourn in California. During a few short weeks in March 1931, John Brown would have his final opportunity to walk the campus with his daughter, seeking her advice and encouragement before he was once again off to California for an evangelistic campaign.

That campaign began in Fullerton, California, on Sunday, April 12. Brown finished the day's revival services with a feeling of great confidence that the meetings were going to have powerful results. The next morning, after going for a walk, he returned to his hotel and learned from the clerk that someone from Siloam Springs had been calling for him long distance. "That announcement carried with it an awful threat," Brown later said, and it took him some time to secure a return phone connection and find out the news.

His oldest daughter, Jean Elizabeth, came on the line and told her father that Helen had been sick for a week. They had not thought it was serious, and indeed she had seemed to be getting better, but that very morning she had suddenly taken a turn. Jean told her father that the doctors did not expect Helen to live.

John Brown no doubt had a frantic, worrying few hours as he tried to determine how best to get home. First, he drove the few miles north to Los Angeles, stopped by his western office, and put in another call to Siloam. This time, he was able to speak with the doctors, who told him even graver news—they did not think Helen would live through the afternoon. He headed for the train station and bought an 11:00 a.m. ticket headed east. By 6:00 p.m., with the sun lowering behind him, and a darkening sky ahead, his train stopped in Yuma, Arizona. There he was handed a telegram. His wonderful Helen had died a few hours before.

For a moment, everything went black. "Returning to my train, I sat for some time questioning whether it was not all a dream, a horrible dream that would pass," he recalled. "I need not tell those who have passed through similar experiences what happened in that hour. What an unspeakable weakness comes over one. How the whole world seemed to reel." Then Brown struggled with the question in his mind: "After preaching to others a Christ sufficient to every hour of need, . . . will the faith you have preached with such confidence to others sustain you?"

Letting what Brown called an "unnameable loneliness" grip him, after a short while "there came a great surge of strength! . . . Then, out of the calm and quiet peace of that hour, there came the assurance, doubly sure, 'Helen is just a little way ahead!'"

Thursday morning, a service was held on the lawn in front of the Brown home, where Mayfield women's dormitory stands today. Pastors and faculty stood on the home's front porch, speaking of Helen's sweet, unselfish life. John Brown himself spoke, and on that glorious spring day, with bright sky, flowers blooming, and birds singing all around, the evangelist and father proclaimed the hope of the resurrection.

About sixty girls of the student body, wearing the blue uniform Helen had designed, carried flowers in a procession across the road to the mausoleum, where Helen's body was laid to rest. The flowers had been sent in as condolences by friends from a dozen states, but before the girls could place them around Helen's casket, John Brown said, "No, were she alive, I know what she would want. Let all the flowers be carried to the dormitories and sent throughout the rooms, that the students may enjoy their beauty and fragrance." To him, Helen's life had been as beautiful as any life could be, this side of eternity.[2]

For the young husband, Richard Hodges, a love for the school and the community that his wife had loved surely sustained him. It wasn't long before he was seen helping others enjoy life there, even dressing up as an unlikely farmer to drive other recently returned newlyweds around the campus in a hay wagon. And in 1933, Richard took perhaps the first moving-picture footage in the school's history and provided an entertaining show of scenes about the campus. In 1938, more than seven years after Helen's death, Richard Hodges remarried. He remained closely involved with the school into the 1940s.

A new building on campus, already underway at the time of Helen's death, would soon be named the Helen Brown Hodges Memorial Building, and would later be adorned by a great tablet over the entryway inscribed, "Helen—the First." The building was itself a symbol of resurrection, as it was constructed largely from the carefully demolished remains of the original white building, whose time had finally come to an end. The new structure would provide dormitory and classroom space, and a chapel for the student body for much of the next twenty years. It would eventually become known in later decades simply as the "MO Dorm." In front of it, other memorials would be erected over the years, including a sundial established in honor of Dr. Isaac Lowe, and the stone from Lone Elm where young ministerial student Paul Loescher had prayed every Sunday morning before his death in the summer of 1927. The Memorial Building stood for more than four decades at the heart of campus. When it was finally demolished in its turn in the 1970s, it made way for the modern-day open quad of grass and tree-lined sidewalks, where new generations of students would relax and play.

***

In fall of 1931, English citizen Howard Keech arrived as a twenty-four-year-old married student. As was so often the case in the early years of the college, the skills he brought with him resulted in his quickly taking on a junior staff role. Keech had already spent time working professionally as a printer in California, and he had spent his childhood in Central America, where his English father was a missionary and distributor of Christian literature and tracts.

Keech's mother was American, and his two siblings were born during the family's mission terms in El Salvador, but Howard was born in England during a family furlough in his father's native country. After his father died during Howard's high school years, Howard and the rest of the family took up permanent residence in California.

Howard and his wife Helen arrived at JBU in the fall of 1931, and within weeks he became the assistant manager of John Brown's printing department. In January 1932, he began teaching a printing course for the high school students. Miss Boudinot recorded one inventive display put on by the printing students that semester: "A unique program was given at the chapel hour telling in a clever way of the work in the shop and immediately after the program, the paper, the *Astonisher*, was distributed as though just from the press as an extra."[3]

Howard interrupted his time at JBU when he had to return to California for a few years in the mid-1930s, but he and Helen eventually returned, and Howard served several years on staff as a faculty member, yearbook advisor, and director of University Press. Later, he became vice president of the JBU alumni association.

The Keeches participated together in musical programs at the school, and on one occasion Howard was part of a group of male faculty and staff members who, with great fanfare, donned dainty aprons and served the ladies of the school a Sunday breakfast.[4]

***

The year 1934 brought the watershed moment of the school's becoming a four-year degree-granting institution, and thus John Brown University was officially and enduringly established.

The decision to expand the John Brown schools' offerings into a four-year degree program was based on several considerations. Many of the students who had been attracted to the college because of their limited financial resources ended up with few options to continue their education beyond the two-year junior college program they had taken at John Brown. And since students filled so many of the working roles within the many campus industries, there was the problem of constant turnover, where the best-trained and most effective workers departed every two years. The founder realized that there was both an economy of scale and a greater impact on ministry and professions that could be achieved by applying for approval from the state of Arkansas to offer bachelor's degree programs.

The John Brown schools thus became a university of three colleges, as well as the associated high school academies where students in the state-authorized teacher-education program could practice what they learned. The three colleges were a liberal-arts-oriented John E. Brown College; a hands-on, technically oriented John E. Brown Vocational College; and a Bible training school called the Siloam School of the Bible, which had been in existence as a part of the John Brown campuses since the earliest days of the institution. With these 1934 amendments to the institution's articles of incorporation, the university was now authorized by the state of Arkansas to grant bachelor of arts, bachelor of science, and bachelor of theology degrees. The high school academy programs, in various forms, would continue at the Arkansas JBU properties until the early 1950s.[5]

That first year after becoming a university, 1934–1935, produced thirty-five members of JBU's inaugural graduating class of seniors. These were students who had attended the two final years of the school's existence as a purely junior college, as well as taken advanced junior-level classes that had been introduced the prior year, and thus were able to complete the requirements for a bachelor's degree within the first year of JBU's existence as a four-year college. The graduation speaker that day in May 1935 was Dr. Louis T. Talbot, president of the Bible Institute of Los Angeles—known today as Biola University—and pastor of Los Angeles's Church of the Open Door. The founder's relationship with this Southern California church went back several years, and he had spent a month in 1929 as a featured speaker at the church every Sunday. The church itself traced its lineage back to Dwight L. Moody, whose evangelistic methods were held in such high regard by Brown during his own early days of evangelistic ministry.

A week after JBU's momentous first senior graduation, John Brown dedicated his newest radio venture, the newly acquired one-thousand-watt radio station KUOA. That first broadcast was an all-day program hosted in Fayetteville, Arkansas, but within a month, KUOA began broadcasting from Siloam Springs, with new JBU graduate Storm H. Whaley—son of the Sulphur Springs banker—as the station manager. The station would be owned and operated by John Brown University for the next seventy years, providing a strong new vocational program for students in radio.

The history of the KUOA call letters does indeed originate, as it might seem, with the "U of A"—University of Arkansas—since the state's flagship university originally owned the station. But the station later passed into the ownership of the Fulbright family of Fayetteville, who in turn sold the station to John Brown.

It wasn't until a year after the purchase, in the spring of 1936, that JBU received permission to move the KUOA transmitter to Siloam Springs and increase its power to twenty-five hundred watts. The founder was able to raise $40,000 in the space of just one week to make the move happen. Soon, the school broke ground on the KUOA building—a simple structure with hints of art deco style on the outskirts of campus—which would house station operations for many years; and in November of 1936, the accompanying 450-foot-tall "Rod of God" radio tower began sending JBU's Christian programming across the airwaves.

Perhaps symbolically, John Brown the evangelist held the last major citywide revival meetings of his life in California in July 1936—just a month after breaking ground on the KUOA radio building. As one era of his ministry life ended, so another was beginning with hardly a moment's pause.

As an AM radio station (FM radio was in its infancy in 1936), KUOA had the power to be received and heard well beyond the horizon, especially at night. KUOA had "pre-sunrise" authority for the start of their broadcast day, and so John Brown could begin his teaching broadcast as early as five in the morning and be heard literally all across the midwestern United States.

One story provides a glimpse of the impact Brown's radio ministry had on the future of the university. A Texas oilman named Murray Sells was sitting in his car early one morning, listening to the radio while watching an oil rig, when he heard John Brown preaching on KUOA about the value of Christian higher education. As a result, Sells included JBU in his estate for a substantial gift that helped to build the Sells Gymnasium on campus, which for nearly fifty years was the main intercollegiate athletic venue for JBU's basketball and volleyball teams. Though a much larger gymnasium—the Bill George Arena—was built adjacent to the older gym in 2010, the Murray Sells gym stands today and continues to be used for a variety of athletic activities.

***

John E. Brown Sr.'s vision for a college that maintained both high academic standards and a robust vocational program to prepare students for the world of work was sometimes a difficult balance to explain. Students were required to work in vocational training positions on the JBU campus for the first several decades of the institution. At the same time, the university was seeking to recruit faculty with strong academic preparation in major fields and in the liberal arts.

There was a constant tension in the early years between a somewhat derogatory idea—that the school was just a place for poor students who had to work to earn their seat in the classroom—and the actual vision of the founder—that work was noble, and the chief earthly aim of an education was to equip youth to be productive with their lives in all respects. Newspaper articles from the time frequently showed this misunderstanding, and Brown spent much time over the years making speaking tours where he emphasized a more accurate view of his threefold educational ideal.

One important part of winning this reputational struggle was to grow a corps of quality faculty and staff on the JBU campus who brought keen minds and compassionate hearts, along with their credentials, to the academic program. Many of those early faculty were drawn to the campus by the founder's personal charisma and vision for what would someday be realized, but was not yet fully in place.

The establishment of John Brown's college in Siloam Springs as a full-fledged university in 1934 brought increased attention to the need for a highly educated faculty, and one addition that year in the Mathematics Department was a woman with a PhD from the University of California, Dr. Nina Moore. While she did not remain at JBU for long, she would leave an impact on one of her brightest students that year—Roger Cox, who would go on to be an integral part of the university for more than forty years.

Cox had grown up and gone to high school in Gentry, Arkansas, a few miles north of Siloam Springs. He entered John E. Brown College in 1930 and graduated from the junior college program two years later. But even though he wanted to continue pursuing an engineering degree, the Great Depression found him back at home after graduation, working as an auto mechanic. Two years later, when John Brown University was established, he eagerly returned, hoping to finish all of the required engineering courses for a bachelor's degree in just one busy year. Unfortunately for those dreams, JBU wasn't offering the courses he needed, so he opted to finish out a mathematics degree under Dr. Nina Moore's instruction instead.

Roger Cox

He passed, with high marks, a number of Dr. Moore's classes during that school year, and was successfully on track to earn his mathematics degree in May 1935, before he had yet turned twenty-one. Cox tended to think of himself as "young, frightened and ignorant" as a college student, but the faculty and administration of JBU saw in him something that went well beyond his modest self-perception. Before the end of the spring semester, JBU invited him to pursue a graduate degree in mathematics and then return to teach.

Just weeks earlier, Cox recalled, "under the ministry of Dr. John E. Brown, the founder, many of us were challenged to surrender our lives to Jesus Christ to serve wherever He should lead us." When the offer came to join the JBU faculty after a course of advanced studies, Cox said, "This was taken as the leading of the Lord and gladly accepted."

Cox made quick, brilliant work of his master's degree, completing all of the mathematics courses at Oklahoma A&M (the future Oklahoma State University) in just one year. Then, a mere twelve months after leaving JBU with his bachelor's degree, he was back and teaching mathematics at JBU for the summer term in May 1936, at just twenty-one years old.

"I was still young, still frightened, and surprisingly ignorant," he recalled, but "I loved this work and gave myself to it." His graduate advisor in Oklahoma had told him that he was better prepared for his graduate study than most of the graduates of Oklahoma A&M itself, thanks to the quality of the education he had received at JBU. He humbly insisted, "Many thanks were due Dr. Moore." For the next forty-four years, until his retirement in 1980, he would become a key contributor, both as a professor and administrator, in making sure this same quality education was provided to future generations of John Brown University students.[6]

In the fall of 1937, Cox joined the school's famed Ozarkians male singing quartet. The group had formed in 1932 with four students, including founding members Robert Jackson at second tenor and Storm H. Whaley at bass, and over its first five years they became a radio sensation, often traveling with the founder on his speaking tours. A few different students had taken the first tenor and baritone slots over the years, but by late 1937, the group had been disbanded for a few months after two of its members graduated. When one of them, first tenor Donnis Turner, returned to join Jackson and Whaley on the JBU staff, Cox became the fourth and final member of the reconstituted quartet as its permanent baritone singer. Together, the 1937 roster of the Ozarkians would become a fixture of the JBU experience for almost fifty years.

***

Among the PhD's recruited to join the newly constituted university was thirty-year-old biologist Dr. Irvin A. Wills. He and his wife Ruth—who had taken advanced studies in the Latin language and violin—joined the faculty of the academic college in 1935. They had each studied at the University of Iowa, where the couple met while completing their graduate degrees, and when they arrived on campus after their journey, the only money they had to go along with all their worldly possessions was three cents.

Their teaching contract with JBU allotted them a salary of $100 per month, with an apartment and meals provided for them on campus. Ruth Wills did not have a glowing first impression of the buildings of the school—they seemed to be "all wood." In fact, fires were a recurring hazard during the early decades of the school, some of which would prove to be quite costly.

During the Willses' first semester on campus in the fall of 1935, two tragedies were narrowly averted. R. C. Abraham, a vocational department head who had sent three of his sons to the schools for the last several years, was seriously injured while setting dynamite to tree stumps that were slated for removal behind California dorm. Two years earlier, Mr. Abraham had endured another grizzly accident at the campus sorghum mill, which had resulted in the amputation of his hand. After the dynamite accident, he was hospitalized for several days.

The second emergency arose in the first few days of November. The weather had begun to cool, and heavy

Dr. Irvin A. Wills

Students and staff work to control a fire that destroyed
the small mechanical shop building.

rains had soaked the campus. On November 4, as the student body was finishing
supper in the California basement's dining hall, a cry of "fire!" came from outside. Those who rushed out of supper saw smoke and flame rising from a small
outbuilding that sat at the rear of the quadrangle formed between the "Helen
the First" memorial and the mechanical buildings. The outbuilding was near a
tall water tower that had been erected the year before. In this burning structure
was the campus's auxiliary power plant, an acetylene welding shop, and the auto
mechanics shop, along with other machinery. Above the work floor was a storage
attic filled with additional combustibles, where it was later thought the fire had
started.

The campus fire brigade began their work to extinguish the flames, but the
night's winds made the firefighting hard and put the campus's other wooden
buildings at grave risk. Soon the flames were threatening to leap across the short
distance to the Memorial Building, and the difficult decision was made to begin
evacuating valuables from it, in anticipation of its loss. Students and staff marched
into the chapel at the rear of the building, saving pictures and art—including a

painting of Helen gifted to the school at the building's official dedication the year before—and a new Cable-Nelson Concert Grand Piano. As volunteers carried the school's important possessions out into the cold night air, the wind suddenly shifted. Fortunately, the danger to "Helen the First" had passed.

The fire had burned the small mechanical shop building to the ground, and the recent heavy rains had probably prevented fires in the surrounding structures. As the flames were brought under control and the campus fire crew set up their overnight watch to monitor the smoldering rubble, the season's first frost set in. The next morning, student crews picked through the cold wreckage, salvaging what machinery they could and hauling off the debris.[7]

***

In the spring of 1936, another of the new generation of university professors, possessing strong academic credentials and destined for a long tenure with the university, arrived in Siloam Springs with his family. Calling the move an act of "foolhardy faith at the call of God," Dr. Earl C. Smith brought his wife and their six children—ranging in age from high school graduate to one-year-old baby—to John Brown University from their home in Abilene, Texas. "Our whole interest in the move was the John Brown Schools," he wrote many years later. "We had six children to educate, and they were too precious to us to trust to non-Christian schools."

Dr. Smith was a Bible scholar, experienced in New Testament Greek, and by the time of his retirement from JBU in 1961 he had been the chairman of the school's Division of Bible and Religion for more than half the history of the university. He was to become an anchor for the school's convictions on the divine origin and authority of the Bible, and the simplicity of true Christian philosophy without any denominational bias.

But in 1936, he was just a forty-two-year-old man in a new town, with a family to feed, an aspiration for his children's education, a strong faith in God, and no job. "We must stay here twenty years until our baby finishes college," he told his wife. Soon John Brown University found a place for him among the faculty.

In his scholarship, Dr. Smith would come to emphasize the difference between Christian faith and Christian systems of theology, and he was firmly in line with the founder's wish that the college remain nonsectarian. "It is my conviction that any church or Christian school that commits its people to a system of theology does them a disservice," he wrote. John Brown University had never done so, and had committed only to the faith itself. Smith expressed the freedom he felt during his more than two decades of service in the school's Bible Department when he

John Brown orchestra; printing press; Arkansas building; Helen the First building; Simon Sager Cabin

Clockwise from top left: The Women's Drum Corps; vocational training; early uniforms; dorm life; auto mechanic shop; the cannery

Clockwise from top left: The electrical shop; members of the Ministerial Club; a girls trio from the 1930s; Jesse Jones Day in 1938

Clockwise from top left: students, faculty and staff from 1930; women's dining hall; California building dedication; students in the 1930s; graduating class of 1935

Siloam Springs Main Street in the 1920s; students in the 1920s and 30s; John Brown Sr. and Juanita Brown

Dr. Earl Smith teaches class in the Memorial Building.

wrote, toward the end of his career, "We are Bible-centered, not theological-system-centered. No place on earth could I have been freer to express what I think the Bible teaches on any subject, nor is there any place where I could have been freer to change my opinion about what it teaches without losing my standing in the University, as long as I am committed to Christian faith."

He grew close to John Brown Sr., and in later years it was said that as Smith's hair whitened with age, he seemed to mirror both the appearance and the philosophy of the founder. "I learned to know Dr. John E. Brown Sr., close up," Smith wrote a few years after the founder's death. "He was a man of great courage and perseverance, wrought of a profound love for God and men."

Perhaps Smith's earliest opportunity to marvel at the strength of the founder's character came in the summer of 1937, around the time Smith was brought onto the faculty.

Sunday, July 11, 1937, was the opening day of the twenty-fourth annual Summer Bible Conference, held that year in both Sulphur Springs and on the JBU campus. At the time, Brown's wife and youngest children were in California, while he carried on in Arkansas with his many obligations to the conference and the schools. During his first sermon that day, John Brown spoke on a series of "alls" found in the Great Commission—how Christ provided "all authority" to go into "all nations" and teach "all things" of his gospel. After Brown's talk, one of the visiting speakers, Dr. Harry M. Lintz of Moody Bible Institute, took to the podium to give an uplifting message on immortality through Christ. Had those in the audience listened intently enough during a pause in Lintz's sermon, they might have heard a telephone ring in the distance. Turning, they might have seen Brown quietly step out to take an urgent call.

As Lintz brought his message to a close, he quoted from the book of Job the poignant question, "If a man die, shall he live again?" At that, Brown emerged and stepped to the front of the meeting hall. His countenance was serious, his face pale. But he was calm. He quietly began, "I believe that and have preached it." But his faith and reliance on that truth was about to be tested once again. Brown told the audience he had just received a long-distance phone call from California, bearing the news that his youngest daughter, twenty-two-year-old Juanita—named after her mother and known in her childhood simply as "Little Sister"—had given premature birth to a baby boy and was suddenly lying at the brink of death.[8]

Soon after, Brown retired to his room, where he sat alone all night, Bible in his lap, telephone at his side, waiting for word. If ever it had seemed cruel to him that he had lost one of his daughters to a sudden illness while he did God's work a thousand miles away, surely it must have seemed unbearable to face such loneliness a second time.

But in the morning, with no news yet of his daughter's condition worsening, Brown determined that he must continue in the work God had put before him. He continued with the Bible conference, preaching a few more times during the week. A planned business meeting with students and staff was held as scheduled, and the founder stood before them, as Miss Boudinot recalled, "with great fortitude." He told them the work was larger than anything he personally faced, and it would not be neglected.

Only when the summer Bible conference had closed did he journey to be with his family in California. Young Juanita lay in a near coma, and for more than a month there was great uncertainty as to whether she would ever recover. During this time, Brown continued his work, meeting his appointments and conducting his regular radio ministry. It was an extraordinarily busy summer, since it had been only a few months since he had acquired two new institutions in Southern California, which would soon join the John Brown schools system. His steadfast faith in God carried him through, and his messages over the airwaves during these weeks of anguish were later compiled into a volume he called *The Why of Suffering*.

In time, Brown's youngest daughter regained her health. For a new Bible faculty member such as Dr. Earl C. Smith, who had himself walked in such extravagant faith to bring his family into the community of John Brown University, the steadfast courage displayed by the founder in this time must have been inspiring to behold.

***

Brown's busy slate of obligations during that trying summer of 1937 was due in part to the acquisition of two schools in Southern California—The San Diego Army and Navy Academy for Boys, and the Girls' Collegiate Institute of Glendora, California. He had been asked somewhat frequently over the years to open other schools under his ideals, but he had always resisted the requests, even when existing school properties were offered to him. He felt that John Brown University in Siloam Springs needed to be "definitely and permanently established," Boudinot said, "before he could have part in others." With Brown feeling that the time was finally right, and with the promise of additional income to be generated for the school system from these two Southern California preparatory schools, Brown closed on the deals in April 1937.

The San Diego Army and Navy Academy for Boys had been in existence since 1910 and had gained a reputation as "The West Point of the West," but its forty-acre campus was in foreclosure, and as Brown took over its ownership and administration, the news came that it had lost its ROTC charter from the War Department. This school, which was still in operation when Brown acquired it, was renamed Brown Military Academy.

The Glendora school had been dormant for a few years by 1937, though its history extended back to 1892. The scenic fifty-acre campus was owned by friends of Brown who were in poor health, and they sold the school property to him for a bargain price. This school was renamed the Brown School for Girls and would reopen, along with the Brown Military Academy, in September 1937. Both institutions were pay schools, generating income for the overall John Brown schools system.

Less than two weeks after returning to Siloam Springs in April 1937 with the news of these school acquisitions, Brown was off again to Houston to meet with Jesse Jones, now a powerful figure in the administration of President Franklin D. Roosevelt. It would be this old friend who used his influence in government to help get Brown Military Academy reauthorized as an ROTC school with the War Department. Within a few years, the school's reputation as a quality preparatory academy for military officers would be resoundingly affirmed—by 1944, it had set a record for the highest marks achieved in its War Department evaluation, and after the war it earned the Military Institute rating.[9]

Brown maintained an active role as the president of each of these schools in

Brown Military Academy in California

both Arkansas and California for two years. Miss Boudinot, as well, split her time between the two states, helping to establish the libraries of the California schools. By early 1939, President Brown relinquished his active presidential duties over the western schools, and he entrusted them to administrators who had several years of association with JBU and who could take over the larger duties in California.

***

In early March 1938, Brown stepped off the train in Siloam Springs and returned to JBU, having spent the past two months in California supervising the western schools' first year of progress. He urgently desired to see JBU gain accreditation as the first university of vocational study in the nation, and taking action in this direction was firmly on his mind. Students of JBU who wanted to transfer to the University of Arkansas or enter its graduate school were often finding that some or all of the work they had done at JBU counted for nothing toward a degree from the state school. He soon went to Little Rock and met with Governor Carl Bailey and state education officials, including the leadership of the University of Arkansas, impressing on them the unique virtues of the college he had founded. The meeting was generally positive, but upon leaving, it was clear that Brown still had work to do for the accreditation process to gain any momentum.

As he had done on so many previous occasions when his schools needed help, Brown turned his thoughts to his old friend Jesse Jones. But beyond simply asking Jones for his assistance, Brown envisioned something—an event—that would both honor his dear friend, who had been such a faithful supporter of the schools, and also elevate the public's impression of the Siloam Springs campus on a scale never before attempted.

But to bring such an event about, he needed the help and support of surrounding communities. To lay this groundwork, Brown gathered the Ozarkian Quartet—composed of former students and current staff members Donnis Turner, Roger Cox, Robert Jackson, and Storm H. Whaley—and set off on a goodwill tour of music and speaking throughout Northwest Arkansas and parts of Oklahoma. For several weeks he visited local towns, stirring up interest in the university and for the grand event he had planned, while behind the scenes countless administrative details were attended to, and invitations were sent to notable figures. Finally it could be officially announced that the school's nineteenth commencement day, to be held on Thursday, May 12, 1938, would be a gala spectacle for the public known as "Jesse Jones Day."

The campus was spruced up for the occasion throughout the spring. A giant star-shaped layout of hedges and bluebonnet flowers was tended to, having been planted by the students of the Texas Club in 1931 and featuring the name of Jesse H. Jones in the center of the landscaping; the college seniors, as their class gift, laid down a fresh concrete sidewalk leading to the new recreation building and gymnasium that had opened at the start of the school year; and the high school seniors erected an attractive rock gateway at the entry to the campus. As the day neared, the young men of the Brown Military Academy band loaded up their instruments and parade-ground uniforms and boarded the train that would bring them to Arkansas from San Diego.

Then, in the predawn hours of Thursday, May 12, a light rain fell. State police officers gathered at key points on the roads near the JBU campus and along the Tulsa highway. Newspapermen from distant metropolitan cities roused themselves from their hotel beds in town and made their way to the campus, perhaps riding on the small Dodge bus JBU operated between campus and town, where a trip down the newly paved West University Street cost a nickel's fare.

A great tent, able to hold some five thousand people, stood at the brow of the hill where a cathedral would one day be erected. As the rain lifted and dawn broke, cars began to arrive—hundreds of them. People from the surrounding areas, rich and poor, all having experienced their own trials during the recent hard years of the Depression, were coming to see President Roosevelt's "New Deal banker"—the man who, according to America's Vice President John Garner, had loaned out more money "than any other man in the history of the world." For in 1933, at the depths of the Great Depression, after thousands of banks had failed and millions of Americans had seen their life savings vanish, newly elected President Roosevelt had given Jesse Jones the chairmanship of an entity called the Reconstruction Finance Corporation—and with it, the power to distribute literally billions of dollars to keep banks afloat. He had been featured on the cover of *Time* magazine, and would soon be hailed in other publications as the one-man "fourth branch of government."

And now, Jesse Jones, staunch friend of JBU, convert to Christianity under the ministry of its founder, and shepherd of the nation's economy into its gradual recovery, had arrived in Siloam Springs, finally to be welcomed to the campus he had given so much to.

The special train, pulled by a Kansas City Southern engine to the depot in town, disembarked not only Jones but also officials of the railroad and its president Harvey Couch, himself a great friend of the university. With them to offer special invocations for the day was Dr. William Bell Riley, the seventy-seven-year-old Minnesotan Baptist minister, frequent speaker at John Brown's summer Bible conferences, and founder of the Northwestern Bible and Missionary Training School (a school that, nine years later, Riley would, on his deathbed, personally hand over to the leadership of the great future evangelist Billy Graham).

Arriving also to hear Jones give the commencement address were Arkansas Governor Carl Bailey and Ernest W. Marland, governor of Oklahoma, with their police protection details. The weather cleared, and the day became perfect. Some fourteen hundred automobiles had made their way toward campus and were systematically directed by state police into parking areas. The tent filled to overflowing, with additional thousands of people gathering nearby; it was estimated that eight thousand people were on campus that morning.

More than fifty college graduates entered in cap and gown, the Brown Military Academy band from San Diego provided music, and as Jesse Jones finally stepped to the lectern to give the commencement address, radio microphones carried his speech across a network of twenty stations. Jones provided a message that paid tribute to John Brown University and its vocational, God-honoring ethic. He spoke on the large issues facing the nation, and in a time where fascism was rising in Europe and war was engulfing the Far East, he emphasized the need in America for leaders who respected God and were trained to work.[10]

Before the morning's ceremony closed, whimsical gifts constructed by the university's various vocational shops were distributed in a humorous presentation to several of the day's distinguished guests: Dr. Riley received an enormous pencil; Mr. Jones was presented with a five-foot-tall screwdriver; the visiting governors were each given a commemorative gavel; and a Mrs. James from Louisiana, who was recognized with an honorary degree in home economics, received a huge rolling pin.

The ceremony concluded, and the crowd dispersed. Some visited the vocational departments and the special exhibit hall that had been set up in the new recreation building. The vast tent was rearranged for the serving of a luncheon banquet with tables

Jesse Jones and John Brown Sr.

and seating for twelve hundred. In the afternoon, another program was begun for the formal dedication of the three-year-old KUOA radio station, recently increased in power to five thousand watts. Praising the use of this technology to spread the gospel and educational programs throughout the region, Dr. Riley gave a talk called "The Spirit of Invention," highlighting the important need for practical men who could apply the gifts of scientific theory; he marveled that over the previous half century, inventions had become so bewildering that the public had ceased to be surprised by the advances.[11]

***

After the rousing success of Jesse Jones Day, President Brown kept up his efforts to gain state accreditation for JBU. He was frequently campaigning on the issue from his radio platforms, and in June he made an astounding series of cross-country trips to press forward on the issue as well as sustain all of his other obligations. He had returned to California shortly after the May 12 commencement gala, then was back in Sulphur Springs in mid-June to open the summer Bible conference. A few days after the conference opened, he was in Washington, DC, to meet with Dr. John Ward Studebaker, the United States Commissioner of Education. After this meeting, he raced back to Siloam Springs for the second half of the Bible conference, then went right back to DC again. On this second trip east he convened not only with Dr. Studebaker but also with Arkansas governor Carl Bailey and Jesse Jones.

If the sheer pace of travel could translate directly into institutional momentum, then perhaps John Brown's tireless motion during June gained some concrete results. On July 11, Governor Bailey sent the state's commissioner of education Dr. T. H. Alford, along with an examining committee, to study the curriculum, policies, and practices of John Brown University. Before the month was out, the committee had delivered their recommendations for further development of the university, including improved equipment, faculty, and library holdings. Through this JBU gained conditional state accreditation.

While the state's accreditation finding would unfold over the course of two probationary years, the University of Arkansas at Fayetteville continued to resist full recognition of transfer credits until 1941.

***

Among the requirements of Alford's examining committee in 1938 was for JBU to provide a practice school for its teacher-education majors. The school at Sulphur Springs fulfilled a part of this role. But just after New Year's Day 1940, the Sulphur Springs academy suffered its worst setback, which would necessitate John Brown's high school programs being once again consolidated on the Siloam Springs campus until after the end of World War II. Around eight in the morning of January 2, fire broke out in the large, three-story, rock-walled building that was the centerpiece of the Sulphur school and summer resort.

Mabel Whaley of Sulphur Springs, long a supporter of the John Brown schools, witnessed the fire and wrote to President Brown the next day of what she saw. She was the widow of Storm O. Whaley, the Sulphur Springs banker and later Arkansas state senator who had facilitated John Brown's acquisition of the Sulphur properties more than fifteen years earlier. Mr. Whaley had died after a car crash in 1933.

Mrs. Whaley wrote to President Brown, who was at the time in California, "I want you to know that the men of the town led by the Mayor fought hard for hours in the freezing weather, many of them drenched and their clothes frozen. . . . It was the coldest morning of the winter and the water would actually freeze as it hit the stone on the outside while it was burning on the inside." Being the postmaster of Sulphur Springs, Mrs. Whaley periodically ran outside her office throughout the morning to watch the battle. "I fear the whole attic was on fire before it was discovered. . . . There was no wind and it just ate the roof away like a corrugated paste board box."

After the fire, Mrs. Whaley's son announced on KUOA's evening broadcast that the building had burned, and his mother said, "Storm expressed so much better than I can . . . that while there is a catch in our throats at the damage to a beautiful structure which has been the pride of the whole area since the early part of the 20th century, so far overshadowing this is our thankfulness to God that no child, staff member or townsman was injured." She no doubt recalled the time, seven years earlier, when a fire had broken out in the teachers' cottage at Sulphur before dawn one morning. The teachers had barely escaped on that occasion, and all their possessions were lost. Mrs. Whaley continued, "Fear grips our hearts when we think what might have been if it had come in the dead of night with all the children back from their holiday vacation."[12]

The following day, as snow fell, one of the town's old-timers, a stonemason who had helped erect the building decades earlier, saw that the fire had caused little damage to the two-foot-thick walls, though the interior was gutted. Restoring the building was possible.

In the near term, the loss of the Sulphur Springs building as a home for the academy would become a blessing in disguise. When America joined in fighting World War II, the JBU campus would see a drastic decline in the male student population. With the Sulphur Springs high school academy forced to return to the Siloam campus—less than a year before the first military conscription measures were signed into law—the university's vocational industries would still have an ample supply of male student workers even when, late in the war, the men enrolled at the college level dwindled to a handful.

Another fire struck the Siloam campus later the same year, which would be especially memorable in the mind of Ruth Wills. On a Saturday night in May 1940, two weeks before commencement, fire broke out in the top floor of the alumni building where the science laboratories were housed. On the floor below was the campus laundry. Dr. Irvin Wills, in addition to his teaching duties as the school's biology professor, was the academic dean of the college at the time, a role he took just two years after his and Ruth's arrival in 1935. Ruth knew her husband loved his biology work, loved nature, loved gardening; but if he had any hobby, it was his work at the university. He was known for keeping long hours, and on at least one occasion, Ruth had to walk from their home up to the campus in the middle of the night to retrieve him from his lab, where he had fallen asleep.

The fire on that Saturday night was first discovered in the chemistry lab. Chemicals and lab equipment burned, and members of the campus community rushed to save machinery from the laundry below. Smoke and water filled the upper floor. And at the side of the building, with a ladder rising to the upper windows, was Dr. Irvin Wills, going up and down the ladder saving his books. Ruth would have the mental picture of her husband—so devoted to preserving his science that night—vividly in her mind for years to come. The building was ultimately saved, and other than the destruction in the chemistry lab, most of the damage was due to water and smoke. The floors were eventually fully remodeled, and the building endured for another seventy-one years.[13]

Les Wright, Roger Cox, and Harry Lehman broadcasting a high school ball game on KUOA in June 1937.

CHAPTER 6

THE CRUCIBLE OF WORLD WAR II

As the 1930s drew to a close, the financial needs of the university became ever more urgent. The fact that many loans from the earliest years of the school were now coming due, some twenty years after its founding, was beginning to weigh heavily on the founder.

In the 1930s the school began publishing a monthly pamphlet called the *John Brown University Bulletin* (the forerunner of the modern *Brown Bulletin* magazine), which was sent to thousands of donors, radio listeners, friends, and alumni of the John Brown schools. While some issues did present the occasional notable piece of news or update on campus happenings—such as the growth of JBU's aviation program—the bulletin was usually dominated by President Brown's discussion of the school's financial and equipment needs, with frequent entreaties for donors to join in the school's good work.

As war spread across Europe and American society began shifting from an isolationist stance toward a sense of inevitability that the United States would become directly involved, John Brown's writings in the *Bulletin* began to reflect his sense of the war. He had received criticism from some for acquiring a military academy, "on the ground that a military school repudiated Christ and everything for which the Christian church stood."[1] He responded to this criticism in 1940: "I stand just where I have always stood and pledge our schools to the same ideals to which they were pledged twenty-one years ago, and that is, the highest standards of Christian training to protect the nation, whatever the crisis the nation might face."[2] He likened the training of police officers to the training of an effective military force—both existed to protect innocents from evil. "And just there I challenge the pacifist, whoever he is, or the peace-at-any-price advocate to stop and face facts. . . . If it is patriotic and Christian to build schools in America to train courageous men for every department of law enforcement . . . then it is ten thousand times more patriotic to build great schools—great military schools— for Christian leadership to protect this nation against the plunderer and the kidnapper and the murderer who may come from other lands!"[3]

He extended the question of his wartime educational ideals even further, asking what would happen to thousands of college-age men after the war's end. He commented optimistically at one point, over a year before Pearl Harbor had drawn America fully into World War II, that it seemed likely the war in Europe could end before America's mobilized young men ever had a chance to fire a shot in anger. How would these boys, who had been trained up to be fighting men at a young age, find their way back to productive service in society? The answers were bound up in his philosophies of vocational education: Those who were already trained to work productively would surely be needed in the reconstruction of a devastated Europe; those boys whose only adult experience was in the training regimen of Army life would need schools, such as JBU, where they could be "trained to live."[4]

And so, in the season of war's gathering storm, with a vision for how threefold education would be vital to both the youth of America and, by extension, the world, John Brown urgently sought the financial support his university needed to avert its own looming debt crisis. He would later write of the period that it was "probably . . . the darkest period of my life and the hardest."[5] With ordinary fundraising work failing to bring long-term financial security into view, he addressed the university's friends and alumni with a triumphant message of trust: "God can."[6]

Brown launched two measures to firm up the university's financial footing. First, in January 1941, he announced the formation of a donor society called the "Master Builders of America," where participants could pledge as little as $1 per year. Membership soon exceeded his goal of ten thousand new contributors to the endowment of the school. Second, in July 1941, the university took advantage of the federal Chandler Act—a revised bankruptcy law passed a few years earlier—which allowed institutions to restructure decades-old debt at the much lower interest rates of the day under supervision of a federal court. It was this latter course—seeking government oversight and approval of a restructuring scheme—that he said was the darkest, hardest period of his life and of the history of the schools. But late in 1941, the courts approved the restructuring plan and, true to his ideals, John Brown insisted that every old debt be paid off at 100 percent of its original value.

Progress was also finally being made toward fuller academic recognition in Arkansas, as in January 1941, the dean of the graduate school at the University of Arkansas in Fayetteville finally announced that for transfer students and graduate degree candidates, the credits they had earned at JBU would be accepted on an equal standing with those from any other college.

During this period, when war still remained over the horizon from America, John Brown wrote often in his bulletins about what he believed a Christian

American patriot stood for—"God, motherhood and honest toil." And when President Roosevelt spoke of America's becoming the "Arsenal of Democracy," John Brown wrote of democracy's need for a God-honoring people if it was to endure.[7] As to the "Arsenal" the nation was suddenly and rapidly building, John Brown firmly placed his university at the forefront of that effort through the fruits of industrial, vocational training.[8]

He did not crave war, of course. Yet "peace at any price" was not an option for him either, given the sad conquest of so many nations by the totalitarian enemy. "Look at Finland! Look at Norway! Look at Denmark! Look at Holland! Look at France! Look at Czechoslovakia! Look at Poland! Look at Ethiopia! Look at England! Does America want that?"[9]

***

As an institution, the most significant contribution the university at Siloam Springs made to the war effort was its pilot training program, which would ultimately be selected by the War Department as an introductory flight training facility for aviation cadets. Beginning in 1938 with the development of a small airstrip along Holly Street, on the far side of Oak Hill Cemetery from the campus, a fledgling aeronautics program took shape over the next two years. The Engineering Department acquired a wind tunnel and laboratory equipment, and the salvaged remains of a forty-five-horsepower Curtiss Junior were brought in for students to practice their aircraft fabrication and repair techniques. The little Curtiss two-seater was soon restored, with great pride, into certified flying condition.

Ground schooling for aviation and engineering students progressed during the program's first year. A second, larger airport was established across the Oklahoma state line about a mile from campus, and by the end of 1939 JBU had become the first school in Arkansas to earn the authorization of the federal government's Civil Aeronautics Authority (CAA) to offer pilot training. The CAA funded the first class of ten student pilots, who started their flight training around the beginning of 1940. A young man named Woodrow Wilson, a college senior, was JBU's first student pilot to make a solo flight. By the end of March 1940, all ten of the first class of students had successfully earned their civilian pilot's license, and over the next two years, more than one hundred additional JBU students would join these first ten as licensed pilots.

The school's flight program, consisting of two planes, narrowly escaped serious disaster near the end of the semester. On April 30, 1940, a powerful wind blew across town. At the small airport along Holly Street, the planes were secured inside the hangar, where three students also took shelter from the storm. Suddenly, the

Ten student pilots began their flight training at JBU in 1940.

roof of the hangar was ripped away. As it sailed across the road, the exposed planes were in serious danger of being tossed by the roaring winds. Two of the hangar's walls collapsed, and the three students grabbed hold of landing gear and wing struts in an attempt to manually tether the planes to the ground. The gale passed, the students were uninjured, and the only serious setback for the aviation program was the loss of the Holly Street hangar. It's replacement would soon be under construction by student vocational laborers at the large airport.

As these first student pilots were completing their training, the school secured the appearance of a famous aviation figure as a guest of honor during the upcoming 1940 commencement ceremonies. World War I fighter ace Eddie Rickenbacker, the top scoring American ace of that war, agreed to be a guest of the school and perform the dedication ceremony for the larger JBU airport across the state line.

Commencement day, May 24, 1940, saw forty-two college students graduate. In the afternoon, Eddie Rickenbacker spoke to a crowd of more than two thousand people at the airport, which now encompassed 120 acres, and had three runways up to a half mile in length. But before he had finished speaking, a heavy rain began to fall, according to the memory of one professor who was there.

That professor was Dr. John H. Panage, forty-year-old English instructor, and teacher of Greek for the Bible Department. Panage was from the Mediterranean island of Cyprus, and was just finishing his first year as a professor at JBU after having earned two master's degrees and a PhD during studies at universities throughout the United States—including Princeton. He was a confirmed bachelor, indeed would be so all of his life, and had lived in the boys' dorm during his first year at JBU. He would soon move in to the Park Hotel in downtown Siloam, where he could have a small space to himself for $16 per month, walking every day to campus. Panage had herded goats as a boy in the Cyprus mountains, stood in line waiting for bread during World War I, loved classic literature as a student, and had the soul of a poet-philosopher. He never managed to shed his exotic accent or feel like he had fully mastered the English language—though he had a PhD in English literature and would teach it till the day he retired. He yearned to contribute a major original work to the universe of English literature, but never quite found a starting point for any magnum opus. Instead, he kept diaries. Beloved for his wittiness, his occasional mangled idioms ("You hit the nail on the neck!"), and his pithy philosophical insights, he seemed the most unlikely of men to be drawn into service for the war.

Half a world away from the celebrants listening to Captain Rickenbacker at the JBU airfield, the German army was advancing deep into France, the British forces were retreating into a defensive perimeter around Dunkirk, and the United States was edging ever closer to the need for able-bodied young men to take up arms.

The draft for all men ages twenty-one to thirty-five was enacted in September, and later that fall, the government required that all students taking CAA-authorized pilot training courses, such as the one at JBU, to commit to joining the military after their training. October 16, 1940, saw many of the male students and several faculty members go downtown to register for the draft. These included academic dean Irvin Wills, printing professor Howard Keech, and Donnis Turner, one of the Ozarkian quartet.

The 1940–1941 school year unfolded with forty-nine university seniors pressing on toward graduation, and President Brown pressing forward with his Master Builders of America campaign and the plans for financial reorganization of the university under the Chandler Act. The aviation program had expanded to six aircraft, and the good news came in the middle of the year that the University of Arkansas was now recognizing JBU credits. Yet the looming prospect of war could not have been far from the minds of the campus community. In the summer of 1941, four young staff members, all former students, departed to enlist in the Marine Corps.

The start of 1942 should have been a time of great celebration for the JBU community with the immense relief that came from a successful financial reorganization under federal protections. Indeed, a "Victory Days" dinner was held on January 3, 1942, where slides were flashed on the screen proclaiming triumphantly, "Bills Payable: NONE. Salaries Payable: NONE. Notes Payable: NONE." John Brown Sr. told the audience, "We enter the year 1942 in the best financial condition of our history. That is to say, we have more assets and better recognition amongst the schools than at any other time since the first nail was driven."[10] Yet in the aftermath of the Japanese attack on Pearl Harbor of December 7, 1941, and the resulting declarations of war against Japan and then Germany, the celebration—dampened as it was by one of the worst Northwest Arkansas blizzards in years—surely must have felt bittersweet.

In fact, one high school graduate of the John Brown schools had already died in the service. Billie LaRue's ship, the *S.S. Astral*, had been carrying fuel oil on December 2 when it was attacked by a German U-boat in the Atlantic, exploding with the loss of all hands. And as America followed the saga of the fall of tiny Wake Island in the Pacific during the days leading up to Christmas, probably no one in the JBU community knew that two of the school's alumni, Corporal Winford McAnally and Private Roger Dorman, were Marines defending that besieged atoll. They were taken captive by the Japanese upon the surrender of the island on December 23, beginning a nearly four-year-long ordeal as prisoners of war before their eventual liberation.

Dr. John Panage

Upon America's official entry to the war after Pearl Harbor, the draft was expanded. Now all men ages twenty to forty-four had to register. On February 16, 1942 a group of more than three dozen students and faculty members went downtown to register for the draft. Along with them that day was forty-two-year-old Dr. John Panage.

With his name now officially among those who could be called at any time to join the Army, all Dr. Panage could do about the war was wait to see if his number got called. Over the next several months, Panage confided to his diary his fears of being selected for the service. He wrote, "Fear is the worst enemy of mankind. . . . Last year I was worried by financial difficulties. This year I am vexed by the fear of being drafted into the Army. I guess there is no rest for the weak and the wicked. It is best, therefore, to enjoy the present without fear of the future or regret of the past. After all, what can a man do, being caught in unusual times brought about by forces he could not control?" With the soul of a pacifist, he focused on his teaching, striving to instill a love of language and literature in the hearts of those under his guidance. He once said, "Since I was born, there has never been a time when there wasn't any war." And he knew that in the aftermath of any war, intelligence, art, and beauty must endure.

By the end of the summer of 1942, with male college enrollment starting to fall precipitously as men went to war, President Brown was presented with the opportunity to make John Brown University a government-designated vocational training school for men headed into technical aspects of the service. The move would have brought a substantial revenue stream, but Brown and the rest of the leadership of the school recognized that the effects—erecting barracks and accepting a student body whose admissions requirements were established by military necessity rather than agreement with the ideals on which the school was founded—would essentially end John Brown University as they knew it. Thus Brown wrote at the time that the mission of the university for the duration of the war would be to continue along the path the school had always followed—vocational education under a Christ-centered ethos that made its graduates capable, productive, and willing to work.[11]

Even in a time of war, the mission of the well-rounded university to enlighten the mind and the soul could not change. Brown wrote, "Boys may be skilled in the use of their hands, but unless trained to appreciate great literature and art and music . . . the trained hand in skilled production might prove the greatest sort of a disappointment. My conviction is now and always has been that a cultured mind and a trained hand should never be separated."[12]

Dr. Panage lamented "this madness of war and race for armaments," and he wrote in his diary of the urgent need for preserving the arts in higher learning. "Scholars feel out of place in a war-torn world, and yet the scholars in these dark days must keep the torch of learning burning bright and transmit it to the coming generation. Otherwise the world will plunge again into another long dark age." And again he wrote, "The more the war rages, the more I think of Goethe who said, 'The end is everywhere, art has still truth; take refuge there.'"

***

Summer 1942 was hot, dry, and unwelcoming in Siloam Springs. Nothing about it appeared to be a refuge for the arts, especially to a newcomer recruited to teach music and voice. One day in August, a woman who had just completed a long, sweltering, three-day car ride from New York stepped out into the center of campus and immediately had second thoughts about her agreement to join the faculty. Her name was Mabel Oiesen, and she had recently completed her master of music degree at the Cincinnati Conservatory of Music.

"It had been one of those summers that had burned the grass to a veritable crisp," she recalled many years later, adding, "the roads were unpaved and dusty. . . . It was a picture of absolute desolation." Looking toward the site of the ill-fated Oklahoma building, she saw the "unfinished foundation, obviously started some years past and abandoned," and her heart sank. "My mind was made up at once to return East."

But before turning around and going back home, she went to see Bob Jackson, the vice president who had invited her to join the university. "He sold me on the fact that the physical aspects, the buildings, etc., had little to do with the success of the educational program. He sold me on Dr. Brown's dream of educating young people for their life's work."

Convinced by Mr. Jackson, Oiesen stayed at JBU, and in her second semester she was appointed chair of the Music Department. She was an exceptional person for the role. Oiesen had spent many years studying with Yeatman Griffith, one of the preeminent vocal coaches in New York City, and she had focused her graduate research on a scientific method for teaching voice.

Dr. Mabel Oiesen

But as the 1942–1943 school year wound down, she found the experience at JBU not only challenging but also frustrating. With other personal obligations pressing on her from home, she decided to resign at the end of the spring term of 1943.

"I spent the summer on the tip of Long Island, and much of the day I was alone—alone to reflect and to evaluate," she recalled. "Again and again, fragments of Dr. Brown's sermons and his compulsive power of expressing his educational dream pursued me." By the end of the summer, she wrote President Brown, not to ask for her job back, because it had already been filled, but to thank him for what he had done for her personally. Soon, President Brown invited her back, and she would spend more than thirty years as the chair of John Brown University's Music Department, beginning the traditions of ensemble groups, great spring musical pageants, and the enduring and deeply moving Christmas Candlelight Service.

***

In the fall of 1942, JBU's aviation program was sufficiently established that the War Department selected it for military training of ground crew and pilots. With JBU seeing a drastic drop in male student enrollment, a portion of the Memorial dormitory was now turned over to rotating groups of military aviation servicemen. Every two months, a new group of 20 Army Air Force reservists was brought in for flight training in an aviation program that now boasted eight trainer planes for flight and ground instruction. Over the course of the next year, roughly 175 officers would be assigned to take their primary flight training at JBU.

November of 1942 brought the news that Dr. Panage had been selected in the draft. After months of worry, he now trusted his future to God with an attitude that he would express often in his diary over the coming years: "Let His will be done." Upon his induction to the Army, he wrote hopefully, "The stars and the winds are always with us, and there will be books and newspapers and magazines and fellowmen everywhere I go. God has probably given me just what I need to develop my personality and character. He will provide me with means and ways of profiting by this new experience and will lead me with strong hands through the dangers that will face me."

Panage was fortunate to spend his years in uniform stateside, serving in the Signal Corps at Camp Crowder near Neosho, Missouri. But hundreds of other alumni and former staff of the John Brown schools had far more dangerous and deadly assignments.

By the start of 1944, May Boudinot, who had spent the past few years serving as the librarian at Brown Military Academy in San Diego, returned to her duties as alumni secretary for JBU, and began chronicling the names, locations, and fates of hundreds of former members of the John Brown schools family. The pages of the monthly *John Brown University Bulletin* soon became a clearinghouse for astonishing details, updates on service members abroad, and sad reports on friends

JBU choir in the 1940s

lost in the war. The longest update, in the September 1944 *Bulletin,* contained over four hundred names.

Some twenty former ministry students served as military chaplains throughout the world. A number of men served as doctors and medical corpsmen in battle zones. Dozens of women served as nurses, WACS, and WAVES both at home and abroad. And Miss Boudinot chronicled the responsible positions of many young men who were putting their vocational training to use in the armaments industries.

In the Pacific, boys who had lived and studied at Siloam Springs died in the assaults on Tarawa, Iwo Jima, and Okinawa, or aboard destroyers, cruisers,

Storm Whaley

submarines, and transport ships that were sunk in naval battles or ravaged by kamikaze attacks. Men were lost to the sea when their long-range bombers were shot down between the myriad islands of the vast Pacific Ocean. While flying on routes through China and India, men were killed when their planes ran out of fuel or crashed into a mountainside. Over Europe, bomber and fighter pilots died in the frantic carnage of huge dueling aerial armadas, or were shot down only to spend the rest of the war in German POW camps. Alumni soldiers died in combat in Italy, on the approach to Normandy on D-Day, and across France and Germany as the Allied armies made their long, final push toward Berlin. And at home, several pilots died when their planes suffered accidents during training or ferry service. In all, more than forty men who had attended the John Brown schools in Arkansas—including two pairs of brothers and one pair of cousins— died as a result of the war.

***

For a brief period at the outset of war, JBU implemented a regimen of military drill for the remaining boys. As the population of college-enrolled men dwindled, enrollment was opened to more boys of high school age. The campus culture soon took on a different tone, as the oldest men in residence were now the aviation cadets who were there for only short stretches on orders from the War Department. The high school boys laboring in the vocational industries were restless, as so many of their older brothers, friends, neighbors, and classmates had now gone off to war. Miss Boudinot wrote that these restless spirits "created some serious problems" for a time.

KUOA director Storm H. Whaley launched an *Ozarks at War* radio program in 1942, part of the station's "up-to-the-minute" news service for listeners throughout the region. Whaley became the Benton County chairman of the Red Cross, and he used time on the airwaves to publicize Red Cross fundraisers and War Bond drives. In the radio studios of the red brick bungalow, a United Press teletype clacked away with news from the war, which could be read on air within moments of its arrival.

***

In January 1943, John Brown Jr. entered service as a naval officer. He had completed the first semester of his senior year of college at JBU the previous fall, but

John Brown Jr. as a student at Brown Military Academy

when the draft was expanded in early 1942, new federal rules were also handed down for young men in college who were entering the service. Seniors could now be granted their diploma one semester early.

The only son of JBU's founder had grown to maturity just as the university itself had, being born in 1921, less than two years after the school's founding. As a boy, John Jr. had often been a fixture on campus, mixing with the college students and acquiring the nickname Buddy. He grew up milking cows and working on the family farm, which by 1935 was located a few miles west of the college campus on a new property the founder had bought along Flint Creek in Oklahoma.

After Brown Sr. bought the California schools in 1937, John Jr. went to the newly named Brown Military Academy in San Diego for a portion of his high school years, then returned to JBU for college. During his sophomore year at JBU, John Jr. met an attractive Siloam Springs coed, Caroline Trahin, who was majoring in English. After a proper courtship, John and Caroline's wedding in November 1941 was held in the campus chapel in the Memorial Building, with the campus pastor Dr. Vincent Bennett officiating. John was twenty; Caroline was nineteen.

The Pearl Harbor attack was just sixteen days later, and in 1942 John Jr. determined to join the Navy. He had learned to fly at JBU's airfield, and opted to take Naval flight training. But after he was commissioned as an ensign in the Naval Reserve at the start of 1943, he served stateside for a time, then was assigned to amphibious assault command ships in the Pacific, participating in the campaign to liberate the Philippines.

***

John Brown Jr. and Caroline Brown

Late 1943 saw the end of JBU's pilot training program for the War Department, as military training was concentrated on larger military bases. All of JBU's aircraft were commandeered for further war service, bringing a temporary end to flight training at the JBU airport.

One of JBU's few college sophomore men in the fall of 1943 was Bruce Garda Biddle. He was a skilled radio student, having a substantial part in running the operations of KUOA. In November, on his eighteenth birthday, Bruce registered for the draft.

By the summer of 1944, Bruce was the highest-ranking junior in the vocational college. Perhaps Bruce did not want to be at the mercy of the draft board; perhaps he was eager to apply his intimate knowledge of radio operations in a service role where he knew he could be used to his proper potential. Whatever his motivation, Bruce withdrew from JBU in July 1944 and joined the merchant marine. A month or two later, he was the nineteen-year-old radio operator of the *S.S. Lewis L. Dyche*, a transport ship used to ferry ammunition in the Pacific.

During the bitterly fought campaign to liberate the Philippines in late 1944 and early 1945, kamikaze attacks were frequent. Bruce Biddle's life ended, along with those of the seventy other men aboard the Dyche, on January 4, 1945, less than six months after he had departed the JBU campus. A kamikaze struck his ammunition transport, and the resulting explosion vaporized the entire ship in a flash.[13]

Three months later, another beloved member of the campus community was lost in battle, his body never to be recovered. Howard Keech, the printing professor who had been a student and faculty member over a span of ten years, had been drafted at age thirty-six the previous year, and entered service with the Army. He was killed in the brutal fighting on Okinawa on April 29, 1945, a day that saw a small band of enemy holdouts make a suicidal banzai charge against Keech's unit. For his actions on Okinawa, Keech—a thirty-seven-year-old Army private—received the Bronze Star.

Victory in Europe was declared days later, and the May 1945 commencement ceremonies at JBU were marked by another important groundbreaking. Mrs. Emily Biddle, mother of the young radioman Bruce Biddle, was given the honor of pushing the first shovel into the earth on the site where a great cathedral would one day stand. The Cathedral of the Ozarks and its two companion buildings, having been envisioned for several years, would now begin construction as the Memorial Group, and the cornerstone of the cathedral would one day be inscribed, "In Memory of Our Boys."

***

When the war finally ended with Japan's surrender a few months later, the long process of returning home began for countless men and women of JBU's distant and recent past. Several had spent months or years as prisoners of war, many had been wounded, a large number of women had served under the trying conditions of war zone hospitals, and untold numbers of others came home bearing deep, invisible scars.

Dr. Panage returned to teaching at JBU, walking every day to campus from a new downtown apartment, and John Jr. rejoined the campus with a vice-presidential role in his immediate future. A few former students who had left for war service and been discharged before the end of the war now returned to continue their studies. But soon, a vast number of young men—many of them married— would flood the campus as new students, matured and hardened beyond their years after their military service.

Since virtually all able-bodied young men in America had served the war effort in some capacity, John Brown University's campus population had seen male attendance dwindle to as few as eleven college-level students during the war. Due to wartime printing restrictions, the yearbook had been discontinued for three years, but it returned in a smaller, staple-bound pamphlet format at the end of the spring semester of 1945. The *Pioneer, Jr.*, as it was called, depicted just 155 total students, with a mere 63 enrolled in college. There were only eight college seniors shown in the yearbook that spring, of whom only three were men.

Before the war, the largest graduating classes of college seniors had numbered in the forties. With the sudden and dramatic increase in enrollment immediately after the war, due in part to the tuition assistance of the GI Bill, the first graduating classes for those who had started their college career after war's end ballooned to eighty in 1949 and more than ninety in 1950. Government surplus buildings were used to rapidly expand the campus facilities and provide married-student cottages during this period, and special efforts were made to provide the wives of the new married students with opportunities to become a part of the campus community.

***

In California, the Brown Military Academy (BMA) had earned high marks from the War Department for the quality of its ROTC training, and after Pearl Harbor the graduates of BMA were authorized to receive direct commissions as second lieutenants in the Army. One such cadet was reportedly commissioned having just barely turned eighteen, and another alum of BMA was Chester Nimitz Jr., the son of America's commander in chief of the Pacific fleet.

The private schools in California that John Brown Sr. had acquired continued to operate for many years after the war. In 1947, a third school was purchased in the area, the Southern California Military Academy in Long Beach. This school was aimed at elementary- and middle-school-aged boys. In the coming years, these California schools would see some consolidation. In the 1950s, the aging campus of BMA was put up for sale, Brown School for Girls in Glendora was closed, and the military academy was moved to the Glendora campus. As years went by, it became apparent that the primary need of the university at Siloam Springs was to maintain its own buildings and keep costs affordable there; this limited the university's ability to commit capital funds toward the aging facilities at the academies in California. Also, by the time of the Vietnam War and its aftermath, society's interest in military-school enrollment for young men of good character had declined significantly across the country. In 1967, the Glendora campus was sold to Azusa Pacific College, and the Long Beach military academy acquired in 1947 was sold off a few years later.

The Brown School for Girls in Glendora, California

Cadets at Brown Military Academy

Dr. Panage teaching class in the 1940s.

Men's chorus from 1945

CHAPTER 7

A NEW PRESIDENT AND
THE FOUNDER'S FINAL YEARS

Even before John Jr. returned to JBU's campus after the war, plans were in motion for him to take on a vice-presidential position with the school. The 1945 yearbook showed a dashing portrait of him in his Navy uniform, with the title "First Vice President," alongside other relatively young leaders of the administration such as Stewart Springfield, Storm H. Whaley, and Roger Cox. Upon his return from active duty in the Pacific, John Jr. set about completing his bachelor's degree in business while still remaining active in the Naval Reserve, where he ultimately achieved the rank of lieutenant commander.[1]

In 1945, the man who had officiated John Jr. and Caroline's wedding, Dr. Vincent Bennett—a "vivacious little Englishman" in Miss Boudinot's recollection[2]—decided to leave his position as JBU's campus pastor, which he had held for several years. Bennett contacted a twenty-five-year-old preacher he knew to see if the younger man was interested in taking over the role. Stuart Schimpf was, at the time, the assistant pastor of Linwood Presbyterian Church in Kansas City, Missouri. He was already familiar with the JBU campus, since his wife, Madge Grove, had graduated there in 1939. On one occasion in 1943, Madge brought her then-fiancé Stuart to see the college she had attended and loved, but, as Stuart recalled, "I was unimpressed."[3]

Still, by 1945, Schimpf was interested in the campus pastor role, and Dr. Bennett passed the news on to John Brown Sr. "He was never one to let any grass grow under his feet," Schimpf recalled of the founder, for he contacted Schimpf about the job right away.

Schimpf was amply qualified, having earned his master of divinity degree from Princeton Theological Seminary. But when Brown Sr. interviewed him for the job, the questions were simple, fundamental, and reflective of the founder's interdenominational philosophy. As Schimpf recalled it, the conversation went something like, "Do you believe the Bible is inspired?" Schimpf answered, "Yes."

"Do you believe Jesus Christ is the Son of God?"—"Yes."

"That He died for our sins?"—"Yes."
"Rose again the third day?"—"Yes."
"Believe in the new birth?"—"Yes."
"That He's coming again?"—"Yes."
Schimpf recalled, "And that was about it."[4]

Stuart Schimpf

Soon after Schimpf arrived on campus, Brown Sr. acquired a war-surplus twin-engine Cessna Bobcat. With the war over, JBU's aviation program was now in the position to acquire several aircraft and resume flight training at the airport, both for students and for the general public. Brown Sr.'s traveling schedule, meanwhile, was as busy as ever, and so travel by private plane became his routine for a couple of years. He could be a cantankerous passenger, however, especially when he was less interested in flying safely than were his pilots—at least one of whom had been an Army Air Force flight instructor during the war. One tale from this period involved a flight into northern Saskatchewan in the dead of winter. With weather conditions marginal, Brown grew frustrated that his pilot "could not accept the high level of faith he expressed and refused to venture into adverse weather." The founder soon hired a different pilot.[5]

Brown Sr. had recently joined the board of a new ministry organization called Youth For Christ, and by 1946 had been named one of the organization's national speakers. During Rev. Schimpf's first year at JBU, he was invited to go along with Brown Sr. on a speaking tour for the organization, and it would prove to be a whirlwind introduction to the pace of activity John Brown Sr. kept in his ministry.

"I have a vivid recollection of flying with him to Chicago in his twin-motor Cessna during my first year as university pastor," Schimpf said. "He spoke at Chicagoland Youth for Christ on Saturday night, then at Midwest Bible Church on Sunday morning, where Torrey Johnson and Bob Cook were serving as co-pastors, as well as in Moody Memorial Church Sunday night where he introduced me to Dr. [Harry] Ironside and insisted that I sing the solo before his message. The next day I recall being ushered into the office of Dr. Will Houghton, then president of Moody Bible Institute."

Brown Sr.'s personality and charm made an impression on Schimpf in these early days, no doubt influencing his decision to remain at JBU for seventeen years. "I shall never forget the first sermon I heard him preach," Schimpf said. "At a Youth For Christ meeting he preached on Pilate's timeless question, 'What must I then do with Jesus, who is called the Christ?' With his shock of unruly, iron-grey hair listing to one side, he reminded me of an Old Testament prophet."[6]

Schimpf also recalled that given the founder's tireless pace of activity and speaking, "if you woke him up suddenly in the middle of the night, he would come up waving his arms and preaching threefold education!"

***

While John Brown Sr. was known for his evangelistic gifts, John Jr. was known as a gifted and competent administrator. Still just twenty-five years old, John Jr. held an important vice-presidential role on campus in 1947, leaving his father free to do the work of raising support for the university and also continuing his radio and traveling ministries.

In February 1947, the largest and most disastrous fire in the school's history struck while the founder was in California. On the evening of February 10, Mechanical Building 2—a large, two-story structure northwest of the original Mechanical Building—caught fire in the woodworking shop on its second floor. This was no small building, but was in fact just as large as Mechanical 1 and the Memorial Dormitory to the east. Along with the gymnasium built in 1937, Mechanical 2 was one of four buildings that formed a large rectangle at the center of campus, with a spacious quad, paths and roads, and numerous outbuildings and structures in between.

The fire spread throughout the upper story of Mechanical 2, and the campus fire crew and Siloam Springs Fire Department fought the flames for hours. The building housed the campus machine shop, the auto garage, and the aviation laboratory with all of their heavy equipment, in addition to classrooms and a drafting studio. While students and staff rushed to save equipment from the ground floor as the upper story burned, the fire spread to two smaller outbuildings that included the campus fire truck's own miniature station. A considerable amount of light equipment was saved, but as the entire building collapsed in the conflagration, much of the university's heavy vocational equipment was lost.

Later that night, John Jr. placed a long-distance call to his father on the West Coast. Distraught, John Jr. told his father of the destruction, but the founder encouraged his son to trust in God's plan. "Go to bed and rest, son," he said. "Everything will be fine! You will see this is a blessing sent by God. I am going back to bed and to sleep!"[7]

John Jr. went home to take his father's advice, while behind him the smoldering remains of much of the college's vocational industries cooled in the winter night.

Over the next few days, the surviving engineering laboratory equipment was shifted next door into the gymnasium building—which would be transformed into teaching labs—and the salvaged production machinery was trucked over to the original airfield on the far side of Oak Hill Cemetery, where a government surplus steel building had recently been erected. Indeed, war surplus material would soon replace the spaces that were lost due to the fire and the tools needed to keep up the workshops.

Throughout the remainder of 1947, the campus continued to take on the shape that would be familiar to later generations of students. Excavation of the cathedral site had been completed, and now the bottom floor was finished, providing the campus a new large chapel and performance space, along with housing for the expanded library and Music Department offices. Concrete work continued across much of the campus, providing roads and sidewalks, the famed one hundred steps down the hillside behind California dorm, and the opening of a swimming pool and tennis courts in the valley. Next to the new pool was erected one of the government surplus metal buildings, providing a new gymnasium for the campus. Government surplus buildings were also assembled together alongside the road opposite the cemetery to form a new science building that would serve the campus's needs for the next few years.

On Sunday night before commencement 1947, the cathedral basement's new auditorium was dedicated with the seventy voices of Miss Mabel Oiesen's Cathedral Choir singing Handel's *Messiah*.

By the fall of 1947, beginning the campus's twenty-ninth year of continuous operation, and the fourteenth since its official designation as John Brown University, the institution at Siloam Springs was now for the first time completely collegiate. As part of the renewed effort to gain accreditation in the postwar years, JBU had been advised to eliminate the high school academy from the campus as soon as possible. With the Sulphur Springs property now completely rebuilt after its own disastrous fire several years earlier, all academy activities were now concentrated there under the name Brown Military Academy of the Ozarks.

Before the end of that school year, another great transition occurred when, on Founder's Day, April 2, 1948, John E. Brown Sr. announced that he was stepping aside as president of the university he had founded. At the young age of twenty-six, John E. Brown Jr. was named president of JBU by the Board of Trustees, making him—like his father had once been—the youngest college president in the nation at the time.

Dr. Brown Sr.—who had begun to be called by the honorific "Dr." in the 1930s for his many years of writing and teaching—became chairman of the Board of Trustees, but the sixty-nine-year-old educator and evangelist didn't take the move as an opportunity to enter into retirement. He simply devoted more of his time to preaching the gospel and raising money to provide for the salaries and expenses of the university.

John E. Brown Jr. became president in 1948.

Two of the 1948 graduates who witnessed this historic change in presidential leadership would one day become stalwarts of JBU history in their own rights.

A young Pennsylvanian named Bill George—business major, athlete, and Cathedral Choir member—would soon become a faithful manager of JBU's California operations, and in 1954 would begin more than a half century of service as a member of the Board of Trustees. But as he watched this first-ever transfer of the university presidency, he surely had no inkling that, forty-six years later, he would himself be called on to serve as president of JBU during one of the school's most uncertain times.

One of George's fellow choir members, Ida Mae Adolphson, was the editor of the 1948 yearbook, graduating with an English degree, and already a standout member of that year's *Who's Who in American Colleges and Universities*. A decade later, she would return to JBU as California dorm's resident director for a time before becoming the dean of women, influencing the lives of countless students. Beginning in the 1980s, she became a pioneer of female leadership in other ways, serving as the only woman among the Psychology Department faculty, and becoming the first woman in JBU history to teach a Bible course. Her impact on the culture of JBU would span six decades.

***

In 1948, the college corporation acquired radio station KGER, in Long Beach, California, which had carried Dr. Brown's daily broadcasts since 1930. Much of the later years of the founder's life were spent in Southern California, raising funds for JBU and sharing the truths of Scripture on a daily *John Brown Hour* broadcast over KGER.

During those later years, Brown Sr. also became a very close friend of the pastor who followed Dr. Louis T. Talbot at the Church of the Open Door—Dr. J. Vernon McGee. Dr. McGee began his own local Bible-teaching program on KGER in 1949. By the time McGee had retired from the pastorate in 1970, his *Thru the Bible* broadcast was being aired across the nation by a network of sixty stations, and upon his death in 1988, *Thru the Bible* continued to be aired in over forty languages around the world.

McGee was not only a friend of JBU's founder; he was a regular visitor to the Siloam Springs campus for many years, often leading the traditional Spiritual Emphasis Week services that began each academic year. During his lifetime, Dr. McGee also made a substantial gift to the school that established the J. Vernon McGee Chair of Biblical Studies at John Brown University.

Another friend of the founder was R. G. LeTourneau, who established a Christian university in 1949 that shared many of the ideals of John Brown University. LeTourneau was a prominent Christian industrialist whose nearly three hundred inventions in earthmoving machinery revolutionized the practice of site construction and roadbuilding in the twentieth century. LeTourneau's factories produced as much as 70 percent of all the heavy equipment used by Allied battlefield engineers during World War II.[8]

LeTourneau had been a frequent visitor to the JBU campus over the past several years, first serving as the commencement speaker for JBU's graduation ceremonies in 1939. There, LeTourneau told the crowd of how John Brown's evangelistic meetings in Stockton, California, many years earlier, had greatly influenced the course of his life.[9] LeTourneau returned for commencement week four more times throughout the 1940s, often leading an evening Vespers service during the last week of school, and in 1947 he gave a commencement address titled "God Runs My Business."

In February of 1949, LeTourneau invited Dr. Brown to participate in the dedication of LeTourneau's new university in Longview, Texas. LeTourneau introduced Dr. Brown to the crowd by saying, "What I am offering to Texas is nothing original with me, for I was taught this idea of education thirty years ago by a man who is on this platform with me, John Brown of Arkansas."

Brown graciously replied, "If I had any part in the thinking and doing of the man, R. G. LeTourneau, whose work reaches throughout the world in this three-fold demonstration for the training of youth, my reward is a large one."[10]

***

By the spring of 1949, much progress had been made on the cathedral building, with walls enclosing the unfinished second and third floors of the rear of the structure. The grand cathedral sanctuary itself, however, remained just an open concrete slab. The environment, it turned out, was the perfect setting for Miss Mabel Oiesen's spring music festival, which featured a dramatic outdoor performance of Hansel and Gretel.

In the evening dark, fourteen actors dressed in the white robes and golden wings of angels descended an ethereal stairway from the third-floor roof in front of a tall, curtained backdrop. They each carried black lights, giving the effect of a ladder descending from the clouds to the earth below.

The dramatic effect on the audience was one of the fondest memories of another of JBU's long-serving professors, Dr. Dorothy Woodland, who had designed the set and costumes. Woodland was Oiesen's dearest lifelong friend, but the two were not both professors of the dramatic arts. Woodland was actually JBU's chemistry professor, with a doctorate from Ohio State, and she had the career distinction of having participated in the Manhattan Project—the effort to develop the nuclear bomb—during World War II.

In 1944, a thirty-six-year-old Woodland came to JBU at the urging of her friend and former classmate Dr. Oiesen. Much like Oiesen's first reaction upon arriving at the campus in 1942, Woodland's initial impression of College Hill in 1944 was summed up with the word "dreadful." So many of the buildings were made of wood, and in her early years, her science labs were in the Alumni Building above the campus laundry and utility plant. During her lectures, she competed with the loud huffing and clanking of a steam engine outside the window, and the lab equipment provided by the dean and Science Department chair, Dr. Irvin Wills, was crude to say the least.

"Dr. Wills couldn't see spending money on anything," Dr. Woodland recalled. Feed sacks were her towels, and empty jars were her chemistry lab's beakers. Yet she remained as one of the brightest and most respected members of the JBU faculty for thirty years, drawn in part by the "vision of the founder" and the people she worked alongside. "There was a feeling of being in a great enterprise together," she later said.[11]

Oiesen and Woodland shared a special bond for the rest of their lives, and together they designed a home

Dr. Dorothy Woodland

overlooking Sager Creek and the JBU campus, which uniquely blended science and art. It featured a spacious living room that provided an ideal space for musical performances, with acoustic design and a raised stage platform at one end.

∗∗∗

More changes came to the schools in the early 1950s. The associated high school academy in Sulphur Springs came to an end as the properties were sold to Wycliffe Bible Translators, and enrolled students were invited to attend the affiliated military and girls' schools in California. The vocational aspect of John Brown University had been gradually shifting away from the scheme where students worked half of each day in one of the industries, and now vocational training consisted of ten hours per week.

The fall of 1950 saw the Helen Brown Hodges Memorial Building completely renovated as a men's dormitory, and for the rest of its days, until it was dismantled in 1973, it was known most commonly as the MO Dorm.

The lengthy work of building the cathedral sanctuary began in earnest in the spring of 1951, when the cornerstone was placed with an inscription—fulfilling a promise made at the 1945 groundbreaking—that read "In Memory of Our Boys." The following year, John Sr.'s older brother Ben, with whom the founder had first come to Arkansas a half century before, arrived on campus to lead the work on the cathedral, and several months later, the second building of the Cathedral Group was begun on the long-dormant Oklahoma Building foundation that had been poured two decades earlier. The original Mechanical Building was completely renovated by the spring of 1953, and was dedicated anew as the Arkansas Building.

Dr. Gordon Palmer, a pastor and radio teacher in California, was a friend of the founder and had been the president of a Baptist seminary in Philadelphia during the 1930s and 1940s. He provided JBU with a substantial gift—anonymous at the time—that allowed construction to begin on the Cathedral Group's Library and Science buildings. Palmer would be an instrumental member of the JBU Board of Trustees in the years to come.

∗∗∗

Another type of change came to the school's culture in 1953, when campus pastor Stuart Schimpf began using the newly published Revised Standard Version of the Bible in his sermons. When word of this got to the founder in California, it did not sit well with him. Schimpf recalled, "From California he wrote me a blistering letter of rebuke, indicating that JBU had never tolerated modernism in any shape or form and was not about to do so now, or words to that effect. I felt like I'd been punched in the stomach."

But Schimpf knew that Dr. Brown was a persuadable kind of man who could recognize if he ever made an ill-informed judgment, and so he wrote back to the founder, asking him to talk the new translation over with someone the two of them both admired—Dr. Gordon Palmer. "I was sure such a conversation would help clarify his thinking," Schimpf said.

A few days of silence passed, and Schimpf carried his wounded spirit to the office of President John E. Brown Jr., where Schimpf slumped in a chair, hoping for some advice or consolation. "As he was trying to smooth the troubled water," Schimpf recalled, "the phone rang. It was Dr. Brown."

President John Jr. answered, and after a moment said, "I've got the preacher right here in my office." Schimpf undoubtedly strained to hear what was being said over the phone, waiting to see if he was to be called to speak with the founder on the issue of his break with tradition. But after a few moments, John Jr. hung up the phone.

"Dad told me to tell you he's *for* you!"

Schimpf brightened, and later recalled, "What a boost to my sagging ego!"

A week or two later, the founder was back in Siloam Springs, speaking in chapel, where he made an announcement to the whole college community. "Now I want everybody to know," the founder said, "that whatever Brother Schimpf quotes from, I endorse!"

Schimpf would remember the relief he felt and the increased admiration he had for the founder for many years. "If Dr. Brown ever felt he had made some hasty judgment or was wrong in any way, he did not hesitate to say so," Schimpf recalled. "I have seldom witnessed such a 180-degree turn, but it was certainly a most gratifying experience!"

On April 2, 1954, a great celebration was held in honor of John and Juanita Brown's seventy-fifth birthdays. The date had long been celebrated at JBU as the annual Founder's Day, and the occasion had been used in 1948 to announce the passing of the presidency from father to son. At the birthday banquet, the founder told the campus family, "God willing, we feel many years of service are lying out ahead, and, we hope and pray, the best service we have ever known."[12]

Even in the eighth decade of his life, Brown Sr. remained fixed on the mission of "training youth to live." In late 1954 he traveled to Washington, DC, to attempt to gain legislative support for a great program of military-style camps that would bring discipline to the growing numbers of juvenile delinquents that were running the streets at night and introducing "gang warfare" into the schools. He even asked General Omar Bradley, famed for his leadership in the European theater in World War II, to be the director of his plan. While his proposal gained no traction with General Bradley or elsewhere in the halls of power, the effort revealed that Brown still had the energy and the will to attempt to take on new, grand ventures in his mission to educate the head, heart, and hand.[13]

***

In 1956, two of John Brown Sr.'s great friends passed away, Jesse Jones and May Boudinot. The pinnacle of Jones's government work had been serving as President Roosevelt's secretary of commerce during the majority of the war years. He returned home to Houston, where he spent the last decade of his life pursuing his business ventures and engaging in much public philanthropy. The Houston Endowment he established in the 1930s grew to become one of the nation's largest such endowments by the 1970s.[14]

Miss Boudinot had retired for health reasons in 1953 at the age of seventy-four, having spent more than thirty years working in the libraries, teaching history, and documenting the life of the John Brown schools, both in Arkansas and California. She was the last remaining and longest-serving member of the John E. Brown College's early faculty. Although she had concluded the typing of her unpublished manuscript about the history of JBU, *The Magnetic Power of Dreams*, around 1950, she continued to make pencil notes in that great trove of JBU historical records until early 1952, logging the activities of special banquets, commencement activities, and campus changes. In April 1956, six months before her death, the second building of the Cathedral Group was completed and dedicated as the campus library, a function it would serve for almost twenty-five years, until it was remodeled to become the engineering building.

A tribute to Miss Boudinot in the December 1956 JBU *Alumni News* mailer said, "It was the delight of her heart when the new library was completed last spring. She had spent many, many hours trying to protect the books from fire, rain and other enemies."

At her memorial service, one alumnus who had served in World War II recalled how Miss Boudinot spent countless hours writing letters to JBU's servicemen abroad, "encouraging them, strengthening their faith in the Lord, and sending out rays of sunshine into the dark clouds of doubt and despair."

May Fidelia Boudinot was laid to rest in Oak Hill Cemetery, across the street from the JBU campus, where she had devoted the majority of her adult life in the service of training youth to live. As the writer of her obituary said, "God alone knows all the lovely things she did, for she was one who literally did not let her right hand know what her left hand did. Praise and honor from men were the least of her desires."

***

The year 1957 began with John Elward Brown Sr. residing in San Diego and still tirelessly spreading the gospel and working on behalf of the university he had founded. Then, in the early morning hours of Saturday, January 12, he fell and broke his hip.

"I was getting ready for a red-letter day when I was to have our Board of Directors with me at that beautiful spot by the seaside," the founder said in a radio address a short time later. President John Jr. and several others of the JBU administration were in California at the time, and they were to meet with the founder that morning at a beautifully furnished home on the coast that friends of the university had given him to use a few months before.

That early Saturday morning had been dark and rainy, and when Brown Sr. went out to get his morning paper, he misjudged the steps leading down from the house. "I did not know one could fall as hard as I fell," he told his listeners. "I lay there, practically in the gutter, with the rain coming down from the eaves of the house." He knew something was broken, but he either could not or dared not move, being unsure how bad his injury was. "Is this to be the end?" he thought, "as I lay there on that dark morning, suffering, of course, horrible pain. When I called for help, help did not come."

After a short time, a housekeeper who lived with him and cooked his meals heard his cries and brought help. John Sr. was taken to Scripps Memorial Hospital, and John Jr. was telephoned with the news.

JBU's president spoke with his father as doctors prepared the elder John Brown for surgery. The founder's thoughts were not on himself, but on the future of his school. "Things look good out here, don't they? I will be here only a week or ten days, and then we will go full steam ahead on completing our campaign for the funds needed to finish the Cathedral sanctuary," the founder told his son.[15]

John Brown Sr. responded well to the surgery, and remarkably, he arranged for a microphone to be brought to his bedside so that he could continue his daily radio broadcasts. By February 5, he was permitted to return to his seaside home, where he could continue broadcasting from his radio studio there. He told his listeners the story of his fall and praised the skills of his doctors, and continued on with his ministry. The next day, John Jr. was persuaded to return home to Arkansas, having spent the past four weeks tending to his father's needs.

A month after his fall, and six days after John Jr. left his father's side, word came that Dr. Brown had suddenly died, struck down by a blood clot on February 12, 1957, at the age of seventy-seven.

Dr. Stuart Schimpf officiated the memorial service a few days later in Siloam Springs, and Dr. Mabel Oiesen led the Cathedral Choir in providing a moving musical tribute to the founder, his work, and his Lord.

In their 1966 biography of the founder, *John Brown of Arkansas*, Ralph C. Kennedy and Thomas Rothrock wrote a touching passage, reflecting on the events surrounding the funeral and final laying to rest of the founder's body. "Hundreds of expressions of sympathy were received from all over the country, but amidst the sorrow at his passing, one was also aware of the impression that he had completed the work which God had assigned to him. . . . The final note of triumph in his great life seemed to be sounded as the John Brown University Cathedral Choir sang his favorite anthem, Luther's 'A Mighty Fortress is our God.'"[16]

John Elward Brown Sr. was laid to rest in Oak Hill Cemetery, across the road from the college he had founded in his family cornfield almost four decades earlier.

Two months after his passing, the Cathedral of the Ozarks, which had been a work in progress for more than ten years, was dedicated with a completed sanctuary, filled with pews made in the campus furniture factory, and decorated with rows of stained-glass windows. Each glass depicted not only a key moment in the life of John Brown and his university, but also, above each of those images, a key moment in the life of Christ, whom the founder had served faithfully for so many years. Thus the symbolism for JBU's motto and mission, Christ Over All and Head, Heart, and Hand, were beautifully presented in the sanctuary's art, just as the founder had envisioned.

Construction of the Cathedral of the Ozarks

CHAPTER 8

THE LEGACY OF THE FOUNDER'S CHARACTER

The deep convictions of John E. Brown Sr. left an imprint on the institution he founded, which to this day upholds essential Christian doctrines and morals, and encourages an environment free of worldly vices. However, rather than being a campus governed by legalistic strictures, John Brown University exhibits the "grace and truth" character of the founder, who was a part of the Christian evangelical movement of the twentieth century, avoiding the fundamentalist and isolating views of some of his peers.

There is no question that Dr. Brown Sr. could at times "preach up a storm" while condemning the wiles of Satan. He would use the language of his day to rail against the temptations of many worldly vices that he had seen destroy lives and families. He was an active leader during the 1930s in the local campaign to establish Benton County, Arkansas—where JBU is located—as a dry county. However, he also knew that there were several sides to the social and religious issues that stirred debate during his lifetime.

In one of his recorded sermons, he quotes Matthew 15:11—"Not that which goeth into the mouth defileth a man; but that which cometh out of the mouth, this defileth a man" (KJV). Brown's sermon goes on to mention an older lady he knew who had the habit of having a "hot toddy" at bedtime each night. His message was not to condemn her for taking a nightly serving of alcohol, but to focus his listeners' attention on a simple question that is just as relevant today as it was for him: What is it that controls the mind and body of the believer—is Christ Lord of our lives and priorities, or are we driven by the prevailing secular values of the world around us?

Brown Sr. was said to sometimes quote St. Augustine's famous phrase, "In essentials, unity; in nonessentials, liberty; and in all things, charity." He also described JBU as being "as narrow as the cross of Christ, but as broad as the love of God."

In his preaching on the question of the origins of the universe, Dr. Brown affirmed God's sovereignty over all we see and know about the universe.

"Everywhere there is system, organization and unification. Back of all, there must be a Higher Power, some Cause of all Causes—and who announces Himself as the author of all." But, as a lay theologian, he also concluded, "In no sense does God intend that we are to take the story of creation as a detailed account, from a scientific viewpoint, of the exact processes through which He moved in creating worlds and generating life."

The founder was open to discussing differences of interpretation, and he was not highly dogmatic about his own understanding of that which he affirmed to be the "inspired" words of the living God in the Bible. Most people familiar with JBU would say that this left room for a balance between "grace and truth," which has remained a vital characteristic of JBU over the years. JBU faculty and staff affirm an evangelical statement of faith as part of the annual contract of employment, but there is a generous latitude of grace given for differing denominational preferences or biblical interpretations.

As Brown wrote in his 1933 collection of messages, *Let There Be Light,* "God's Word does not condition man's salvation on a belief in, or an understanding of the various controversies that center back in what the skeptic calls, 'Old Testament fish stories.' In other words, God's condition is not, Whosoever believeth that man came by the direct creative act of God shall be saved . . . or whosoever believeth that a flood came upon the earth and destroyed all but Noah and his family shall be saved . . . but rather, the declaration of our God is, 'God so loved the world, that he gave his only begotten Son, that whosoever believeth in him might not perish, but have everlasting life'" (John 3:16 KJV).[1]

***

Another issue very important to an understanding of JBU's place in the twentieth century is that of racism and bigotry in the United States. Until the 1950s, the official policy in public school education for most states was the creation of "separate but equal" schools for children of different races. Dr. Brown's death in February of 1957 came only months before the momentous events following a school desegregation case in Little Rock, Arkansas, in which a federal court ordered Central High School to allow nine African-American students to join the all-white student body. The nine brave young students walked fearlessly with armed guards to the school each morning.

While there is no specific statement on racial integration recorded in Dr. Brown's writings and sermons, he was not one to use offensive words or make the kinds of social criticisms about the races that were prevalent in the political circles of Brown's day. From the school's earliest years, there were a number of non-Caucasian students who attended John Brown's college in Arkansas, fully participating in all of the school's activities and student clubs. While it does not appear that any African American students arrived until the 1970s, a black singing group called the Dixie Melody Masters was welcomed to the JBU campus several times in the 1930s.

One of the most egregious examples of racial bigotry in the South during the founder's era was, undoubtedly, the Ku Klux Klan. Although that grotesque organization had first arisen in the aftermath of the Civil War, it was largely dormant as an organized secret society until 1915, when it reemerged as a prominent force. By the 1920s, as John Brown began to hold frequent evangelistic meetings in Tennessee, the resurgent Klan was controversial enough in that state that a violent confrontation was inevitable. A clash between Klansmen and their opponents in November 1924 erupted in the city of Kingsport at the same time Brown was holding meetings. More than a dozen people were shot and wounded, and national guardsmen were called in to restore order.[2]

At one of John Brown's earlier meetings in Chattanooga in 1922, three Klansmen in characteristic garb had interrupted the meeting to march up to the platform and present one hundred dollars in appreciation of Brown's work. While Brown's immediate reaction is not recorded, a newspaper account followed up this startling event by saying that in Brown's later sermon, "he literally kidded the life out of Old Man Gloom and chased him out of the tabernacle."[3]

Despite the Klan's profession of admiration for him, Brown had no love for the them or any other secret fraternal society. In the early years of the twentieth century, the surge in Klan membership, as well as the growth of Masonic lodges and other types of fraternal organizations, led some to call the era the golden age of fraternalism. Apart from the Klan, many of these societies often emphasized organizing good works in their communities and appeared to be generally benign. However, Brown found the trend to be so alarming that he devoted an entire series of messages to his condemnation of the movement, which was rising even among professing Christians, and to emphasize that the church was the bedrock on which brotherhood and good works should be founded.

"These movements often hold up the Christ ideals without holding up Christ," he said. "They seek to magnify the fruits of the Spirit, without recognizing the Spirit. They make a show of religious belief and religious ceremony, but when you look for the 'Redemption that is in Christ Jesus . . .' you look in vain."[4]

Brown's messages on the spiritual failings of the fraternalism movement were collected in a book, *Upon This Rock*, which he published in 1923. Though he generally declined to name specific fraternal societies in his condemnations, the Klan did earn a mention. "Not until the launching of the Ku Klux Klan was the nation awakened to the realization of the tremendous grip which the secret society appeal seemed to have on the national life," he said. Many secret societies' rituals were, he said, "grotesque, ludicrous, and pathetic." He repudiated the idea that the secret societies of the day were in any way based on the ideals of Christ, "because it was written of him everywhere that 'He did nothing in secret.'" Brown took care to emphasize that the evangelists he respected, "including men such as Spurgeon, Moody, Dixon, Torrey," taught that these secret societies were "in direct opposition, and in open violation of the true principles of Christianity."[5]

Brown's aim with the messages in *Upon This Rock* was not only to warn against the lure of fraternal organizations. The volume's purpose was to make clear the role of the church in relation to the kingdom to come after Christ's return. He wrote in the introduction to the book, "If the reading of these messages create[s] a determination in the hearts of those who read, to place the church 'FIRST,' my goal is reached, and I shall be thankful to God."[6]

He made clear that what he believed is the breadth and inclusiveness for all races of Christ's atonement for sin when he said, "God is working toward the golden age of Brotherhood 'where there is neither Greek nor Jew, circumcision nor uncircumcision, Barbarian, Scythian, bond nor free: but Christ is all, and in all.' [Colossians 3:11 KJV] . . . from the beginning to the end, 'humanity is one.' Humanity cannot be broken up into many nations, tribes, or millions of individuals, for men and women around the world must constitute one family [in Christ] when the 'golden age' is ushered in."[7]

CHAPTER 9

GROWTH OF THE UNIVERSITY UNDER JOHN E. BROWN JR.

Even though the daily duties of presiding over the university had been in the hands of John E. Brown Jr. for nine years, the death of the founder in February 1957 was a major event for the leadership of the school. Six days after the founder's death, a special meeting was called of the Board of Trustees. At that meeting, the board passed a unanimous resolution to "rededicate our lives to the ideals upon which the school was founded."[1]

Two months later, during the board's regular meeting in April 1957, President Brown Jr. brought as the first order of business the possibility of reorganizing the JBU Board of Trustees. One of his highest priorities as the institution's second president was to achieve major accreditation for the university, and there was a need to bring the board's structure into compliance with certain requirements of the North Central Association of Colleges and Secondary Schools.

The function of the board was—and is—to be a body of dedicated Christian leaders who could serve as the legal and spiritual guardians of the mission, values, and physical assets of the university corporation. Since the school was founded with a firm insistence that no particular Protestant denomination should be favored, and no particular church should exercise control over it, the board has historically included a diverse membership, representing many denominations, professions, and geographic regions. Being independent of any outside authority, the board is "self-perpetuating" in nominating and electing its own members.[2]

In the early years of the school, the Board of Trustees was largely a family affair, though it was not without objective members. In August of 1919, the founder had established the school's first board out of a close group of his family and friends, but he also made sure to include two local bankers as members of the executive committee. John Brown Sr. recognized the need to handle donor funds with public integrity, writing at the time, "These men will supervise expenditures and those who join me building this great school can rest assured their money will be wisely invested."[3]

The founder was a significant figure in all of the decisions of the board through-out his entire life, and there are many years' worth of board-meeting minutes that contain little more than formalities: the board would hold an annual meeting each spring, reelect board members and officers, and approve the candidates for grad-uation. Clearly, there was little cause for dissent from the founder's decisions.[4]

Much of the board's business, particularly in the Depression years of the 1930s, dealt with the financial needs and obligations of the university. When the col-lege was reincorporated as "John Brown University" in 1934, the board was still fairly small, standing at only nine members. Three of the board members at the time were women—the founder's wife, his sister, and May Boudinot. Three years later, the board had been expanded to include twenty-three members, although it was still largely made up of Brown family members and JBU staff, along with a number of trusted businessmen who were friends or alumni of the school. The reorganization in 1941 of the school's debt under the Chandler Act had been approved at the April 1940 board meeting, and as a signal of the significant bur-dens constantly carried by the founder, the board authorized John Brown Sr. to take a leave of absence so he could focus on the fieldwork required of him as the university's chief fundraiser.[5]

Following the founder's death, and President Brown Jr.'s suggestion of a reorga-nization of the school's governing body, the board took steps to begin implement-ing several changes over the next few years. One of the issues standing in the way of full accreditation was the fact that employees of the university had long been key members of the board—an arrangement that was not acceptable to the North Central Association. A year after the founder's death, at the April 1958 meeting, all salaried officers of the university—including John Brown Jr.—stepped down from the board, and the first person not related to the Brown family was elected to the chairmanship. He was Robert W. Hyde, a 1937 JBU engineering graduate, World War II Navy veteran, and successful highway construction contractor from Mississippi. After the Alumni Building was renovated and equipped to become the home of the JBU Engineering Department in 1959, it was rededicated as the Robert W. Hyde Building. Hyde served as chairman for twenty years, longer than any person other than the founder in the university's history.[6]

Under Hyde's chairmanship, the board soon adopted a new set of bylaws for itself, ushering in a more modern, "corporate" model with several standing com-mittees. The board was naturally loyal to the founder's ideals, even after his death, since so many of its members were alumni of the school. It would be another twenty years before the board chairmanship and committee chair positions were opened up to non-alumni trustees.[7]

President Brown Jr. raised another suggestion with the board shortly after the

Cameron Townsend (founder of Wycliffe Bible Translators),
Rev. Billy Graham and John Brown Jr. in 1959

founder's death—that JBU prepare a doctrinal statement. The board approved of the idea, and in 1959 a statement of faith was adopted. Dr. Gordon Palmer, a member of the board at that time, made a motion that the statement be submitted to new faculty to assure they were "in sympathy" with its essential Christian doctrines and would "agree to work within the framework" of its tenets. The statement has remained firmly in line with the mainstream doctrines of American evangelical theology—the inspiration of the Bible, the eternal triune God, and the need for salvation—ever since.[8]

***

Palmer, whose quiet generosity had made possible the construction of the Library and Science buildings of the Cathedral Group, played an important role in continuing the evangelical spirit of JBU in the wake of the founder's passing. The commencement ceremonies of 1957, just three months after John Brown Sr.'s death, were held in the newly finished cathedral sanctuary, and an air of solemnity at his absence overshadowed the celebration of students whose work was complete. Palmer gave the commencement address with a title that fit both meanings of the day—"Your Destination, Please."[9]

Palmer was invited to take John Brown Sr.'s former role as the leader of the opening week of evangelistic services in the fall for each of the next several school years, continuing the clear, consistent voice of the founder in exhorting youth to put Christ over all.[10]

In the fall of 1959, Palmer was joined in the semester opening chapel program by the most famous evangelist of the day. Billy Graham, whose "crusade" format of evangelism had gained worldwide recognition throughout the 1950s, attended the Wycliffe Bible Translators conference at the former John Brown properties in Sulphur Springs in September. Then, on Tuesday, September 15, in the first chapel service of the new semester, Billy Graham came to the Cathedral of the Ozarks.

"When he came I was an usher," recalled English professor John Panage, "and we didn't have enough seats to seat all the people." In a tribute to the traditional Billy Graham Crusade theme song, Dr. Oiesen led the Cathedral Choir in a special rendition of "How Great Thou Art," and President John Brown Jr. introduced the famous evangelist to an enthusiastic reception.

Graham urged the students to go "all out for Christ" and spoke from chapter 10 of the Gospel of Mark, using the story of the "rich young ruler" to specially address the teenage students in the audience. He said the young, rich man who met Jesus was much like the youth of the day—confused and disturbed about life. Graham's message was, "Had he been willing, in Christ he could have found the answers and goal he needed."[11]

***

Under the leadership of President Brown Jr., the university put in much effort during the 1950s to improve JBU's academic program and facilities, with the goal of securing full accreditation. All three buildings of the Cathedral Group were complete by the end of the 1957–1958 school year. These facilities were important to the accreditation effort because they finally provided the university with a dedicated library and a science building equipped with multiple laboratories. The following school year, intercollegiate athletic programs were instituted for the first time since the interschool competitions of the early 1920s were discontinued. And in 1961, a "general education" core curriculum of liberal arts courses was implemented.

All of these efforts brought about the desired goal when JBU received full regional accreditation in 1962. It was yet another major milestone in the maturation of JBU as a full-fledged university. A decade later, JBU's teacher-education program received even broader recognition when it was accredited by the National Council for Accreditation of Teacher Education (NCATE) in 1972.

Student recruitment in the 1960s received an immediate boost after successfully

In 1961 a new south wing and connecting lobby were added on to J. Alvin Brown Hall.

achieving accreditation, but other issues of financial strength and much-needed facility improvements required attention. These issues became a primary focus for Brown Jr.'s remaining years as president.

In 1961, a major expansion and renovation of the J. Alvin Brown Hall for men was finished. The original brick structure remained as the north wing, with a new south wing and connecting lobby completing J. Alvin's U-shaped layout. The central courtyard created by the dorm's expansion provided a unique sense of community for the men living there, and more than twenty years later it would be enclosed to form the university's popular atrium.

The first married-student duplex of Broadhurst Village was finished in the summer of 1962, and in 1964 the original wing of Mayfield Hall was opened, providing women students with an additional hundred beds beyond the available capacity in the California building.

Also in 1964, the Murray Sells Gymnasium and swimming pool opened, providing a more modern venue for crowds to cheer their new Golden Eagle teams. The facility replaced the World War II surplus gymnasium and concrete pool that had been used for much of the previous twenty years in the valley along Sager Creek.

The 1970s saw new buildings replace old in the heart of the campus. Construction began on the new Mabee Student Center and Chapman Administration building, followed later in the decade by the adjoining Learning Resource Center. With the northern half of the new complex finished in the spring of 1973, the venerable old wooden structures of the Memorial Dormitory and Arkansas Building were razed over the next year. The two-story wood-frame Arkansas Building—originally simply called the Mechanical Building, with its vocational industry shops and auto mechanic garages—had anchored the entryway to the campus since 1922. In later decades it had been remodeled to serve as an executive office suite, business and registrar's office, student coffee shop, post office, print shop, and grocery store. With its demolition, land was now free to begin constructing the Learning Resource Center. It was completed in 1979 with a large new home for the library, and it added new classrooms and office spaces for the Business, Accounting, Teacher Education, Broadcasting, and Journalism Departments. Famed radio personality Paul Harvey was a featured speaker at the dedications of the two halves of the Mabee complex in both 1973 and 1980.

The growth in campus facilities under President Brown Jr.'s tenure was matched by growth of the student body. When he became president in 1948, the campus enrolled 300 students. By 1970, the fall student body exceeded 750 students.

***

One of the factors that surely affected enrollment growth was the lack of intercollegiate sports at JBU during its first forty years. Nonetheless, JBU had always had an excellent intramural program on campus—even holding a campus-wide "Intramural Day" on multiple occasions each school year, when all classes were dismissed and students were divided into Blue and Gold teams for a series of competitions. The day would often end with a nonathletic competition such as a spelling bee or skit contest, judged by faculty and staff to declare a winning team. Still, other small colleges like JBU had intercollegiate league sports, which students had enjoyed in their high school years.

By the late 1950s, JBU needed something more than intramurals to help attract a larger student enrollment. The first intercollegiate men's basketball squad was recruited and began playing in 1958. Later, teams in women's basketball, men's and women's tennis, swimming, volleyball, and men's baseball were added in the 1960s, and in later years several club sports gained the strong support of the campus community, including the Rugby Club, which formed in 1981. Throughout the rest of his life, John Brown Jr. almost never missed a Golden Eagle home basketball game.

The intercollegiate athletic program was instrumental not only in building a stronger campus esprit de corps but also in providing athletic scholarships for

The first season of men's basketball in 1958

recruitment of prospective students. These changes also gave a helpful boost to the university's desire to recruit a more racially and geographically diverse student body.

Several traveling JBU musical groups also contributed to the recruitment of new students from across the country. The most well-known and longest-running of those groups, the Sound Generation, began in the fall of 1967.

After returning to campus from a summer tour in Southern California with the Harmonaires — a JBU singing group of seven members — John E Coates '72 was inspired to start a larger group of singers and musicians plentiful at JBU in the 60s. Using the existing trumpet trio, Rolly Richert '69, Les Kline '69, and Jim Young '70, he quickly recruited trombone players Terry Patterson '70 and Roger Byrd '71, as well as bass player Dick Marsh '70 and Jim Hancock '76, who played guitar. The twelve singers, including wife, Marty '68 on alto and exceptional soprano, Lynda Farley '69, were easy to find and Coates eventually convinced preacher-boy, Bill Hartman, '69, another Harmonaires member, to become their director and emcee.

Hartman wasted no time in entering the group in the channel 8 talent contest at the Tulsa State Fair. After winning the tryouts in their category, the ecstatic group took first place, winning over all categories with their rousing Patriotic Package. That gave them the opportunity to perform live on the channel 8 noon show. Then the word was out, and invitations quickly followed to play elsewhere, from as far away as Iowa. Hartman soon worked with the university administration to make Sound Generation an official musical group representing JBU, and in 1968 the twenty-five-member group found themselves driving across the desert for their first summer tour in Southern California. Living at Brown's Southern California Military Academy and traveling in one of their school buses, Bill George, who was managing California operations, booked them extensively, including Downtown LA Rotary Club, Knott's Berry Farm, Disneyland, San Diego Youth for Christ with Andraé Crouch, on military aircraft carriers, and of course multiple church concerts.

During the eight years of its existence, the group toured the nation, bringing the newest generation of sound to the forefront in America, including an unheard-of two-week run with Minnie Pearl in Las Vegas, and performing nationally with celebrities Pat Boone, Jonathan Winters, Florence Henderson, Ray Stevens, 5th Dimension, with Roy Clark (the star of the television show *Hee Haw*), and many more.

Roger Byrd, who served as the second director of the group, said his favorite Sound Generation experience was when the group partnered with Youth For Christ (YFC) to appear in multiple high school assemblies in Michigan and then invite students to attend an evening program where the group played and shared their testimonies. Several hundred students accepted Christ that night, but Byrd remembers the group being disappointed that it wasn't more. YFC, however, was elated with the response and invited the group back, and they saw most of the remaining students become saved.

In 1970, the Sound Generation received the honor of singing for President Nixon's Prayer Breakfast in Washington, DC, with Pat Boone. Things got a little exciting during the program when Dan Posthuma's bass amp "popped" and the secret service went into high alert.

Over the years the group released four LPs, including national distribution for God's Love, with the Benson Co. in Nashville, Tennessee. After an amazing run, sharing the gospel everywhere they went and recruiting hundreds of students for John Brown University, the historic Sound Generation, from obscure Siloam Springs, Arkansas, performed for the last time in 1975.[12]

***

One of the most significant steps toward financial stability at JBU came with the establishment of the Chapman Trusts in Tulsa, Oklahoma. J. A. Chapman was a wealthy Oklahoma oilman who at one time was the largest individual shareholder in the Standard Oil Company—which later became ExxonMobil. Chapman became interested in John Brown University through hearing the founder speak on radio and meeting President John Brown Jr. in Tulsa, where Chapman's corporate office was located. Brown Jr. would later say that he was able to get in to see Mr. Chapman on those occasions he was in Tulsa because he was always brief—never sitting down, but always standing while giving Mr. Chapman an update on the progress and needs of the campus.

J. A. Chapman

During one of those visits, Chapman expressed a concern that any money he gave to the college in Siloam Springs might be used, instead, for some of the investment properties held by the university in Southern California. Brown Jr. said, "Oh no, Mr. Chapman, just the opposite. Those properties are helping by sending monies to JBU for the costs of the campus program."[13]

With the nature of these properties clarified in his mind, Chapman added John Brown University to a group of several specific beneficiaries that would derive money from three of his family's charitable support trusts that were founded in 1949, 1966, and finally in 1974. These trusts are now worth in excess of a billion dollars. JBU receives 5 percent of the annual distribution from these trusts left by Mr. Chapman and his wife, Leta. Today, this distribution to JBU exceeds $3.5 million dollars each year.

***

In 1961, one of the pillars of JBU's biblical scholarship departed the campus after a quarter century of service. Dr. Earl C. Smith, who had arrived with his six children in 1937, trusting God to provide the means to put all of them through college in a dedicated Christian institution, retired at the age of sixty-seven. Though he had told his wife in the spring of 1936 they would need to stay twenty years to make sure their baby had a chance to graduate, the Smiths stayed on a few years more, and indeed all six children—as well as three of their children's spouses, along with Mrs. Smith and Dr. Smith's sister—were educated at JBU.

Upon his retirement, he wrote of his fear that an institution dedicated to the pure Christian faith, without adherence to any particular denomination, might eventually drift into a more liberal theology. "But in my opinion," he wrote, "observing from the campus, whatever drift the university has made has been in the opposite direction. . . . To my knowledge, there was never a time in the history of John Brown University when the men in the Division of Bible and Religion were more loyal to the divine origin and authority of the Bible or were so well trained as now."[14]

He also recalled the diversity of views in the faculty over his years at JBU, having worked alongside instructors with diverging positions on Calvinist philosophies, dispensationalist views of history, and eschatological topics such as the timing of the millennium described in the book of Revelation. Despite this variety, he said, "we have all worked together in love and harmony as brethren in Christ should. Some think that this is confusion and weakness, but I think it is a strength of the university."[15]

Having seen to the education of their children at JBU, Dr. and Mrs. Smith followed a call to Toccoa Falls Bible College in Georgia, where Earl Smith taught until his death thirteen years later at the age of eighty.

***

America was changing rapidly in the 1960s. Continuing issues of racial injustice highlighted the need for a more inclusive Christian college educational experience. This national mandate was made painfully apparent with the assassination of Dr. Martin Luther King Jr. in 1968. Like many US Christian colleges of that era, JBU was located in a racially and ethnically monolithic region. But JBU was committed to sending its graduates into all the world to make a difference, and did not want to simply provide students a sheltered four-year college experience. A diversity of backgrounds among the student body could only help with this mission.

It had proved difficult for the university to recruit either students or faculty of color into Northwest Arkansas, and even more challenging to give those individuals or their families the assurance of cultural acceptance and support. Many times, it was a local church or host family that met those needs for students who did not identify with the dominant culture at JBU. While the unifying JBU community value had always been Christ Over All, for those individuals who came from a minority group in society, being a "missionary" to a majority culture was all too often a required role.

JBU had always had international students—many of them missionary kids, as well as a scattering of students from differing races and nationalities. In the early decades, there were a number of students from the Philippines and Central America. At least one of them had benefited from the missionary work of Cameron Townsend in Guatemala, and he gained the opportunity to come to John E. Brown College after he helped Townsend translate the Bible into his native tongue. But American-born minority students were harder to attract and retain. There was no special support program or culturally sensitive way of integrating those individuals and families into the campus community and the wider local community in general. The first African American students to attend JBU came in the early 1970s, and even at that time, they were often cautious about leaving campus alone.

As another example of the difficulties JBU faced at increasing the diversity of the student body, in 1975 JBU hired an admissions counselor who was assigned the task of recruiting Native American students from across the state line in Northeast Oklahoma, as well as from farther regions such as Arizona and New Mexico. The counselor's position was developed as part of a grant request JBU submitted to a federal program called Aid to Developing Institutions. This aid program was designed to help with recruitment, retention, and academic support at small colleges, which would in turn make those colleges more stable and their "at-risk" students more likely to succeed.

The university received this grant for a number of years, but the recruitment effort showed limited success. Recruiting students from Native American communities was difficult due to competition with the much larger state university programs, which had a long tradition of serving this population. JBU staff also realized that the few Native American students who did come often felt isolated and alone in the predominantly white, evangelical culture of the campus. While this sincere effort was not successful, many good lessons were learned that would later serve the university well with the launch of the Walton International Scholars Program in 1985—a program that dramatically opened the doors to JBU's becoming a truly global community.

***

President Brown Jr. led JBU during the most socially tumultuous decades of the twentieth century. While major universities across America were wracked by student protests throughout the mid-1960s to mid-1970s, John Brown University endured little of that turmoil. The school did have its share of difficulty, however, and President Brown wrote to the Board of Trustees in his 1969–1970 annual report, "During my tenure as President of this university, this, to my mind, was one of our most challenging years." He concluded, however, that "dissent had, in many ways, made us a better institution."

Dr. Richard Niswonger was a JBU history and Bible professor for over thirty years. He arrived at JBU in 1964 and observed firsthand the influence that a decade of social unrest had on the JBU community.

In 1999, Niswonger wrote a brief history of JBU covering the latter half of the twentieth century, which was published in an updated edition of Kennedy and Rothrock's *John Brown of Arkansas*. He described the mood of the JBU campus during the period of greatest unrest:

Dr. Richard Niswonger

> The social ferment of the late 1960's student rebellions and the restlessness of the Vietnam era made an impact on the JBU campus climate. But it was a very subdued effect when compared to colleges and universities across the nation. Students at Kent State University in Ohio torched an ROTC building and later suffered a National Guard armed assault on an unarmed protest group. After a volley from the Guard some of the students lay dead on the campus lawn. On many campuses students held nearly continuous protest rallies in the spring of 1970. With fists raised in the air, they shouted obscenities into microphones, marched in the streets, confronted police in battle fatigues and riot gear, burned buildings, burned draft cards and burned the flag.
>
> The JBU campus seemed like an island of serenity compared to the shock waves that hit other campuses. Even so there was some restlessness on the JBU campus in the late 1960's and early 70's. Criticism of the administration by some faculty and students, though relatively speaking quite subdued, did create some instability.

***

On Saturday, November 15, 1969, members of the JBU community planted a memorial tree north of Mayfield Hall to commemorate all those Americans who had died in Vietnam. Speaking at the ceremony were a World War II veteran as well as a Vietnam veteran.[16]

After World War II, during which more than forty alumni of JBU died, several more JBU alumni had died in military service, particularly during the Korean War, which began in 1950. Many others had distinguished military careers. In April 1952, one recent graduate, Lieutenant Dene Godwin, paid a visit to campus after having flown one hundred combat missions against Communist forces in the Korean War. Godwin made a career of the Air Force, and flew during the Vietnam War more than a decade later—a war in which many more alumni volunteered or were drafted into the service.[17]

Navy Lieutenant (j.g.) Samuel A. Meiss was one JBU graduate who had a distinguished service record in Vietnam. He had been a radio and television production major at JBU, the son of missionaries in northeastern Thailand, and he joined the naval reserves in 1961, a few years before the United States entered into full-scale combat in Vietnam. By 1967, he was in-country as a river patrol boat skipper in the Mekong Delta, and during one engagement with enemy forces, he earned the Silver Star. President Lyndon B. Johnson personally pinned the award on Meiss during a presidential trip to South Vietnam at Christmastime 1967. Meiss continued his service after the award as an aide to the admiral in command of all US Navy forces in Vietnam.

No comprehensive accounting has ever been made of how many members of the JBU community may have died in combat in Vietnam.

Many of JBU's men served and survived their tours of duty in Vietnam, and after coming home, some of them looked for ways to convert the painful lessons learned in war into something good. One such Marine Corps pilot who served in Vietnam was Ron Maines, who graduated with his mechanical engineering degree from JBU in 1967. As his time in college drew to an end, he knew there were few options to avoid getting drafted once his student exemption expired. After a Marine Corps recruiter visited the JBU campus, Maines said, "I thought I would try to qualify, learn to fly and serve my country." In late 1966, with less than a year before his graduation, Maines hopped aboard a decades-old DC-3 military transport plane at the Fayetteville airport and was taken to Memphis, Tennessee, for a military skills assessment and physical. He was accepted as a USMC officer candidate and pilot trainee, and he eventually did a tour in Vietnam as a helicopter pilot.

Upon his return from active duty, Maines decided he would keep flying, but he sought to use his hard-won skills as a pilot to do good and make a difference in the world. He joined Mission Aviation Fellowship in 1972 and went right back overseas, this time to Indonesia. He was with the organization for sixteen years, and even had an opportunity to fly back into Vietnam on behalf of the Christian humanitarian organization World Vision. Although Maines's time at JBU came after the end of the university's aviation program, his choice to use his wartime aviation experience to serve God was no doubt in keeping with the university's ideals and aspirations for the flight-training era of the 1940s and 1950s. He said, "JBU's commitment to Head, Heart and Hand gave us all the confidence to 'Love God, serve others, work hard and not make a big deal about it.'"

Doug Chamberlain '64 transferred to JBU where he earned a teaching degree just before being drafted in the spring of 1965. He completed the Marine Corp officer candidate program and landed in Vietnam in 1967 as a first lieutenant.

Shortly after his arrival the commander of the 2nd Battalion/7th Marines was killed in an ambush and Chamberlain, the only available officer, was given company command. Chamberlain served in Vietnam for a year and was later honorably discharged as a Captain in 1969.

***

One change to the JBU culture at the close of the 1960s involved community standards regarding fashion trends. "We were in the 'Jesus People' era with an emphasis on making the Gospel relevant to culture," said Earl Larkins, a broadcasting major who attended from 1970 to 1974. By 1972, his junior year, he was the editor of the *Threefold Advocate*. Larkins didn't recall anything resembling a campus protest during his years at JBU, but he was aware that just before he arrived, the question of men's hair length and facial hair had been a controversial subject. "I can't overstate the radical shift that occurred when regulations over hair lengths (and skirt lengths) were relaxed," he said.

Gary Elliott, '73, the president of the student government during the 1972–1973 school year, was at JBU when the men's hair issue became a major controversy. "The hair became a big issue in fall '69," he said. "At some points, they would enforce the No Facial Hair rule as well as the length of hair." He vividly recalled that when students returned to campus after the Christmas break in January 1970, an assistant dean was sitting at the cafeteria line entrance, turning away men whose hair was too long. "An uproar ensued," he said. But the JBU administration recognized that this was one campus standard that could be relaxed with the changing times. "Very soon things were instantly changed and absolutely no hair restrictions anymore! Crazy times," Elliott remembered. "By May, we all had long hair!"

After the summer of 1970, many of the male students returned with drastically different looks. "I always smile when I recall the beginning of school year 1970 after the hair restrictions lifted and everyone had a spring and summer to grow hair," Elliott continued. "Lots of mustaches and sideburns. . . . Everyone wanted to look like a member of Credence Clearwater Revival!"

Larkins recalled that in the early 1970s, the broadcasting facilities available to the students were in need of some rejuvenation, decades after radio's heyday as a cutting-edge vocational training program. In the 1940s, JBU had diversified the broadcasting efforts to include KUOA-FM, the first FM station in Arkansas, as well as a low-powered KJBU station that could be heard in the immediate vicinity of the campus. "Some television equipment was available in the 60's but was outdated, along with the hand-me-down KUOA equipment that was used to start a 10 watt campus station, KJBU," he recalled. But during Larkins's years, a new instructor in broadcasting arrived, former TV anchor Carl Windsor, and Larkins credited him with leading the effort to gradually modernize JBU's equipment and curriculum. "He took advantage of cable TV to broaden the school's out-reach, won permission from the administration to rejuvenate the programming on KUOA-FM with student talent, and paved the way for his successor, former Tulsa newscaster Mike Flynn, and others to carry on the founder's goal of equip-ping others to use modern media in all its forms to share God's plan of salvation."

Gary Elliott lived in J. Alvin, and fondly recalled "playing football in the mud in the quad with Iron Butterfly blaring out of someone's window overlooking it." The "quad" in his days, however, referred to the space between the wings of J. Alvin, which was later enclosed to form the Atrium. The modern-day quad of JBU didn't exist in the early 1970s, since the Memorial Dormitory—"MO" as the students called it—still stood in that space.

Larkins spent his junior year in MO Dorm, being among the last men to make it their college home before it was torn down in the summer of 1973. As newspaper editor, Larkins made sure to pay tribute in the pages of the *Threefold Advocate* to the venerable building's four decades of service. He reported that the old chapel in the north wing, where President John Jr. and his bride Caroline were married in 1941, still had its stage in place until the end.

The men who lived in MO insisted that the nickname stood for "Men Only," as opposed to J. Alvin, which was the "boys'" dorm. "It was an energy-waster," Larkins recalled of MO Dorm, saying, "I remember sometimes having the window open in the winter as the only way to regulate the temperature." During his years there, the rooms were all single-occupancy, "which could be radically decorated in ways not allowed in J. Alvin." He enjoyed the fellowship and broth-erhood of living in the MO. "All I saw was an honorable bunch of guys that han-dled their freedom responsibly."

In its latter years, after the "Helen—the First" tablet adorning the front of the building had passed into history, the dorm had a famous banner hung over its south entrance. It was a simple, flag of dark cloth bearing two large letters, "MO." There was a story that went around among the broadcasting majors in the spring of 1972, that Larkins admits may have grown in the telling, but it involved the sudden disappearance of the banner. In those days, the KJBU station was located in a classroom on the west end of the cathedral's third floor. One of the students looked out the window and said, "Isn't that the MO flag on top of the KUOA tower?" Larkins said, "The story I heard was one or maybe two of our freshman broadcasters took the banner and climbed the tower at night. Fortunately for them the station was off the air at night. Unlike FM, where an antenna cable is lashed to the supporting tower, an AM station's tower is the antenna, and current would flow through the human body."[18]

This legendary prank was not the only time the MO flag disappeared. The rivalry between MO's "men" and J. Alvin's "boys" meant that mischief was often afoot. Garry Friesen, a 1969 alumnus of JBU and the MO dorm, said, "Often the boys tried to steal the men's flag, but we always retrieved it." Still, before the MO was torn down in the summer of 1973, the final MO flag disappeared. Some of the last residents of the spring of 1973 tried mightily to locate the flag, but as summer came and the wrecking crews began their awful work, the orphan sons of the Helen Brown Hodges Memorial Dormitory dispersed from campus, never to know the fate of their noble banner.

That is, until almost forty years later, when a surprising revelation was made. During Homecoming 2011, Friesen, who earned advanced degrees in theology after his years at JBU, then went on to teach at Multnomah University and write a book about making decisions in the will of God, was invited to give a chapel address. Upon mounting the stage in the Cathedral of the Ozarks, Friesen unveiled—with all the reverence owed to an artifact of great historical importance—the MO flag itself, returning it to the university as his gift to be preserved in perpetuity.[19]

***

In 1974, JBU saw the end of an era as several of the school's longest-serving professors retired. Irvin Wills (thirty-nine years), John Panage (thirty-two years), Mabel Oiesen (thirty-two years), and Dorothy Woodland (thirty years) all brought their tenures at JBU to a close, and an employee recognition banquet was held in the spring, in part to honor their combined 133 years of service.

Dr. Oiesen likely captured the feelings of all of the retiring professors in her remarks at the banquet. After describing her decision to remain at JBU despite a frustrating first year, she said, "The next thirty years were fruitful and satisfying beyond words to express. My work with the students has been rewarding, challenging, thrilling, and joyous. I never again hesitated concerning this work. I knew it was the place I was called to serve."[20]

Two years later, having lived a quiet, simple life of education and service, Dr. Panage passed away at the age of seventy-six. Though he never fulfilled his dream of publishing a great work of literature during his life, thirty years after his death, his spiritual heirs in JBU's English Department published a collection of his journals titled *The Panage Papers: From Cyprus to the Ozarks 1942–1955*. In his will, Dr. Panage left half of his life savings to JBU, a gift that was used to help build

John E. Brown Jr. and John E. Brown III

the Learning Resource Center, home to JBU's new library. Upon his passing, his estate consisted of little more than his clothing, a wristwatch given to him in honor of thirty years of service to JBU, and his beloved collection of books.

Dr. Stuart Schimpf, the former campus pastor who had been a colleague of Panage at JBU throughout the late 1940s and 1950s, returned to campus for Panage's August 1976 funeral service in the Cathedral of the Ozarks. Schimpf told a charming memory of one of Panage's humorous plays on the English language, which, though foreign to him, he so loved. "Reverend Doctor," Panage once said to Schimpf, "do you know that in the Greek 'pan' means 'all' and 'age' means 'holy one'?" Having thus suggested an etymology for his own name, Panage concluded, "I am the 'all holy one.' I exude holiness!"

***

In 1979, John E. Brown Jr. stepped aside as president shortly before his fifty-eighth birthday, having served in the role two years longer than his father had. And, just as his father had done, John Jr. made way for his son, then–Vice President John E. Brown III, to become JBU's third president. In its first sixty years, the university had only two presidents—a remarkable period of faithful service and leadership to the campus. Despite many challenges and days of uncertainty, the university was growing larger and stronger with each passing year. One had planted and another had watered, but God was causing that growth to continue.

Upon turning over the presidency to his son, John Jr. was named chancellor by the JBU Board of Trustees and given responsibility for the oversight of the university's endowment programs, which now included traditional investment funds as well as several radio station properties that were still held and operated by JBU. John Brown Jr. fully retired from JBU in 1987, but retained the honorary title of chancellor until his death in June 2011.

In later years, John Jr. had a way of summing up many of his duties as president of the institution for over thirty years. "We had a big debt hanging over our heads, so I probably spent 80 percent of my time or more out knocking on doors and soliciting funds for the college," he said. "When I became president, I didn't really do things much different than my father had, except I intensified the effort to bring the school into a sound financial structure and to receive accreditation." When accreditation was achieved in 1962, John Jr. considered it the "greatest achievement" of his thirty-two-year tenure as president.[21]

In a self-effacing view of the three Brown presidents' roles, John Jr. was often heard saying, "I always say my dad started the college, I came along and sort of held it together, and my son John III took it to new heights."[22] Once, after fondly quoting the humorist Will Rogers's famous quip—"There ain't no good old days and there never was"—John Jr. added, "I agree with him and think these days and the ones ahead are the best because we have solved a lot of the old problems."[3]

John E. Brown III became president in 1979.

CHAPTER 10

THE THIRD PRESIDENT BROWN

John Elward Brown III was born on July 1, 1949, the year after his father took office as the second president of JBU. He was just seven years old when his grandfather, the founder of the university, passed away. Both the founder's son and grandson had the experience of growing up as the only boy in a family of many daughters. John Jr. had five sisters; John III had four.

"I grew up in the president's home adjacent to the campus, the home where my family and I now live," John III wrote a few years into his presidency. "My close friends were the sons and daughters of other college employees. The University was the center of our lives. We went to church together, participated in campus activities together, lived in community together."[1]

Still, during his youth, John III was fairly sure he did not want to follow in his father's and grandfather's footsteps as president of the university that carried his name. Dr. Richard Niswonger wrote of young John III's feelings about the future that seemed to be laid out for him. "Providence and family expectations seemed to indicate that the mantle of presidential leadership would eventually be placed upon the shoulders of the third John Brown," Niswonger said. "This seemingly predestined role disturbed him even at a very young age."

His reluctance was evident as early as the fourth grade. Recalling an essay he wrote that year about his ambitions, John III said, "I wrote that I didn't know, but I definitely did not want to be the president of JBU." Still, given the trajectory his life would take, John III reflected, "but 'God moves in mysterious ways, His wonders to perform.'"

After high school, John III broke with his father's and aunts' tradition and did not even start his college years at JBU, enrolling instead at Hendrix College in Conway, Arkansas. However, it may be that one of the ways God moved in John III's life to draw him into the service of JBU was the young woman he was dating, Stephania Ford of Siloam Springs. John III returned to Siloam and married Stephania in 1968 while the two were still teenagers. He went on to finish his undergraduate degree in business at JBU.

Niswonger wrote of a key moment that moved John III to reconsider carrying on with the mission of his father and grandfather. During one JBU chapel service while John III was a student, he had what he would recall many years later as a moment of epiphany. The guest speaker, Rev. Charles Allen from the First United Methodist Church of Houston, Texas, "gave a stirring message on finding and following God's will," Niswonger said. "Suddenly the conviction gripped him that he had been like the prodigal who selfishly asserts his own will rather than God's. That episode marked the beginning of John III's catching the vision of his grandfather. Now he was open to God's will, even accepting a leadership role at JBU."

After graduation from JBU in 1971, John III decided to pursue an advanced degree, which was an opportunity neither his father nor grandfather ever had. He entered the University of Arkansas School of Law in Fayetteville and earned his JD degree in 1974. He also completed the ROTC program at the University of Arkansas, and was commissioned into the United States Army Reserve.

After finishing his graduate work in Fayetteville, John III began serving at JBU. He worked in administrative roles in development and legal affairs, and also taught classes in introductory business, business law, and criminology before becoming—just as his father had—JBU's vice president while still in his twenties.

Then in 1979, after a series of meetings the Board of Trustees held with an outside consultant, the board chose to appoint John E. Brown III as the third president of the university. At his formal investiture ceremony that October, he spoke to the gathered JBU community and distinguished guests about his reasons for assuming the mantle of leadership of the university his grandfather had founded. He told them that, notwithstanding his name and the tradition established by the two previous presidents, "I came to work at JBU for the same reason as the faculty and staff—I felt called by God to service at JBU." At his inauguration, he was thirty years old.

JBU's founder had often been called a "dreamer" by those who knew him best. His son, John Jr., was regarded as a skilled administrator who had continued building on the dream of his father. John III's mission would be to carry on the work of his forebears by further establishing the university. Among his highest priorities were to strengthen the school's financial integrity, promote international diversity among the student body, and cultivate a fruitful spiritual atmosphere on the campus.

In the financial arena, JBU carried on the heritage of the founder, who had insisted on paying all debts at face value, even when the aftermath of the Great Depression left the college in serious financial jeopardy. In 1979, JBU became one of the charter members of a new organization that had formed—the Evangelical Council for Financial Accountability (ECFA). This coalition of Christian organizations sought to create a basis on which believers could give their money—as

The Brown family (from left): Kathryn, Jessica, John, Laura, Stephania, Ethan and Jenny

unto the Lord—to ministries that would truly put the funds to wise use. In 1982, John III was elected to the ECFA's board, and he twice served as its chairman during the next ten years.[2]

John III led the university toward embarking on the largest capital campaign it had yet attempted, to provide for facilities and scholarships and to build the university endowment. In 1985, the board approved "A Call to Greatness," a campaign that ultimately raised about $20 million over five years. John III recalled that "it was a hard task" at the time, although its success surely contributed to the confidence the Board of Trustees had in later decades when they launched capital campaigns that would each raise more than $100 million in the new millennium.

The physical campus continued to expand and modernize during Brown III's presidency. During his first semester in office, in the fall of 1979, the final expansion of Mayfield Hall was dedicated. A year later, the Learning Resource Center was finished, providing the university a spacious new library and allowing the Division of Engineering and Construction Management to move into the east Cathedral Group building, where it remained for three decades. Funds were raised to renovate the California dormitory, and it was announced in 1981 that it would once again be configured so as to provide a unique coed living space, with the north wing, nearest to J. Alvin, housing men and the south wing, nearest to Mayfield, housing women. The married student duplexes in Broadhurst Village were also remodeled after two decades of use.

***

In the spring of 1982, two of JBU's longest-serving faculty members, who had both retired in 1974, passed away and were honored in memorial services in the Cathedral of the Ozarks.

On May 6, 1982, Dr. Irvin A. Wills died at the age of seventy-seven after a period of declining health. He had served for several years as JBU's academic dean in addition to teaching biology courses. After retirement, he and his wife, Ruth, served for three years as missionaries at a Christian school in Jamaica before returning to Siloam Springs. The man known for being excessively frugal in equipment expenditures, falling asleep at night in his lab, and being devoted and daring enough to climb a ladder up the side of a burning building to retrieve his books, was remembered as a beloved mentor to generations of JBU students. Irvin and Ruth had always taken a special interest in students, with many finding a college home at the Willses' house after the Willses' three children had grown and moved away.

"He left on the wings of a warm spring rain," Irvin's daughter-in-law Marty said at the service. "He would have chosen it that way—a gentle going at the change of a season—a quiet parting at planting time. He was a man of simple things. He shall have to adjust to his present splendor."

Six weeks later, Dr. Mabel Oiesen, the founder of JBU's Cathedral Choir, passed away on June 19, 1982, at the age of seventy-eight. She had been ill for a long period. Her dearest friend, Dr. Dorothy Woodland, paid tribute to Dr. Oiesen's legacy in the lives of her students. "We will no doubt have tears but let them not be for Mabel. And in a way, we should not weep for ourselves, for Mabel has left us too many memories of beautiful things—and not just of beauty but memories of courage and devotion—and above all, of absolute dedication to our Lord."

Dr. Woodland noted that every music program Mabel worked on had as its sole aim bringing the hearer into worshiping God. And, thinking of her entry into eternity, Woodland said, "I know she went immediately from the pearly gates to the podium of an angelic choir. The sopranos are now less shrill and strident, the basses have somehow gotten the mush out of their throats, and all the choir now sings beautifully, powerfully, victoriously, in praise of our Almighty God."

Both professors were buried in Oak Hill Cemetery across from the campus they had each served for over thirty years.

***

As the university pressed on into its seventh decade, several means of

The campus store; Hansel and Gretel outdoor performance in 1948; students in the 1940s; the Ozarkians quartet

Vocational training in the Hyde Building; Dr. Oiesen directing the Cathedral Choir; the JBU Hospital

The woodworking shop in 1937; machine engineering; sledding on the hill behind the president's house; a graduating class in the 1940s

Student life in the 1950s; Brown Military Academy in San Diego, California

Student life in the 1950s; musical group, the Harmonaires; John Brown Jr. presents an award to a Brown Military Academy cadet

Services inside the Cathedral of the Ozarks before completion; student life in the 1950s; graduation ceremony in 1945

Construction of the Cathedral of the Ozarks; service inside the basement of the cathedral

KUOA broadcast; students in the 1950s;
Siloam Springs Main Street in the 1940s

The flagpole entrance plaza, built in 1982, is a popular
photo spot for visiting prospective students.

commemorating the legacy of those who had founded and built the school were
undertaken. A few months after the cathedral memorials to Wills and Oiesen, a
time capsule was enclosed within the newly built flagpole entrance plaza during
the homecoming celebration of October 1982. The capsule's contents, known
only to a few at the time of its burial, were to be left untouched until the university's centennial homecoming celebration of 2019.

In another tribute to the history of the university, in 1984, during the school's
sixty-fifth anniversary year, John Brown III worked with Dr. Ed Nichols of the
English Department to publish a book on several important faculty figures from
the school's history. The compilation, *By These Stones*, featured stories and reminiscences on Wills, Oiesen, Woodland, and others, as well as many pieces of their
original writings.

"Many changes have taken place over the years," John III wrote in the book's
foreword. "In spite of the nostalgia to which we are sometimes too vulnerable,
most of these changes have been for the better. But the history of change and
development at John Brown University has been, first and foremost, a history of
persons. It was not the buildings or program which sustained our work; it was the
dedication and perseverance of humble servants of God who responded to the
founder's call to educate the 'Head, Heart and Hand.'"

***

Three professors who joined the university faculty in 1969—beginning their careers at the same time as the faculty featured in *By These Stones* were winding theirs down—were Drs. Jim Walters and Andy Bowling of the Bible Department, and Dr. Shirley Forbes Thomas, professor of English and one of the founders of the university's Honors Department. All became popular, deeply respected, and beloved by their students—becoming true giants of the institution in their own right until their retirements around the turn of the millennium.

Dr. Andy Bowling

These professors saw their share of campus pranks. Jim Walters's bicycle was perhaps the first object to be mischievously hoisted up the new flagpoles at the entrance to the campus one cold day in January 1983. And Dr. Bowling himself was said to have played a prank when he put a bottle of beer in the refrigerator of a public campus lounge bearing the handwritten note, "Please do not drink this. I am saving it for my lunch. Thank you, Dr. Shirley Thomas."

In the late 1980s Dr. Thomas was asked to lead in establishing a new Honors Program for especially gifted and motivated students. While an earlier version of an Honors curriculum had been attempted in the 1960s, it eventually met with roadblocks as it proved difficult to integrate with certain degree requirements. Dr. Thomas had some trepidations about accepting the task, but she held to the Scripture, "The fear of the Lord is the beginning of wisdom," and she trusted God to establish the new endeavor.

The program offered its member students alternative core curriculum courses that experimented with nontraditional methods of integrating various fields such as visual art, classical music, and literature; by the early 1990s Dr. Thomas was introducing new Honors students to the local Arkansas and Oklahoma region through a syllabus that used "place as text" in a memorable freshman Honors Composition class. She has often told of her greatest moment, when, at a student writing competition, she overheard a faculty member from a large university say, "Oh, the kid from John Brown will win it! They always do!" JBU's Honors

Dr. Shirley Thomas

Program soon provided national leadership in the honors movement, and Dr. Thomas became the first faculty member from a small Christian university to be elected to the Executive Board of the National Collegiate Honors Council.[3]

***

Jim Walters's bike was hoisted up the flagpole by pranksters more than once during his thirty-five years of teaching. By the time the flagpoles were installed in 1982, Walters was into his second decade with the Bible Department. He had actually joined JBU a year before his appointment in 1969 as a Bible professor—in 1968, he was recruited out of the pastorate as JBU's director of admissions.

The recruitment no doubt had to do with Dr. Walters's family connections. In 1964 while he was studying at Dallas Theological Seminary, Jim married Lynda Springfield, daughter of JBU's business manager, Stewart Springfield, who had been with the university since the 1930s.

As a Bible teacher, Jim saw his calling as existential. "I felt a responsibility to teach God, not just about God," he recalled. "This is my life—not just a job. It is a call to ministry, where the vehicle is teaching Bible."

For many years, Jim taught two of the Bible courses that were required as part of the core curriculum, and so he had virtually every student to enter the campus sitting in one of his classes during those years. His memory of the names of those students could seem uncanny, decades later. He had a powerful memory, too, for his carefully crafted spoken words. Jim would spend many hours preparing full lectures, ensuring their timing, and meticulously fashioning them anew each year. He had an endearing mannerism when delivering some deeply potent insight—closing his eyes, gesturing with a gently curled hand near his forehead, and raising his countenance as if he were reading from heavenly pages far in the unseen distance. In many cases, his eloquent phrases of wisdom were no doubt born of immediate thought, rather than recalled from a prepared text.

God's character and being, he once said, was "the ultimate dictionary of all true meanings, the ultimate and final truth which sets us free from the untruths that finite and feeble minds have conjured up." It was his and Lynda's reliance on God's character and love that carried them through many physically difficult years of their marriage, making them a living example of patient, selfless,

Dr. Jim Walters

Christlike devotion before countless witnesses among the JBU family. Since 1977, Lynda had been diagnosed with multiple sclerosis. Speech and vision difficulties and loss of her dexterity had gradually become more pronounced throughout the 1980s until, ten years after her diagnosis, Lynda was no longer able to drive. Another ten years, and she was unable to walk. Though verbal communication ultimately became very difficult for her and a wheelchair was her constant companion, whenever Jim brought Lynda to chapels or Christmas Candlelight Services, the two of them both had seemingly endless smiles and loving greetings for the many friends who stopped to wish them well.

Through all the difficulties Jim and Lynda faced, their testimony made Jim's teaching all the more vivid when he would say, "All of life can be an act of worship as we respond appropriately with our minds, hearts and hands to God's glory."

***

The fall of 1983 brought the beginning of a new campus institution that would expand JBU's ministry via radio in exactly the way the founder had once dreamed. Campus station KLRC made its first broadcast—albeit as only a one-hundred-watt station with a small local reach—on October 1, 1983. Named after the Learning Resource Center in which its student-run studios were located, KLRC broadcast contemporary Christian music as well as syndicated preaching and talk programs with increasing reach over the coming years. By 2013, after almost thirty years of operation, it would grow into a 100,000-watt powerhouse, simulcast over three additional FM translator towers, and streaming live on the internet, providing uplifting and Christ-centered music to tens of thousands of listeners.

Five years after its small local beginnings, in 1988, KLRC received permission to increase its power to three thousand watts, and the famed radio broadcaster Paul Harvey, whose wife, Lynne, had joined JBU's Board of Trustees in 1980, was invited to perform the ribbon-cutting for the new station. However, by the end of the 1989–1990 school year, the station was facing a difficult choice. Down to its last $1,200 in operating funds, and with no dedicated full-time staff, it was announced over the air that KLRC would be shutting down as its student DJ's went home for the summer.

Over the month of May 1990, KLRC received over one hundred calls from avid listeners who wanted to contribute funds to keep the station going year-round, and as a result the station conducted its first on-air telethon to raise the funds needed for continuous summer operation. The three-day fundraiser brought in enough money to keep the station on the air and started the annual "Sharathon" tradition that, fifteen years later, was so successful that over a third of a million dollars in pledges could be received in just sixteen hours.

A few months after its first fundraising success, KLRC doubled its power to six thousand watts and was well on its way to becoming one of the most influential Christian radio stations in the country. In the new millennium, it would win a Dove Award in three different years as the best small-market station in the country, becoming the only college-owned radio station to win the award. What the founder had only dreamed of, KLRC ultimately achieved: a college-owned, student-operated, maximum-wattage radio station bringing the hope of the gospel to millions and a vocational training program to hundreds of alumni.[4]

***

During John Brown III's tenure, the student body grew from an enrollment of about 750 students at the end of the 1970s to over 1,000 in 1991. The goal of sustained international diversity finally came to fruition in 1985, when Walmart founder Sam Walton and his wife, Helen, created the Walton International Scholarship Program. This scholarship recruited outstanding Central American high school students and provided them with full-ride scholarships to one of three faith-based Arkansas colleges. John Brown University was selected as one of these colleges and enrolls sixty Walton scholars each year. In 1994, the program expanded to include students from Mexico.[5]

As recruiting got underway for the inaugural class of Walton scholars, John III traveled to Central America to meet with potential students. In Costa Rica, one of those prospective students of the first class, Rolando Chaves '89, described the events surrounding his application for the scholarship. "The year was 1985, and I had been praying for five years that God would allow me to study full time and to study science," he said. Due to his family's economic situation, he eventually came to the conclusion that God's answer to his prayer was a definite no.

"Then, the most amazing thing happened," Chaves continued. "I was working for World Vision and my boss had gone to the main office in California where his best friend, a JBU alumnus, had heard about the Walton Scholarship." Chaves's boss returned with a copy of the application form, and Chaves eagerly completed it and sent it off to JBU within two days.

"That very same week," Chaves said, in what must have seemed an amazing coincidence, "a missionary friend of mine told me that the JBU president, John Brown III, was going to her house that night!" Chaves was sure he was the only person in Costa Rica who had ever heard of JBU. "That night I went to the meeting with President Brown and at least twenty students who were applying to the

Walton International Scholarship Program students visit with Sam Walton (center, back row) at Walmart Headquarters.

scholarship were there. Only four of them were going to be chosen."

Chaves had fortunately kept a copy of his Walton Scholarship application, and he had it with him when he went to the missionary's home to meet President Brown III. Chaves handed it over for the JBU visitors to review, then left. "I received a phone call the very same night that I had been given the scholarship."

As it turned out, his meeting with John III was no mere coincidence, but providence. Chaves said, "As if I needed confirmation of God's will about me going to JBU," he found out later that "my original application and papers that I had sent . . . never made it to JBU."[6]

The origins of the Walton program developed fairly rapidly during 1985, and there were only a few months between its announcement and the arrival of the first Central American students on campus. In its haste to make the necessary arrangements, the JBU administration at first planned to house all of the Walton scholars in the California dorm.

One JBU student who had grown up in Ecuador as a missionary kid thought this was a bad idea. That student was Skipper Pickle Jr. '85, the assistant coordinator of resident life for California.

"I don't believe these students should be arbitrarily moved into California dorm," he wrote in a letter to the JBU administration. "If they are placed all together in this dorm, as small as it is and as removed from the rest of the campus as it sometimes seems to be, then this will become a 'safe' place for them which they need rarely leave." He noted the disadvantages of racial and cultural segregation, and the reality that even at JBU, people would have prejudices to overcome. "If we block these foreign students together, they will be seen as a block, unapproachable. Them against us." He continued, "If they should be [offered] the same education, the same degree, then they should be given the same living requirements and opportunities given any resident."[7]

Pickle's letter likely played a role in the JBU administration's adjustment of the plan, resulting in the much wiser approach of integrating the Walton scholars throughout the residence halls. In the coming years, this vibrant part of the campus culture would see many of its members take on significant roles as student body leaders throughout all aspects of academics and social activities, being welcomed as valued and important members of the JBU community.

When Sam Walton first envisioned the scholarship program in the 1980s, several Central American countries suffered under authoritarian regimes or were torn with civil war. More than one Walton scholar had the harrowing experience of being robbed on the way to or from the application interview. Others held childhood memories of seeing the death and violence of civil war on their very doorstep. Sam Walton aimed to bring bright young students to America, where they could experience life in a land of free enterprise and civil liberties, and gain an education that would build their character and equip them to return home to make a difference in their countries. The courage to stand for change as a Walton graduate was built, for many of the Walton scholars, before they even won the scholarship.[8] Many have returned home to open a school or an orphanage, to serve as engineers in improving the standard of living in their communities, to work and provide for their younger siblings to attend school, or to serve in their nation's government.

For over thirty years, JBU has carefully selected students for this scholarship program from low-income families across seven different Central American countries and Mexico. With the commitment of each scholarship recipient to return to their home countries after graduation, JBU's Walton scholars have had a profound impact in Central America and Mexico.

***

Another avenue for enhancing the cultural diversity of JBU's student body came in 1987, when an anonymous $1 million gift established a scholarship specifically for MK's—missionary kids—who had grown up as the children of Christian workers on diverse mission fields. In its first year, the scholarship was awarded to forty new students whose life experiences and unique, "reverse culture shock" views of American society provided enrichment to the campus culture.

As Niswonger observed, "The Founder's vision had included ministry in other lands, especially through use of practical vocational skills, such as radio broadcasting and construction. JBU graduates used technical skills to operate missionary radio stations, to build useful structures in remote areas, and to solve practical problems in underdeveloped regions of the world. They preached the gospel, but they could also repair the jeep or airplane that took them into the interior."

By 1989, at least 233 JBU alumni were actively serving in mission work, with at least 136 of them serving overseas. With the long history of mission service among JBU's alumni and the dedication of the special MK scholarship, now many of JBU's alumni serving abroad could send their children to the same college that had given them such a formative experience.

As the international diversity of JBU's student body increased in the 1980s, a tradition emerged in which one chapel service each year would be dedicated to celebrating the many nationalities on campus. One student from each of the represented nations would carry his or her country's flag to the front of the cathedral in a ceremony that, by the late 1990s, included more than thirty foreign flags.

Toward the close of Brown III's tenure, a missionary-in-residence program was started, where missionaries who were on sabbatical from their work in the field could spend a year contributing to the student community. These missionaries would teach special classes and serve as guest speakers, but also fill the vital role of providing support to missionary kids who were feeling out of place.

In the late 1980s a house near the university had been donated to the school and later was furnished to be the home for the missionary-in-residence families. The home had been built by a longtime employee of JBU, Harold Ward, a mechanical "fix-it" man who ran some of the school's vocational departments. He was the son of 1920s professor Dr. Artemus Ward. The Ward family had been a vital part of campus life in the early decades—Harold was one of eleven children, a number of whom attended and worked for JBU. After Harold married, he and his wife Mildred became a beloved part of the JBU community for sixty years. After living much of their lives in a house on Holly Place, next door to the president's home, Harold built a new home along Holly Street in the 1960s for his and Mildred's retirement years. After both of them had passed away, the home was presented as a gift to JBU. Since then, about twenty missionary-in-residence couples have lived there. Since many of them have themselves been both MKs and graduates of JBU, they have been a great encouragement to MK students who needed an occasional hot meal or a welcoming place to feel at home in the house that Harold Ward built.[9]

***

Sam Walton (middle) attends the dedication of the
Walton Lifetime Health Complex in 1988.

President Brown III had a priority of establishing deeper spiritual life on campus. During his tenure, the position of campus chaplain was reinstated, providing a single pastoral voice that could provide leadership to many student-led ministries and the twice-weekly chapel program. The J. Vernon McGee Chair of Biblical Studies was established, bringing in evangelical scholars as visiting professors. These included Dr. Kenneth Kantzer, former editor of the magazine *Christianity Today*, and Dr. Vernon C. Grounds, the former president of Denver Seminary.

Academic development was another of President Brown III's priorities throughout the 1980s. By the fall of 1991, almost two-thirds of JBU's faculty held PhDs in their teaching fields, and that number would increase to 70 percent by the end of the decade. A sabbatical leave policy was also adopted for all faculty members.

Scholarships for students showing high academic excellence were expanded throughout John III's tenure, and John Brown University crossed the one-thousand-student threshold for the first time in the fall of 1991. In 1992, the school achieved its highest-ever freshman student retention rate of 94 percent. The achievement was a significant one, since two decades earlier the admissions staff found themselves needing to recruit some three hundred new students—about half the campus population—every year. At the beginning of John III's presidency, admissions consciously focused on recruiting "more of our own students to return." Toward the end of his presidency, with success in this area achieved, admissions focused on recruiting "1,001 by '91."

The steady growth and maturation of the university under President Brown III eventually led, in 1994, to JBU's being recognized for the first time as one of the top colleges in its category in the annual US News and World Report Best Colleges rankings. JBU has been highly ranked in the annual survey ever since.

***

Many additional facilities improvements took place in the latter years of John III's presidency. In 1985, the great atrium was enclosed at the center of J. Alvin, providing an informal and sometimes raucous gathering space for student concerts, worship meetings, and Super Bowl parties. In 1987, the now-familiar chimes from the cathedral were first heard after an electronic carillon was installed. On Homecoming Weekend 1988, the Walton Lifetime Health Complex (WLHC) was dedicated, providing a new fitness center for both the campus family and the local community. The WLHC also provided a popular late-night snack shop and grill called the Eagle's Nest, introduced the sport of racquetball to many students with its four enclosed courts, and included the largest meeting space ever available to the JBU community—a two-story-tall gymnasium large enough to contain three basketball courts, which would be used for commencement ceremonies for many years to come. Renovation of the cathedral continued in the early 1990s, and a unique form of "suburban" college living was added for upperclassmen as the first townhouses on the slope behind J. Alvin opened in 1990.

***

In September of 1992, John Brown III announced that he would resign from his position as the university's third president at the end of that academic year. He believed that the time had come for nonfamily leadership of JBU. His tenure as president encompassed fourteen years, and he would be just forty-four years old at the time he stepped down from his official duties. Perhaps by virtue of this contrast to the lengthier terms served by his father and grandfather, the announcement was unexpected. Niswonger observed,

> The resignation surprised all segments of the university family, especially since the institution had reached a high point spiritually, academically, and financially. Brown reminded faculty, staff, and students that

he had periodically stated publicly his intention not to remain in the presidential office permanently. The successes of the university seemed to urge him to argue well for choosing that moment for the passing of the torch to another. He did not believe that having the surname "Brown" was the primary prerequisite for a candidate for the president's office. "I have always considered my commitment to this university," he insisted, "to be the result of my second birth, not my first."

John Brown III departed the presidency of JBU and went on to be elected to the Arkansas legislature as a state senator from Northwest Arkansas. He also became the executive director of the Windgate Charitable Foundation, a philanthropic family foundation established by Bill and Dede Hutcheson in 1993 to provide donations to educational programs, the visual arts, and other charities across the United States. In the 2010s, funds from the Windgate Foundation would help to completely renovate the engineering and science buildings of the Cathedral Group, turning them into fully modernized facilities for JBU's ever-growing art programs. The two buildings would be renamed Windgate Visual Arts East and West. The Windgate contributions to these projects, as well as to others on campus over more than twenty-five years, have provided significant support for JBU's scholarships, facilities, and endowments.

Niswonger reflected on John III's relationship with JBU in the years since his departure from official duties: "His commitment, concern and support for the university continued undiminished despite his choice of a new vocation."

The year 1993 drew to a close a remarkable seventy-four years of continuous executive leadership by the three generations of John Browns. As it turned out, the first year of change to new, outside leadership would not be an easy one for the university community. But by the school's seventy-fifth-anniversary year, in 1994, the legacy that had been built in the first three-quarters of a century at JBU would be carried forward faithfully into the next quarter century under the new leadership of President Lee Balzer and, a decade later, continued by President Charles Pollard. Those following years would be filled with unprecedented growth in campus facilities, university endowments, gifts received, student enrollments and retention, and a continuing belief in the importance of educating the head, heart, and hand.

As John III observed, "Under the banner of Christ Over All, God's providence and blessings have been evident in multiple ways."

Or as the founder might have said, "That old bass drum of the Salvation Army is still beating!"

Built between 1990 and 1992, the six townhouses are divided into two sections. Each section contains four-bedrooms, two bathrooms, a kitchen, and a living room and houses eight upperclass students.

An aerial view of campus from the mid-1990s

CHAPTER 11

THE BOARD OF TRUSTEES' LEADERSHIP IN A YEAR OF TRANSITION

With the announcement of President John Brown III's intent to resign, JBU's Board of Trustees faced an unprecedented task—searching for and selecting a new president of the institution who was not a descendant of the founder. Soon, however, the mission of the board was to address an even bigger concern—the fact that their newly appointed choice for president felt it best to resign midway through the 1993–1994 school year, his first year in the post.

The board was well-equipped to deal with the unforeseen challenge of this school year. John Brown III had worked with the board in the latter years of his presidency to strengthen its role in the guidance of university affairs. He had encouraged the board—now thirty members strong—to carefully define its own role, and commit to spending more time on campus. Niswonger wrote, "This preparation proved to be invaluable as the university made the eventual transition in 1993 and 1994 to the first presidents from outside the Brown family since the founding in 1919. The board members stepped forward to truly become the legal and spiritual trustees for the campus."[1]

***

After Brown III's announcement of his impending resignation in September of 1992, the board began its search for a new president over the 1992–1993 school year. The chairman of the Board of Trustees at the time was Don Soderquist, the widely respected chief operating officer of Walmart. Soderquist appointed a search committee and designated as its head the long-serving trustee and alum of JBU Dick McCartney '47.

Working with a search consultant, McCartney's search committee identified the board's presidential choice by the end of the spring 1993 semester. He was Dr. George F. Ford, the vice president of development for Roberts Wesleyan College in Rochester, New York.

During Ford's brief tenure as president of JBU, the university successfully launched the Advance Degree Completion Program, which provided a vast new opportunity for JBU's educational ideals to reach beyond the traditional undergraduate model. The program began by offering a major in organizational management, and it provided a curriculum designed for working adults who wished to finish their college degree while still maintaining a career. Program applicants had to have previously completed at least two years' worth of college credits to enroll. The first classes were held in Siloam Springs, and spread to several other nearby cities in the following years. In an era before the emergence of the internet and the proliferation of online college courses, this program positioned JBU as an educational leader throughout Arkansas.[2]

Dr. George F. Ford

Unfortunately, the appointment of Ford was soon followed by a series of issues that raised concerns from several corners of the campus community throughout the summer and fall of 1993. Ford's more formal, Northeastern demeanor and autocratic leadership style did not mesh well with the consensus-style leadership, Southern friendliness, and family orientation that the JBU community had come to expect under the Browns' leadership. Ford forbade cabinet members from speaking to board members without his permission or outside his presence. He was absent from campus for long stretches of time, and he made decisions with little consultation with others. A leading faculty member began questioning first the direction of the university and later the integrity of certain of Ford's statements, which led a few faculty to contact key board members to raise concerns. One of the trustees who had served on the search committee was Mark Simmons, a business executive from the Siloam Springs community. Together, Simmons and Soderquist spent time on the JBU campus meeting with Ford, members of Ford's executive committee, and concerned faculty and staff. They found the faculty and staff concerns to be legitimate, and after further conversations between Ford and the board members, Ford resigned prior to the spring 1994 meeting of the Board of Trustees.

With the presidency so suddenly vacated, the board's search committee returned to the list of names they had originally considered during the prior year. But in the meantime, John Brown University needed someone to step into the role of the president immediately.

Longtime trustee E. William "Bill" George was asked to step in as interim president. George was a JBU graduate of 1948 and had been a trusted friend and advisor to all three of the Brown presidents, joining the Board of Trustees in 1954. He had worked for several years managing the university's California interests, such as the military academies and radio station KGER.[3] He held the respect and confidence of the campus community, and his presence was critical to calming and reassuring the JBU faculty and staff that all would be handled well.

Bill George

George fully understood the fact that he was serving only in an interim capacity, and he symbolized this understanding by choosing not to sit at the president's desk. Instead, he set up a folding table in the middle of the president's office, where he could do his work.

"Bill George became the healer," Soderquist said. "He called people together, he nurtured the staff—he was the right person at the right time for the campus."

Years later, on the occasion of JBU's ninetieth anniversary, JBU's director of parent and alumni relations Jerry Rollene, a 1975 graduate, researched the history of the school's presidents through original interviews, and he reflected on the lessons to be learned from Ford's brief tenure. "What I found is that during [that year], the JBU community drew closer together, and it helped us realize that we had an identity which defined who we were, and what we were not."

One of the search committee's finalists during the prior year's presidential search was Dr. Lee Balzer, then president of Tabor College in Hillsboro, Kansas. Balzer had a strong academic background, a servant-leadership style, and a graceful personality. The board agreed that he was a candidate who deserved consideration again, and a call was placed to see if Balzer was still interested in the position. Balzer made a follow-up visit to JBU's campus late in the spring of 1994, and he soon agreed to come that fall and become the president of John Brown University. His arrival on campus brought a renewed confidence to the JBU community, as well as to the Board of Trustees.

***

JBU's Board of Trustees was strengthened during this period of presidential uncertainty. One result of this time was the creation of a new standing membership committee of the board. The presidential crisis had shown the important role individual trustees could have on campus, and the great value in having trustees who were a good fit for the mission of the university.

The membership committee would establish policies related to the composition of the board, as well as to evaluate prospective trustees and the performance of incumbent trustees. The committee would also oversee the board's officers and administer self-assessments and presidential evaluations. It would also be responsible for recommending the president's compensation and benefits.

Today, the board membership "reflects the diversity of the JBU campus," in the words of former chair Don Walker, who served in that role from 2002 to 2007 and was an Arvest bank president in Arkansas and Oklahoma. Walker believed that a strength of the board was in having a healthy mix of men and women, alumni and nonalumni, younger and older members, and, significantly, a multicultural membership. In recent years, one trustee position on JBU's board has been specifically reserved for a Walton Scholar alumnus.

Walker described the character qualities of a good JBU trustee. "I think the primary quality of a good JBU trustee is for the person to be a Godly leader in their church, their business, and in their family," he said. "They need a love for the Lord and a love for higher education." He also noted that, in addition to a "servant heart" and a "belief in the mission of JBU," many trustees are "sacrificial in giving of their time and resources."

Robert Cupp, teaching pastor at Fellowship Bible Church in Lowell, Arkansas, served as JBU's campus pastor for a time in the late 1990s, and was chairman of the board from 2007 to 2012. "I think commitment to the heritage and history of JBU is critical to being a good trustee—Head, Heart, and Hand," he said. Also, Cupp pointed out that effective trustees understand that they deal in "policy governance," not in micro-managing issues on campus.

The board chair enjoys a close relationship with the JBU president, not just for the purposes of reviewing decisions made on campus, but also with a heart for encouraging the president and his family in their critical role. Said one former chairman, "The most important thing we do as trustees is to select, advise, and nurture the JBU president."

With the arrival of Lee Balzer, the board would continue to nurture and advise JBU's president as he led the university through a decade of increasing growth, stability, and success.[4]

1966 baseball team; classroom in the 1960s; Broadhurst Village duplex

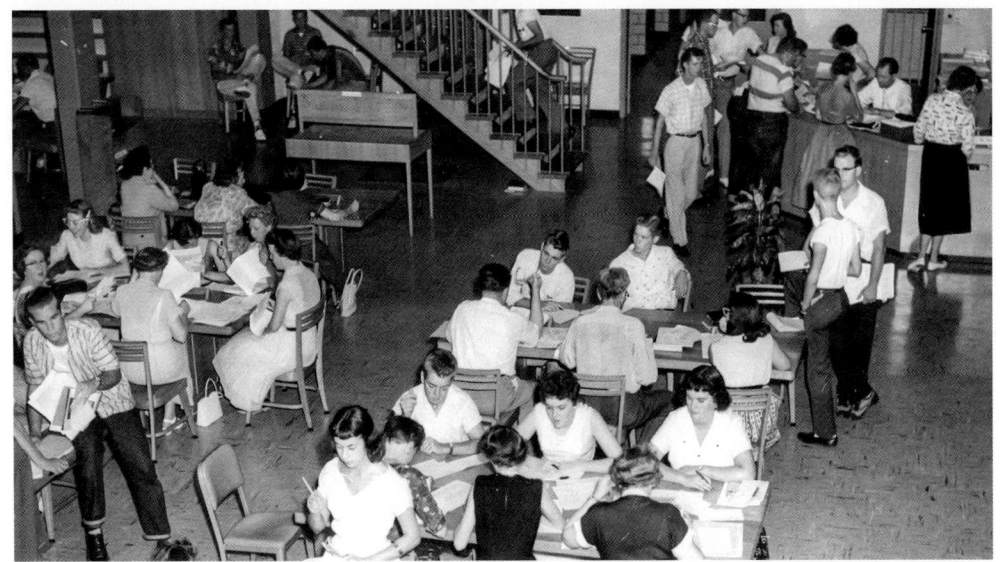

Student life; R. G. LeTourneau
visits campus; Mayfield
ringlighting ceremony in the
1980s

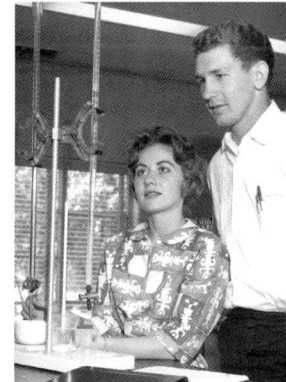

Campus coffee shop in the 1960s; Mayfield Hall; 1950s student life; Dr. Gil Weaver teaching Bible class; student life

Clockwise from top left: Library; student life; dorm lobby; engineering competition; graduates walking the 100 Steps; student life; chemistry lab; the Learning Resource Center under construction

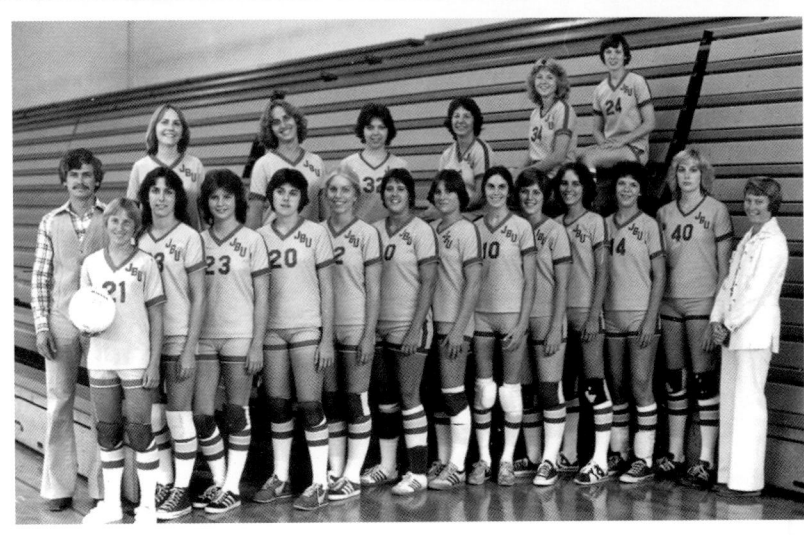

Clockwise from top left: the 1979-80 women's basketball team; 1980s tug of war contest; 1970s aerial view of campus; education major in the classroom; 1970s volleyball team; 1970s track and field

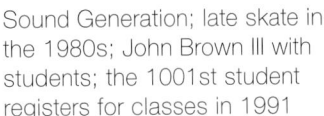

Sound Generation; late skate in the 1980s; John Brown III with students; the 1001st student registers for classes in 1991

CHAPTER 12

THE BALZER ERA

Newly appointed president Dr. A. LeVon (Lee) Balzer and his wife, Alice, arrived at JBU on August 1, 1994. They would serve as president and first lady of John Brown University for ten years until Lee's retirement in 2004. In contrast to the Brown family presidents, who were each known for their surprising youth when they first took office, Dr. Balzer was a genial fifty-seven-year-old with white hair and four young grandchildren.

Lee and Alice met in the 1950s while they attended Meade Bible Academy, a Christian high school in Meade, Kansas, and they were married two years after graduation. Lee attended Grace Bible Institute for two years. He and Alice both graduated from the University of Oklahoma, and Lee also earned a master of natural science degree there. He taught high school for four years in Shawnee Mission, Kansas, before moving to Columbus, Ohio, where he earned his PhD at Ohio State University in 1968.

The Balzers had extensive experience in Christian higher education before coming to JBU. After completing his PhD, Balzer served on the faculty at Western Washington State University in Bellingham, Washington, for seven years. The family then moved to Seattle, where Balzer served as a member of the faculty and dean of arts and sciences at Seattle Pacific University (SPU), a distinctly Christian university of the Free Methodist Church denomination. For a time Alice served as administrative assistant to the director of the Music Department at SPU, and later she was office manager of the campus church. The Balzers were active in the First Free Methodist Church adjacent to the SPU campus during their thirteen years there.

During these twenty years of teaching and college leadership, the Balzers raised a son and a daughter and became grandparents for the first time.

Lee & Alice Balzer

In 1988, Balzer was invited to the presidency of Tabor College of the Mennonite Brethren denomination in Hillsboro, Kansas. This call presented the Balzers with a very difficult decision because their daughter Tanya was to be married in Seattle that summer, and their son Cary, his wife Tracy, and their new daughter, Kelsey, had just moved to the Seattle area to serve in full-time church ministry.

However, given Tabor's needs and the Balzers' experience, Lee and Alice interpreted the move as God's calling for them, no matter how emotionally difficult it was for the family. As Lee put it, "There were many tears before and after the move."

Tabor College, the Balzers' local church, and the community of Hillsboro were all very warm and welcoming, and the Balzers found their six years there to be deeply enriching. Alice became a very active first lady, and with the helpful and encouraging Board of Trustees, and excellent support from the faculty, staff, and community, Lee led the college effectively for six years.

The Balzers did not have any intentions of moving on from Tabor, but the invitation in April 1994 to the presidency at JBU was compelling, and the Balzers accepted the somewhat urgent request.

Soon after coming to JBU, the Balzers' family joined them in the area. Cary and Tracy joined the faculty and staff of JBU in Christian ministry roles. Tanya and her husband, Todd Reichert, moved to nearby Tulsa, Oklahoma.

***

The Balzers arrived into a campus environment where there was concern about the future direction of the university, given the leadership tumult of the previous academic year. Dr. Balzer heard this concern from many members of the campus community in their general sentiment that "it should be like it used to be."

During those first weeks of the new president's tenure in 1994, Balzer and the Board of Trustees initiated a strategic, long-rang planning process, which was announced after the first board meeting that fall. Under this new president, a welcome commitment was made to preserve the historic identity of John Brown University and to affirm the mottos of Christ Over All and Head, Heart, and Hand with all of their historic meaning and content.

With the university now rededicated to these core commitments, Balzer invited the JBU community to provide active input. Committee structures were made to be broadly representative of the campus community, frequently including a student representative, and the administration provided open reporting to optimize such input and communication.

This process urged everyone, including the board, administration, staff, and

Dr. A. LeVon (Lee) Balzer served as JBU president
from 1994 to 2004.

faculty, to actively envision the future in challenging ways, with a new mandate to seek "God's highest and best" and earn a recognition of "world class" status for the university.

An important result of these early strategy meetings was the creation of a new Campus Master Plan. This guiding document established priorities for repairs and updates of existing facilities, and identified the most urgent needs for new facilities. The plan's overarching objectives were to support Christ-centered content and community on campus, and ensure top academic quality and competent, Christian servant leadership. Discussing these priorities for the future soon became a regular part of faculty, staff, administrative, and board meetings. The results of these open discussions were then shared with the Board of Trustees as part of the long-range planning process, and the board stayed active in developing this road map for the future. Within a few years, JBU had developed a strategic plan that included fifteen to twenty major objectives and more than sixty direct action plans for the future.

A disappointing and painful discovery was made in the summer and fall of 1995. In a surprising revelation, JBU and hundreds of other Christian and nonprofit organizations learned that a foundation they had invested in, New Era

Philanthropy, was actually a fraudulent Ponzi scheme. That summer the scheme collapsed into bankruptcy, with two million dollars of JBU funds potentially lost. Though JBU was eventually able to recover most of its investment, it was a difficult experience for all involved, and the fallout required months of deliberations and negotiations.[1]

***

One of the most dramatic societal shifts that coincided with the beginning of Balzer's tenure was the rise of the internet. Although JBU had been a charter member in 1991 of ARKnet—a precursor to the internet that linked colleges in Arkansas[2]—significant infrastructure upgrades were required to bring JBU's computer systems up to date. So, a Department of Information Resources—later renamed Information Technology Services—was formed.

Some students arrived on campus with desktop personal computers, and could access the internet through dial-up phone connections in their dorm rooms. The ubiquitous AOL promotional CDs of the day, which provided a certain number of free hours of internet browsing when signing up for the service as a "new" customer, were sometimes hoarded by a cash-strapped student with a personal computer, allowing a limited amount of "free" internet access in the dorm. It quickly became clear that the needs of modern higher education in the mid-1990s required more modern, internet-connected computer labs to be installed throughout the campus for student use.

One lab in the upper floor of the Learning Resource Center was, during Balzer's first year, still equipped with decades-old terminals that all functioned off a central mainframe, housed in a closet and connected to a single dot-matrix printer in the room where students could output their work to hard copy for handing in to their teacher. Freshman engineering students taking their introductory computer programming class would often crowd the lab late at night as they worked on a programming assignment due the next morning. Periodically, someone would call out loudly, "Compiling!" as they prepared to send their code to the mainframe, and the rest of their classmates would hurriedly save the current stage of their work at their terminals, just in case the mainframe should crash during the compiling task. It was a hazardous process. Hours of work could be lost if two students attempted to put the mainframe to work at the same time.

In the next few years, networked computer labs with access to the web sprung up not just in the LRC but also in various corners of the dorms and Cathedral Group buildings. There was also an inevitable debate—PC or Mac?—that had partisans arguing the merits of each competing platform. Eventually there was a separate Mac Lab established for the Apple computer enthusiasts to do their work, while the majority of the campus infrastructure adopted Microsoft Windows machines.

By the fall of 1996, JBU had its first website online. Computer science professor Ray West had set up the initial site in 1994 on a desktop machine in his office, viewing it as a useful learning project for his computer science students. Soon, mathematics professor Dr. Cal Piston lent a hand in designing the layout of the university's first homepage, and Carlos Avrard—a graphic design student and JBU basketball player—replaced the basic text links with graphical buttons. Lucas Roebuck, '97, recalled, "I made a graphically rich version of the website with even a video in 1996 which Ray posted for like a day or something, before he pulled it down because it took too much bandwidth."[3]

The rapid cultural shift toward internet-based research, news consumption, and social interaction brought its share of thorny questions. Early on, the campus community struggled with how to address the issue of illicit material available online, and whether it was appropriate for the administration to effectively censor access to the internet, versus simply encouraging students to use the web in an environment of personal responsibility and accountability.

Roebuck wrote, in his September 28, 1995 opinion column in the *Threefold Advocate*, "Should we allow unrestricted access to the Internet if students can use the web to receive pornographic materials? The answer is yes. If JBU administrators decide to limit web access because of potential porn access, then they should get rid of all VCRs as well. . . . If students want porn they can get it, Internet or not. Fortunately, the administration staff has done an excellent job in selecting students with high moral qualities who are mature enough to choose not to partake in these lusty mediums." The question did not go away easily, however. JBU both embraced the technology and developed an accountable community that was attuned to its perils. The internet was a technology that was as socially transformative as the electric light bulb or automobile. Proper Christian stewardship of this resource meant guiding the heart more than walling off the outside world.

***

In the fall of 1995, the Walton International Scholars Program (WISP) reached its ten-year milestone. Hundreds of Central American students had earned their degrees at JBU and then returned to their home countries to apply their education in meaningful ways. To celebrate the anniversary, Helen Walton took several Walmart executives and several members of the JBU community aboard a private Walmart jet to a beautiful rural setting in El Salvador. (Also attending were representatives of the two other participating colleges, Harding University and the University of the Ozarks.) There, many of the JBU alumni who had participated in WISP joined in a happy reunion that recognized all the trials and triumphs of the past ten years, and looked forward to the great successes surely still to come.

Ron Johnson

In the early years of WISP at JBU, the scholarship program was led by Brad Rudd and, later, David Sanford. But in 1996 a new director—a radio engineer and missionary to Ecuador named Ron Johnson— was selected to lead the program.

Johnson had spent fifteen years working in radio engineering support throughout the Caribbean and with radio station HCJB in Ecuador. But that year, some health issues in the family had led Ron and his wife, Sue, to begin considering a return to the United States. Their sons, Chad and Scott, were students at JBU. "I will never forget the Sunday night phone call from Billy Stevenson, international director at JBU, and my youngest son, Scott," Ron wrote many years later, when telling the story of how he came to direct WISP.

"Dad," Scott said on the call, "they are looking for someone who has international experience, in his 40's and is familiar with Latin culture. They have an open position called the Director of the Walton International Scholarship Program. I think you would be great for the job."[4]

Soon, Ron was offered the position, and Johnson's family—his wife, daughters, father-in-law, and two dogs—joined the two sons at JBU. Johnson became a beloved figure to twenty years' worth of Walton Scholars, many of whom simply called him Mr. J.

Johnson organized and managed the yearly visits to Central America, accompanied by Dr. and Mrs. Balzer and other JBU administrators, meeting with alumni in social settings and often in business seminars. Local Walton Scholarship alumni and Walmart executives frequently coordinated the seminars jointly and served as seminar leaders.

Johnson developed serious health issues in early 2007 that resulted in his receiving a pacemaker. Still, he remained active in the recruiting process of the program, making many trips to Central America in the coming years, although returning to a traveling schedule after discovering his health problems was a fearful prospect for him at first. "Over the summer [of 2007] I continued to struggle with fear and was unwilling to even drive to Tulsa," he wrote. Recalling Deuteronomy 31:6, "The Lord will never leave you or forsake you" (NIV). Johnson said, "I reached a critical point where I could go forward or be defeated by my illness. I started memorizing all the scriptures I could find on fear and anxiety and by God's grace stepped out in faith and made my first trip back to Central America in November 2007."[5]

In 2012, Johnson wrote a book filled with reminiscences and student testimonials drawn not only from his sixteen years (at that time) as WISP director, but also delving back into many stories from the previous years since the program's inception. *Our Story: The JBU Walton International Scholarship Program* captured the triumphs as well as some of the tragedies that had marked the program's history, all told through the voices of many of the hundreds of Latin American students who had seen their lives change because of the generosity of the Waltons and the welcoming embrace of John Brown University.

"When I was first hired for this position," Johnson reflected, "I told Dr. Lee Balzer that I was coming from overseas ministry and that my primary investment as WISP director would be to invest in the lives of the Walton students. I have tried to live up to this commitment over the years and have been blessed to play a small part in [their] lives."[6]

Through the years of his health difficulties, Johnson said, "it became crystal clear to me what the Lord has done in my life. . . . One of the Walton students asked me why so many students came and visited my office each day? Without hesitation the words came out of my mouth, 'I guess they know that I love them.'"[7] After a long period of declining health, Johnson passed away in 2017, having touched and guided the lives of hundreds of Walton scholars, so many of whom carried the lessons learned at JBU to influence their homelands in profound ways.

***

In the early years of Balzer's presidency, JBU made significant strides in expanding and improving the academic quality and offerings of the university. The 1995–1996 academic year saw the initiation of the first master's degree programs in JBU's history, in the arena of professional counseling. The first specialties were in school counseling, licensed professional counseling, pastoral counseling, and family counseling.

Graduate programs in other majors became available in the following years as demand increased and JBU refined its excellence in those areas. The new position of provost was created in the spring of 1997, and Dr. Mel Fratzke, a former associate dean for research and graduate studies at the University of Arkansas, was brought into the role. He had two daughters who were graduates of JBU. Fratzke was a highly respected educator in Arkansas, and in his new role—effectively the second ranking officer of JBU behind Dr. Balzer—he became very active in the refining and implementation of these new programs.[8] By 2003, JBU offered master's degrees in business administration, community counseling, leadership and ethics, marriage and family therapy, school counseling, and ministry. At the end of Balzer's tenure, enrollment in JBU's graduate programs was 202 students, with classes offered at both Siloam Springs and on satellite campuses in Fort Smith and Springdale.

The engineering and construction management programs had a long history at JBU because of the founder's Head, Heart, and Hand commitment. However, at the time Balzer took office, the engineering programs were not yet recognized by the Accreditation Board for Engineering and Technology (ABET), even though accreditation applications had been submitted over the years. JBU's engineering programs had a strong history and a long lineage of successful alumni who had earned their undergraduate degrees at JBU over many decades. With Balzer's arrival, there quickly developed a new passion to gain ABET accreditation for the large benefit it provided to JBU graduates seeking professional engineering employment and entry into graduate schools. Recognition by ABET would also provide an advantage in recruiting new, bright engineering students.

Jim Barnes, an elder statesman of the university who held the role of assistant to the president, had many years of professional experience as an engineer. His first job out of college had been working on the Manhattan Project during World War II, and he had spent many years as an automotive engineer, serving as president of two companies and also participating in the national leadership of Youth for Christ. John Brown III recalled that, when he hired Barnes in the late 1980s, Jim and his wife, Priscilla, came highly recommended as a couple who would become "a favorite aunt and uncle" to those who worked with them. Barnes joined the administration of JBU after retiring from the business world. Balzer assigned to Barnes the responsibility of leading the engineering programs toward successful ABET accreditation. Preparations for the new application were rigorous and detailed, and after numerous revisions, the updated application was submitted in 1995.[9]

In October of 1996, an ABET review team visited campus for a thorough evaluation of JBU's engineering facilities, laboratory equipment, programs, and personnel. After a year of review, the good news came that ABET had granted accreditation to JBU's engineering program in August of 1997.

Jim Barnes

Balzer continuously emphasized the development of JBU's high academic standards throughout his tenure, as envisioned in some of his administration's earliest goals for the university's future. Much of the transition of JBU's culture into a mature, professional university was brought about by three important changes.

First, capacity limits were placed on courses, reducing class sizes and creating much stronger faculty/student, teaching/learning relationships.

Second, academic budget needs began to be carefully prioritized with specific costs, such as the hiring of adjunct instructors, becoming budgeted according to needs. Such budgeting increased stability in the academic area.

Third, the maturation of the academic culture was directly addressed with several components of both policy and action. An orientation program was developed for new faculty, addressing the history and culture of JBU and its mission. Funding was made available for faculty to attend and participate in professional conferences. Summer faculty workshops were implemented with an expectation that faculty would participate. This sequence of summer programs emphasized JBU's historic principle of the "integration of faith and learning" as well as enhancing teaching skills. These summer programs were funded for several years by grants from the Teagle Foundation, which paid for the carefully selected presenters and also provided stipends for the participating faculty members. After the Teagle grants expired, the Office of Faculty Development continued to offer these faculty training sessions each summer to promote excellence in teaching, scholarship, and Christian mentoring.

These initiatives were implemented in the late 1990s, along with more rigorous faculty hiring criteria and scholarship expectations. The top criteria continued to be teaching and mentoring excellence, while publishing and presenting in academic venues such as the Coalition of Christian Colleges and Universities were also encouraged. Faculty and staff became very active in such intercollegiate leadership circles, and they found that JBU's interdenominational Christian identity was a positive factor in the availability of such opportunities.

***

Following the spring 1996 meeting of the board, with many of the university's most urgent needs now identified and prioritized in the Campus Master Plan, the board and administration moved ahead with a comprehensive capital campaign.

One of the most urgent needs was for a new, modern science building. Since its dedication in 1958, the west Cathedral Group building had provided physics, chemistry, and biology labs for generations of students, but it offered little potential for expansion or full modernization to continue serving the ever larger

Dedication ceremony for the Pat and Willard Walker Student Center
on September 27, 2002

student body.

Another high-priority need was for a new student center that could provide a more central "heart" of the campus for student socialization. The campus had several popular common areas in various buildings, but none were large enough or highly trafficked enough to provide a true crossroads for the student community experience.

In addition, the university had numerous, though less visible, needs, such as endowment growth, academic program enhancement, technology modernization, personnel, and maintenance. With the decision to embark on a capital campaign, much additional research and planning was needed to establish funding goals, procedures, priorities, and timing. Dr. Alan Cureton had joined JBU as vice president for advancement in the fall of 1995. He studied the many opportunities and financial needs rigorously.

A period of private fundraising was initiated before JBU publicly announced the campaign. By April 1997, donations of $5 million had come together into the campaign fund. After further study of funding potential and projected construction costs for the prioritized facilities, an ambitious capital campaign goal of $32 million was announced publicly in April 1998 with the name Campaign 2000: God's Highest and Best.

Responses by foundations, corporations, alumni, donor friends, board members, and university personnel were extraordinary. In January of 2000, JBU announced that the campaign had generated more than $39.7 million, well above the announced $32 million goal. The funding was applied to construction of the Pat and Willard Walker Student Center beginning in 2000 and the Bell Science Hall in 2003, as well as endowments and scholarships. As a result of this successful fundraising campaign, the JBU endowment approached $40 million.

The capital campaign's funds were also applied to the establishment of two academic leadership centers, which would greatly expand JBU's educational and community outreach in the years to come. These were the Center for Marriage and Family Studies and the Soderquist Center for Business Leadership and Ethics.

***

The JBU community had a passionate concern for the stability and health of Christian marriages and families. During the latter years of John Brown III's presidency, a marriage and family studies program provided the nucleus of an undergraduate major. Then, early in 1998, JBU held a public luncheon announcing the founding of the Center for Marriage and Family Studies (CMFS), with initial funding provided through a generous leadership gift from the Windgate Foundation.

At the outset, the CMFS was dedicated to helping individuals lay the foundations for strong marriages and families; to encourage, enrich, and strengthen existing relationships with the goal of building the foundations of healthy, life-long marriages; and thus to help build up families that would be instruments of transformation in society and in God's kingdom. Its unique focus was to be proactive and help educate and equip couples to build strong relationships, marriages, and families, and thus to complement the remedial care provided by qualified counselors.[10]

The CMFS was also dedicated to equipping pastors, church and community leaders, and professional counselors; and it helped JBU launch the graduate program in marriage and family counseling, which would train a new generation of Christian counselors to provide premarital, marital, and family counseling across the country and around the world.[11]

The program would have a campus, local community, and regional focus, but also reach beyond to a national and international scope. The center would provide seminars and retreats for the campus community and beyond, and serve as an information clearinghouse on marriage and family subjects.

Since its inception, the mission of the center has expanded as God has opened new doors of opportunity, leading the center to adopt two new names over its history that were ever more reflective of its core aims. In 2005, it was rebranded as the Center for Relationship Enrichment, then in 2014 it finally became the Center for Healthy Relationships—a name that its leadership felt was closest to the heart of its mission.[12]

Dr. Gary Oliver

In April 1998, JBU announced Dr. Gary Oliver's selection as director of the new center, effective on July 1. Almost a year after the center's announcement, in February 1999, JBU held another public luncheon featuring Dr. Gary Smalley as the keynote speaker, and announced that the initial funding of the center was now complete. The center developed a series of seminars and workshops and compiled a resource library to minister not only to the JBU community but also to other Christian universities, churches, and parachurch organizations, missionaries, Christian leaders, and the business community. The center also placed special emphasis on reaching underserved populations such as the incarcerated, recently released prisoners, those in generational poverty, and lower-income families.

Alongside its core proactive mission to provide relationship education and enrichment, the center was also asked early on to create a counseling center that would eventually be used solely for the training of JBU's growing number of graduate counseling students. Within a year of its establishment, the center was supporting JBU's master's degree program in counseling, with eighteen student scholarships as well as assistant positions for five graduate students at a counseling clinic called PeopleCare. Over time, the clinic was turned over to the direction of JBU's graduate counseling department, and the center's focus became squarely about proactive education.

Under Oliver's leadership, the center organized an annual Relationships Week on the JBU campus and provided regular workshops for dating and engaged couples. The center also provided an array of in-service training for JBU's departments on topics of conflict, forgiveness, communication, and anger management, and offered a Peacemaker Training course for center staff, student development staff, other JBU staff and faculty, and local pastors. The center also joined with the Crisis Care Network to offer critical incident response training.

Beyond its impact on a regional level, the center provided seminars and workshops at national and international conferences. In 2003, Oliver was appointed senior fellow in the Council for Christian Colleges and Universities (CCCU) in order to share the work of the center with other schools around the country.

By the end of President Balzer's tenure in 2004, the center had influenced well over ten thousand people, including those from a wide range of circumstances—poverty and wealth, young and old, and various levels of education and employment—offering a wide range of biblically based and research-informed resources to help men and women in the building of strong relationships, friendships, marriages, and families.

***

As JBU's influence grew, there was increasing interest for JBU to move into the realm of leadership ethics. With Don Soderquist, longtime Walmart senior vice president and CEO, as chairman of the JBU Board of Trustees, JBU fit such a role exceptionally well. Because of his leadership and reputation, Soderquist was poised to give the proposed venture an immediate, international public identity with his guidance.

In September 1998 the Soderquist Center for Business Leadership and Ethics (SCBLE) was founded and announced publicly. Delia Haak, member of JBU's Division of Business faculty, was named to a part-time leadership position at the center and was given responsibility for the design of a new Master of Science in Leadership and Ethics (MSLE) degree. Haak's design of the new graduate curriculum provided part of her 1999 doctoral dissertation, which won the prestigious Dissertation of the Year Award from the College of Education at the University of Arkansas.[13]

Haak, who came to JBU in 1985 to work as the administrative assistant for John Brown III, took classes on her lunch hour and in the evenings to finish the business degree she had started after high school. Shortly before graduating in 1990, Dr. Doyle Butts, then chairman of the Business Division, encouraged Haak to consider a career in teaching. In 1991 she joined the business faculty part time while finishing her MBA. Haak helped develop the Students in Free Enterprise program from club status to a three-credit-hour class. Under her leadership the team won Rookie of the Year in 1992.

In 2000 the university hired a full-time director for the SCBLE, and Haak returned to her first love, the classroom.

Response to the center was enthusiastic, and within a year, by the fall of 1999, the center's funding goal was achieved. The Soderquist Center and the JBU Division of Business jointly offered the MSLE degree program, and by October 2000, the university's MBA (Master's in Business Administration) degree received full accreditation by the North Central Association. The rapid development of these graduate degree programs showed the collaborative strength of JBU's Division of

Business and the Soderquist Center.

The center held its first leadership conference, The Leadership Expedition, on the JBU campus in September 1999. The conference featured Soderquist and several of his business associates and friends, including Tom Muccio, vice president of Proctor and Gamble Worldwide, Debra Shaw, CEO of Umbrellas Plus, and Dr. Jerry Linenger, a NASA astronaut who had spent several months aboard the Russian space station *Mir*. More than 150 management professionals from the United States and Canada attended that first conference.

The center also created a fellowship program for graduate business students that provided a unique blend of practical and theoretical business education. Under the leadership of Wendy Soderquist and others, the "Soda" Fellows served the customers of the center for thirty hours a week by assisting the center staff with leadership development, strategic planning, and team alignment programming, while at the same time taking night classes in the JBU graduate school of business. In the process, many of the Soda Fellows built relationships with the customers of the center, were hired by them after graduation, and are now serving in leadership positions in Northwest Arkansas and around the region.

"For an undergraduate student, the transition from the structure and security of college to the proverbial 'real world' can sometimes be disorienting," said

A ropes course was added to the campus in 2001.

John Spenst, '04, owner/operator of Chick-fil-A in Midtown Little Rock. "The Soderquist Fellowship served as a bridge for me and gave me a front-row seat to the real-life struggles wise and experienced business leaders consistently face. I was disavowed of the false notion that leadership is dependent on some mythical superpowers that elevate a leader above challenges, but leadership is instead the life-long process of learning how to embrace and address the inevitable dilemmas life throws one's way."

The center also worked closely with several undergraduate departments at JBU, resulting in a cross-disciplinary leadership minor, student development training, and the Leader Scholar Institute. Together these departments, supported by the Center, developed a four-year program with special academic courses, and by the final year of Balzer's presidency, 230 students were involved.

One of the many initiatives of the SCBLE was the leadership training ropes course, added in the woods of the JBU campus in 2001. This facility, including its alpine tower, was one of very few outdoor physical facilities so fully equipped on a college campus at that time. Through its use, the Soderquist Center provided training in team development, leadership, and ethics for corporate management teams, charitable groups, and student groups.

✳✳✳

In October 1999, JBU celebrated its eightieth anniversary during Homecoming Weekend. The celebrations included stories of the founding and history of JBU by John Brown Jr. and John Brown III. The founding of the two new centers was celebrated, and there was much discussion of campus needs and planned new facilities. There was also a celebration of JBU's history of valuing work as a part of learning, and its adaptation over the preced-ing decades from daily vocational work in the campus industries into the modern work-study and student leadership programs. Through it all, there remained a strong emphasis on maintaining, into the new millen-nium, JBU's historic focus of being a Christ-centered institution aimed at developing the head, heart, and hand.

Dr. Steve Beers

In 1999, Dr. Steve Beers and the office of student development took the initiative across multiple departments to fortify the university's intentional focus on Christian growth and development. By 2000, a Spiritual Formation Committee was formed

The 2003 men's soccer team won the Sooner Athletic Conference tournament, won the NAIA Region tournament and made it to the national tournament — quite a feat considering 12 players were new to the team.

to advise faculty and staff in this effort. The Campus Ministries office expanded to become the Office of Christian Formation (OCF). With additional staff and enhanced programming, the JBU communitx`y's commitment to the "integration of faith and learning" flourished. Student-focused programs such as Passion small groups increased domestic and international mission opportunities, CAUSE outreach ministries, and the annual Breakaway retreat were just a few examples of the OCF's attention to student spiritual growth.

Under the leadership of new campus pastor Stan McKinnon, who arrived in the spring of 2000, the twice-weekly chapel program continued to be the centerpiece of spiritual life on campus. Speakers from around the globe and across denominations were selected for their abilities to challenge students in faith and learning. Chapel speakers included such luminaries as Brennan Manning, Dolphus Weary, Palestinian pastor Hanna Massad from the Gaza strip, Terry Mattingly, and Richard Allen Farmer.

In the fall of 2002, a third student-led chapel service was added on Sunday nights called the Gathering. While oversight was given by the chaplain's office, the entire service was organized and led by students, and featured a student speaker. The additional service also allowed students more flexibility in obtaining their mandatory number of chapel credits each semester.

Since many evangelical churches had moved away from traditional worship styles into more participatory and media-involved styles in the 1990s, JBU's chapel services also featured contemporary worship music. In a conscious response to this trend, the music faculty reflected carefully on the modern approach to church music and worship ministries and took major steps to update JBU's music programs. As a result, they developed courses that prepared students in lighting, sound production, song charts, and, importantly, a theology of worship. With these changes students were much better informed in the history and future of worship music.

The athletic teams also focused on Christ-centered service. The women's volleyball team was involved in ministry trips to Guatemala in 1999 and Ecuador in 2000, and the women's basketball team ministered in Brazil in 2000. Men's and women's basketball teams took discipleship ministry trips to Belize in 2001.

In 2002, JBU's men's Rugby team took its first mission trip to Ireland, where they both ministered and played against local teams. Hadden Wilson, an Irishman and longtime employee and teacher at JBU, observed that in his lifetime he had never seen two rugby teams praying on an Irish pitch until JBU's rugby men played the Ballynahinch Rugby Club.

Men's rugby was started as a club sport at JBU in the early 1980s. Steve Beers, who has been the team's faculty advisor since 1998, said the team has always included many of the campus's male student leaders. "As Rugby goes, so goes J. Alvin," Beers said, "and as J. Alvin goes, so goes the male culture on campus. . . . Rugby club leaders were examples of what it meant to be a man of God on campus." The men's rugby team returned to Ireland in 2004 and 2016.[14]

After many years as a club sport, the women's soccer team was established as an intercollegiate program under athletic director Bob Burns in 2002. During Balzer's tenure, the men's soccer team was SAC tournament champion and NAIA Region VI champion in 2002. Men's and women's basketball teams both made their first trips to the NAIA National Tournaments in 2002–2003. There were modest facility upgrades for athletics, such as new tennis courts in 1996, club sports field upgrades in 1997, and upgrades to the Hub White pool with a dedication ceremony in 2002.

***

Another long-running student ministry opportunity that began during President Balzer's years was the Chicago Immersion trip. Since the late 1990s, a group of students has embarked on an immersive experience living and serving in a neighborhood of Chicago's west side each fall break. Facilitated and hosted by co-pastors Derrick Rollerson and Mark Soderquist, eldest son of Don Soderquist, the annual trip has left a profound impact on hundreds of students across nearly twenty years as they learn about the opportunities and challenges of the church from brothers and sisters in Christ who live in an urban, ethnically diverse community.

Members of each year's team may eat in Pakistani neighborhoods, meet with immigrants from Mexico and the pastors who care for them, share a meal on a street corner with someone experiencing homelessness, or spend the night in an African American neighborhood with a history of white flight and economic neglect.

"The trips offer students opportunities to visit various neighborhoods around Chicago and encounter a variety of experiences with different cultures and socio-economic classes," said Frank Huebert '00, alumnus and JBU's director of disci-pleship. "Students wrestle with finding God and his kingdom work in an urban setting marked by issues of poverty, systemic neglect, diverse cultures, segrega-tion, and racial tension, and how the church has hope to offer in all this broken-ness—but it requires the work of the gospel in our lives."

The social issues of American city life gain a human face for the many alumni of the program during their "intense, long weekend," as Huebert puts it. "Our students encounter a variety of stories that are quite different from the 'normal' of their experience at JBU in Siloam Springs."[15]

Gunnar Shaffer was a JBU senior when he went on the Chicago trip in 2013. Martin Luther King Jr.'s "I Have a Dream" speech about the sons of former slaves and the sons of former slave owners "sitting together at the table of brotherhood" became very personal. "During the introductions, Pastor Derrick Rollerson shared his family's difficult past and I decided to open up for the first time and share my family's Arkansas and South Carolina plantation ownership history," Shaffer said. "Through the course of the dialog we all began to weep together, Pastor Rollerson and I had a long tearful hug in the middle of that living room surrounded by Mark Soderquist and so many other students. That short fall break trip turned out to be one of the most powerful life experiences I have ever had the privilege of witnessing. Together we sat at the table of brotherhood 50 years after MLK's famous speech. From that day forward, my opinions and understanding of the African American community drastically changed. I believe there was more healing in those few hours than in hundreds of hours debating the causes of everything that has caused this American nation great pain and suffering."

***

As the calendar wound its way down to the end of the year 1999, a potential global crisis loomed on the horizon. The Y2K glitch in the world's computer sys-tems was feared by some programming experts to be capable of causing massive global disruptions at the stroke of midnight on New Year's Day 2000. Any com-puters that used only two digits to log the year in their internal clocks might shut down, unable to process the transition to a year ending in -00. People around the world speculated that electrical infrastructure would shut down, airplanes would plummet out of the air, and the world financial systems would crash.

Late in the fall of 1999, after a review by an outside consultant, President Balzer assembled a team of JBU staff, headed by Vice President Beers, to generate contingency plans for the campus in case the worst predictions for Y2K came to pass. Beers's committee, including representatives from across many departments of the university, developed a plan to limit the impact of any sudden shut-off of electricity, water, or gas to the campus, as well as prepare means to secure critical information and maintain emergency communications capabilities.

With the turn of the millennium happening over Christmas break, the campus was empty, but Beers's team established a command center in the Walton Lifetime Health Complex, where they would maintain an all-night vigil on December 31. A couple days' worth of food and water were stockpiled for the team of about ten employees and administrators, and a gasoline generator was set up to provide temporary power.

JBU's Y2K response team gathered on New Year's Eve, but as Beers recalled, "The hype leading up to Y2K far outpaced the real experience." With Arkansas in the US central time zone, and with Pacific Islands being the first inhabited land to pass through the stroke of midnight, "we had almost twenty hours to watch as the world rotated through what eventually was nothing," Beers said.

At 11:10 p.m. on JBU's campus, a few minutes after watching the ball drop in New York City's Times Square without a glitch, President Balzer told JBU's Y2K team they could go home. "Everyone was pleased that nothing of substance surfaced," Beers recalled. He added, "Finishing the shrimp platter kept us there a few more minutes."[16]

⋆⋆⋆

By the fall of 2000, students saw more computer labs across campus and internet lines available in many dorm rooms, with twenty-four-hour access to computers in the residence halls. Training classes were available for popular office software systems, and a networked access system called EagleNET was being installed in the residence halls.

A major in computer science became available in the fall of 2001. The related digital media major had first been offered in the fall of 1997 and was seeing an explosive increase that quintupled the total enrollment in the Communications Division, making digital media the single largest major during Balzer's tenure.

Another significant and visible campus improvement was the replacement, during the summer of 2000, of the sixty-four-year-old Rod of God radio tower. The new tower dramatically improved and enhanced JBU's broadcasting operations. The school's FM station KLRC was well received in the extended area, and in 2001, 2002, and 2006, KLRC received national recognition by winning the Dove Award for best Christian radio station in its category. In 2002, the KLRC studios moved out of the Learning Resource Center and joined KUOA in a building west of campus, providing more studio space in the LRC for the Communications Division's burgeoning Digital Media Department.

***

In perhaps the most stringently crowd-controlled and secured public event in JBU's history, the Soderquist Center sponsored a visit on April 17, 2001, from Israel's Benjamin Netanyahu to the JBU campus. The once and future Israeli prime minister was protected by a detail of six Israeli plainclothes officers, and additional security stood at posts throughout the cathedral for the special chapel.

Netanyahu first met with a select group of student leaders in an informal setting in the cathedral's basement lounge, then mounted the stage of a packed cathedral sanctuary for a speech where admittance was carefully restricted to current students, faculty, and staff. He had been invited to speak at JBU by Don Soderquist when they happened to meet a year earlier. As Netanyahu recalled, the last thing Soderquist said to him then was, "See you in the Promised Land." To the assembled JBU audience, Netanyahu quipped, "Well, here we are in Arkansas."

Netanyahu spoke vigorously about the importance of leaders having convictions, values, and a vision, and of his sharing such values with Christians. "Leadership is not about being in a position of leadership. It means being willing to step into the arena for those values." He emphasized the need for democracy to spread throughout the Middle East. "Free societies prosper and unfree societies shrivel up."[17]

***

On a bright Tuesday morning in September 2001, a new day of infamy arrived in American history, much like the one sixty years before. Only this time, rather than the news being read out from a teletype machine in the red bungalow studios of KUOA, the images of crashing planes and collapsing towers in New York City flickered on the television screens in countless cable-TV-connected student dorm rooms.

Tuesday, September 11, 2001, was to be an ordinary day of early classes followed by the usual twice-weekly chapel service. With students, staff, and faculty reeling from the images of the collapse of the World Trade Center south tower, seen live just an hour before, the cathedral carillon chimed for the start of the 10:30 a.m. service.

Campus pastor Stan McKinnon, along with President Balzer and Steve Beers, led a special prayer service during the regular chapel hour. Flags were lowered to half-mast, and Dr. Balzer decided that classes would not be canceled—though students were not required to attend. He said, "We felt it was in the best interest of our predominately residential community of students to interact with each other, the faculty, and to seek counsel if necessary." Beers told the chapel gathering, "Now is the time to be with those you care about and pray together, and that's what we plan to do." Crisis training supported by the Center for Marriage and Family Studies was put into action, and student support groups were established at various places on campus. When President George W. Bush called for a national day of prayer the following Friday, JBU canceled the noon-hour classes and held a special prayer service in a packed cathedral.

"Throughout campus you saw impromptu discussions, group prayer and our faculty and staff members listening to students," Dr. Balzer wrote the week after the attacks. "In fact, one night last week faculty members provided a panel on related historic, religious and cultural issues. Again the meeting area was packed, and students remained for hours with questions."

JBU staff reached out through a network of contacts over the days following the 9/11 attacks, attempting to find out if any alumni, friends, or immediate family members of students had been lost. Ten days later, it appeared there were none, although it was eventually learned that more distant relatives such as aunts or uncles were lost by members of the JBU family. One alumnus had been in one of the buildings of the World Trade Center on that awful morning, but escaped unharmed.

At the time of the attacks, about 10 percent of advance program students were in the armed forces, and several reservists were living on campus. Many other recent graduates were on active duty in the various branches of the military. As American military engagement in Afghanistan, Iraq, and elsewhere played out in the coming years, many JBU alumni—both past and future—served in the war zones, carrying on the legacies of generations of JBU students before them who had served as air crew, foot soldiers, sailors, administrators, and chaplains in times of war.[18]

**

One of President Balzer's early goals had been to establish world class recognition for the university. JBU's heritage of strong academic, spiritual, and financial foundations was increasingly recognized as an excellent value by the late 1990s. JBU was recognized each year of Balzer's presidency by *US News and World Report* as one of the best regional liberal arts colleges in the South, and also one of the best values in that category. The Templeton Foundation had honored JBU as a "College of Character" repeatedly since the inception of the award in 1988.

Dr. Joe Walenciak

In 2002, JBU's business programs under Dr. Joe Walenciak '81 also received specialized accreditation from the International Assembly for Collegiate Business Education (IACBE), giving JBU its first specialized accreditation for business programs in the school's history.

As an active and important part of the business division, the Students in Free Enterprise (SIFE) team won regional championships repeatedly and in 2003 took third place nationally against a field of some eight hundred teams.

Mandy Moore was a member of the SIFE speaker team in 2003. "At one point during a speaker rehearsal, I will never forget when Dr. Walenciak said that he didn't want us to go to competition because he thought our presentation was subpar," Moore said. "My peers and I did not want to disappoint him, so we worked so hard to improve the quality of our work. He challenged us as students to do quality work with integrity. That year, we were the 'juggernaut' team that went from the team from the university no one knew about to the third place team in the country.

Moore said Walenciak laughed about almost not letting the team compete and then having them be one of the best in the country. "Without his feedback and high expectations, we would not have achieved what we did," said Moore.

After one of JBU's winning SIFE performances, one judge commented, "Unbelievable! Absolutely world class! Rivaling anything I've seen in academia or practical work experience!" The 2003 SIFE win was the first time JBU placed in the final four in the nation. Since then, JBU's teams in SIFE—now called Enactus—have consistently placed among the top teams in the nation. In 2017, JBU's Enactus team won the US competition, earning the right to represent the United States at the Enactus World Cup in London, England, where they placed in the top twenty-four teams.

In 2001 JBU's entire speech and debate team qualified for national competition, and in 2004 won first place in Arkansas. Other teams winning honors were con-struction management students in the American Institute of Contractors Ethics Competition and music students in National Association of Teachers of Singing competition. JBU was competing with national teams from Baylor, Pepperdine, Harvard, Dartmouth, MIT, Wheaton, and many well-known universities in many of these events.

The JBU chapter of the Alpha Chi National Honor Society, under its director Dr. Shirley Thomas, was awarded the status of Star Chapter, an honor bestowed on fewer than 10 percent of the honors chapters in the nation at the time. By 2004, JBU's Honors Program had won that honor for eight years. In 2003, the JBU Alpha Chi chapter won the President's Cup, the national top honor in competi-tion with three hundred other chapters.

***

By the turn of the century, JBU faculty and students had also become active in leadership and service in fifteen national and international programs beyond JBU sites.

Dr. Thomas played a key role in establishing the Coalition of Christian College and Universities' Oxford Honors Semester. The program began in the fall of 1998, and enabled honors students to study courses taught by Oxford professors, and also visit and study various historic academic and cultural sites in Europe.

Many international study programs, as well as overseas service and ministry opportunities, became available under the leadership of Bill Stevenson, JBU's director of international programs. In October 2001, members of the art faculty took a group of art students to France. They visited museums, cathedrals, and art galleries, studying art, architecture, and cultural differences for a better under-standing of their own culture as well as a greater appreciation of others.

Also in October 2001, members of the business faculty traveled to Guatemala to provide administrators and leaders of the Toybox Charity with leadership training. The charity had requested basic leadership training for their leadership personnel and for their house parents. In April 2002, five SIFE students and Dr. Walenciak went to Guatemala to work with youth in a small community about an hour outside of Guatemala City.

Thanks in large part to the efforts of Stevenson, a native of Northern Ireland, students and sponsoring faculty increasingly took the opportunity to travel to Northern Ireland on summer mission trips or to take classes as a part of the Irish Studies Program, which was established in 1998. These became life-chang-ing events for many of the students. In 2003 a small group of students initiated a mission trip to the cities of Bangkok and Chiang Rai, in Thailand, managing their own fundraising effort to cover expenses.

The JBU music programs had grown significantly, to the benefit of and enrichment of the university and the community. In 2002, JBU's choirs celebrated sixty years of providing the Christmas Candlelight Service, a beloved holiday event attended by the JBU family, people from the local community and region, and many parents of students. Then the Cathedral Choir took its first international tour to Ireland over two weeks in May 2003. Paul Smith, conductor of the choir since 1987, led the tour to enthusiastic receptions at their numerous concerts, and the tour became precedent-setting. Smith described an "elec-

Renewed Strength

tric hush" that fell over the crowds during the mostly a cappella concerts, since that form of music is not well known in Ireland. "Night after night the choir received thunderous ovations," Smith said. "It was hard to come to the end of the concerts."[19] The cathedral choir toured Northern Ireland again in 2005, and has returned every third year since, making their sixth visit in May 2017—the final tour directed by Smith at the conclusion of his thirty-year career.

***

At the turn of the millennium, the JBU campus would see its largest facilities expansion in twenty years. Since the dedication of the Learning Resource Center in 1980, only the Walton Lifetime Health Complex, completed in 1988, had significantly added to the array of buildings filling John Brown Sr.'s "college in a cornfield." Starting with the spring 2000 groundbreaking ceremony for the Walker Student Center, JBU's campus would see dizzying growth in facilities over the next eighteen years, increasing the entire square footage of campus structures by 85 percent between 2000 and 2018.[20]

In May 1996, the first visible hint of the attractive physical changes to come was dedicated in the small plaza in front of the LRC. Alumni Glen and Lee Sale '68 provided the gift of a sculpture titled *Renewed Strength*. It featured a bronze golden eagle flying before a large replica of the Cathedral of the Ozarks' iconic front window, and it bore the text from Isaiah 40:31, "But those who wait on the Lord shall renew their strength; they shall mount up with wings as eagles, they shall run and not be weary, they shall walk and not faint." With a new capital campaign about to start, Dr. Balzer found it to be a "beautiful pre-campaign stimulus," and "a long-term inspirational presence and motivation in setting and reaching Christ-centered goals."

To adequately provide for the less glamorous needs of the planned expansion, by late 2000, Johnson Controls, JBU's energy consultants, proposed a new, much-higher-efficiency campus-wide power plant. The existing system had long since become outdated, and with the limits posed by the old power plant, each added building such as the new student center and science hall would have needed its own power system. Over the long term, a new power plant would be much less expensive. Thus a new $4.75 million system was installed in time to be incorporated into the construction of those new buildings.

With the successful completion of the God's Highest and Best capital campaign in January 2000, and the successful funding and endowment of both centers, JBU administration's attention shifted to the detailed planning, contracting, and construction of the Pat and Willard Walker Student Center. The vision for the center was that it would provide a core campus and public identity for the university.

Construction of the student center and its attached 165-bed residence hall began in April 2000. The facility was envisioned as housing the Center for Marriage and Family Studies offices, Division of Biblical Studies offices, student development

Bell Science Hall

offices, international and WISP offices, as well as the campus post office, bookstore, a small café, classrooms, computer labs, a prayer room, and a large informal student gathering area. The footprint of this new building was intentionally located at the center of campus as a crossroads for the campus community. The Pat and Willard Walker Student Center was dedicated September 27, 2002.

The facility was immediately popular with students as an informal study area and small-group gathering place. It was an ideal hub for off-campus students between classes to pick up supplies and snacks and find a place to study, and it was a frequent destination for coffee breaks for students, faculty, staff, and administrators. Indeed, it quickly became the "grand central station" for the campus, thus having a significant impact on the JBU community climate.

Maranatha Clock Tower

The increased student housing capacity of the new Walker Student Center made it possible for JBU to finally close the beloved yet outdated California Hall in the fall of 2001, after the residential section of Walker opened. California, after seven decades of service, had become expensive to maintain, constantly needing repairs, and was considered somewhat unsafe. Homecoming 2001 was an occasion for JBU alumni and friends to reminisce, look at old yearbooks, and acknowledge the loss of this great campus landmark.

In April 2000, construction on the second major new building, the William H. Bell Science Hall, was approved. Groundbreaking for the forty-four-thousand-square-foot facility occurred in August 2000. The building included classrooms and labs for biology, physics, chemistry, biochemistry, and microbiology. Funding for the $8.5 million facility was provided primarily by a $6.7 million commitment from the Chapman Trust of Tulsa, Oklahoma.

The science hall was named in honor of William H. Bell, the late JBU trustee who had been very active in the planning and support of JBU during his seventeen

Dr. Jim Krall

years on the Board of Trustees in the 1970s and 1980s. Sharon Bell, daughter of William Bell and member of the JBU Board of Trustees, described the depth of his Christian faith and his character and the appropriateness of naming the science hall in his memory. William Bell had also served as liaison for the Chapman Trust in Tulsa for many years.[21]

Construction of the science hall was completed in late 2002. Students began using the new facility in January of 2003, and dedication took place on October 10, 2003, as part of Homecoming Weekend.

The center of JBU's campus was further beautified when Dr. John Moose, a former member of the Board of Trustees, gifted a fifty-one-foot clock tower in honor of his wife, Joallen, a 1990 JBU alumna. She named the tower *Maranatha*, which means "Come, Lord Jesus." Design, construction, and installation of the tower was largely done by JBU alumni, faculty, and staff beginning in the summer of 2002, with the clock tower's dedication taking place on April 4, 2003.

***

At the end of 2001, vice president of advancement Dr. Al Cureton left JBU to accept the presidency of the University of Northwestern in St. Paul, Minnesota. He would follow a lineage of leadership at that school established by John Brown Sr.'s friend Dr. William Bell Riley a century earlier, and carried on for several years after Riley's death by the evangelist Billy Graham. Cureton had been instrumental in guiding the successful completion of the God's Highest and Best capital campaign. Dr. Jim Krall, an associate in University Advancement since 1996, became the new vice president of advancement at the start of 2002, and in the next seventeen years he too would be instrumental in shepherding to completion two more extraordinary capital campaigns. But among Krall's first tasks would be a short, brisk fundraising effort to address some rapidly arising issues.

Even as the two centers reached their endowment goals by the year 2000, and as the new power plant, Walker Student Center, and Bell Science Hall were being built, new urgent needs became apparent. By the fall of 2002, on-campus residence halls were overcrowded and another residence hall was clearly needed.

In addition, the growing Business Division and the very active Soderquist Center—which as yet did not have a permanent home—needed more space, ideally to be placed in the same facility. The university wanted to bring these two successful programs together into one headquarters where business students would be able to connect with corporate leaders and in turn these professionals could meet highly motivated students.

After vigorous planning, the needs of two new buildings—a new business

In 2008 an additional wing was added to North Hall, and in 2012
the residence hall was renamed Hutcheson Hall (and nicknamed "Hutch")
after longtime JBU supporters Bill and Dede Hutcheson.

center and a new residence hall—plus the resources needed to conduct a major remodeling of the vacated Cathedral Group science building into JBU's first dedicated art center, were combined into a single fundraising campaign. This action was approved in early 2003 by the Board of Trustees under the new leadership of Chairman Don Walker, who had recently assumed the role from outgoing Chairman Don Soderquist.

Numerous foundations, corporations, and donor families were approached, some of them repeatedly, and Krall brought the funding together.

The key gift for the remodel of the science building into the first visual arts center was provided, anonymously at the time, by the Windgate Foundation. The redesign of this iconic Cathedral Group building became a major $2.3 million project, changing eighteen thousand square feet of former science facilities and laboratories into a state-of-the-art building, housing graphic design, digital media programs, an art gallery, gallery lighting, computer labs, theater-style classrooms, drawing and painting rooms, and offices. The building opened to students on January 12, 2004. The dedication and open house celebration took place on John Brown Sr.'s 125th birthday, on April 2, 2004, in conjunction with the spring Board of Trustees meeting.

For Krall, it was an whirlwind of a project, beginning in early 2003 with challenge grants that required the university to raise the balance of the required funds before the end of the year. The renovation was also a difficult project to complete because the major $39.7 million campaign had ended just three years earlier, and the Bell Science Hall was just opening at the start of 2003.

In January 2004, as the new visual arts building was just opening for use,

JBU announced that the brief fundraising campaign for another $12 million to provide the new business building and residence hall had been fully funded. Major donors to the campaign were the Soderquist Family Foundation, the Walton Family Foundation, the Mabee Foundation, and the Windgate Foundation.

Pat Gustavson

Construction of the new North Hall (phase 1) dormitory, which would house 114 students before its future planned expansion, began in the summer of 2003. Groundbreaking for the thirty-four-thousand-square-foot business building took place on April 22, 2004, with a completion date projected for the following year. As Balzer's tenure as president drew to a close in the summer of 2004, North Hall was nearing completion.

***

Balzer's ten-year presidency saw enormous achievements beyond just the successes in funding major new campus construction. The Advance Degree Completion Program for nontraditional students with a major in organizational management grew rapidly. In 1995, a year after its inception, the program expanded to the nearby cities of Rogers and Fort Smith, Arkansas. In 2000, a business information systems degree was added to the program's offerings. Additional class locations in the Arkansas cities of Little Rock, Hot Springs, Harrison, Eldorado, and Springdale were opened in the following years as the program rapidly grew. By the spring of 2004, as Balzer's tenure came to a close, enrollment in the Advance Program was at 422 students.

Various dimensions of JBU functions—income, buildings, personnel, and quality expectations—were changing rapidly near the close of the 1990s. Budgets and financial management had to be adjusted frequently and efficiently to maintain accountability. Vice president of finance administration Pat Gustavson and her support staff adapted and managed the accounts professionally and patiently with resulting black budgets every year.

With a number of timely new degree programs, and refined marketing efforts, Don Crandall, vice president of enrollment management, saw enrollment increase substantially at the turn of the millennium. JBU's annual fall-to-spring retention rates gradually improved among the traditional undergraduate student body during Balzer's tenure, reaching its highest level to that date, at 95 percent in April 2004.

Retention involves many student and parent variables that are not necessarily all within the control of the university, but the measurements of value matched the retention data. JBU's annual total costs for a student to attend in 2003–2004 were at just the 21 percent rank—the bottom quartile—among CCCU institutions, while *US News and World Report* ranked JBU very close to the top 10 percent (89.5) in quality among Southern comprehensive colleges. JBU could credibly say it was still a bargain.

Total enrollment across all of JBU's degree programs gradually increased to a total of 1,834 during the 2003–2004 school year, the highest in history to that date. The total was also the highest ever in each category: residential, traditional undergraduate, advance, and graduate. As adult and married students increased in number, housing for them near campus became especially urgent. The West Twin Springs Apartments south of campus became available for JBU to purchase, and they were available for use by September of 2003.

✳✳✳

For the Balzer family, Siloam Springs and the surrounding towns and cities of Northwest Arkansas became very special indeed. The area and its amenities had also become quite attractive to prospective faculty members, who proved easy to recruit if they could only be brought to Siloam Springs and JBU for a visit. During his years as president, Balzer came to value the enthusiastic participation and supportive spirit of the Siloam Springs downtown organizations, business community, and local citizens in embracing JBU.

Also, over time, the Balzers' children and grandchildren moved to the Siloam Springs and Tulsa region. Cary and Tracy Balzer's daughters, Kelsey and Langley, both graduated from JBU. The Balzers' daughter Tanya and her husband Todd Reichert remained in Tulsa, with their daughter Madison graduating from Oklahoma State University and son Brandon expected to graduate from JBU in May 2019. Lee and Alice realized this family closeness was a special blessing, remembering the sad time when they had moved away from the family many years before as they departed the Pacific Northwest for the presidency at Tabor.

Of course, living in a president's home on campus added its color. The Balzers enjoyed hearing students' voices as they cheered each other on while sledding down the backyard hillside during snowy winter nights. The Balzers were gracious when the inevitable student pranks came, such as the concrete barriers Lee found across the home's driveway one early morning, or the décor of "tee-peed" trees found in the front yard late one night. One day a set of four mounted tires were found on the Balzers' front doorstep. Later in the day it was discovered that the tires belonged to the campus security vehicle. As long as no damage or expenses were incurred, the pranks were well-taken by Lee and Alice.

From the beginning of Balzer's tenure there had been conversation about building a new president's home. However, it did not rise high on the priority list. After hosting a number of campus events, several minor adjustments were made in the long-standing home, which had served the second and third generations of Brown family leadership. The Balzers hosted many events that included students, faculty, and staff. These included hosting the honors students and their families, Christmas Open Houses, luncheons for Board of Trustees' spouses, regular gatherings of JBU women, luncheons honoring commencement speakers, and luncheons honoring chapel speakers along with related faculty and staff.

After a decade at the helm of John Brown University, Balzer found that the gifted and talented faculty and staff, along with their commitment to Christ-centered living and serving, had brought about a remarkable campus atmosphere. The great diversity of very gifted students, in their quest for preparation for life, seemed to thrive in such a welcoming and caring community.

In 2003, a CCCU representative approached President Balzer and said, entirely at her own initiative, "I want you to know that JBU is unlike any of the other Christian colleges I visit, and I visit them all. There is an authentic spirit, a genuine presence of Christian vitality and integrity that I do not see anywhere else."

Lee & Alice Balzer (center) with their family in 2004. Left: Todd & Tanya Reichert with children Brandon and Madison. Right: Tracy & Cary Balzer with children Kelsey and Langley

The Soderquist Business Center is home to the Soderquist College of Business and Milestone Leadership. In 2017 the Honors Center was moved in to the second floor.

Computer lab/classroom in Soderquist Business Center

Dedication of the "new wing" of
Mayfield Hall in 1979; Mayfield
residence life through the years

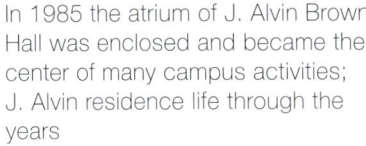

In 1985 the atrium of J. Alvin Brown Hall was enclosed and became the center of many campus activities; J. Alvin residence life through the years

Dedication of the Learning Resource Center Complex in 1980; the first graduates from the Graduate School in 1998; computer labs in the 1990s

2005 Golden Eagles men's basketball NAIA Division I champions; Rogers, Arkansas campus of John Brown University; 2002-03 cheerleading squad; 2002 men's rugby trip to Ireland

The 2003 men's soccer team wins the NAIA regional title; President Balzer kicks off the 2003 women's soccer season; 2004 Speech & Debate team at nationals

2002 Breakaway group photo; JBU receives the 2003 President's Cup Outstanding Chapter Award for Alpha Chi, the national college honor society

Aerial photo of campus from the 1990s; the December 2004 graduates of the Adult Degree Completion program; California is razed in 2002 to make room for the new Soderquist Business Center

JBU student mission trips to Ethiopia in 2004 (top) and New Orleans in 2005 following Hurricane Katrina (bottom)

CHAPTER 13

THE POLLARD ERA

In 2004, JBU again turned to a relatively young person to lead the institution. Dr. Charles W. (Chip) Pollard was forty-one when he assumed the office after President Balzer's retirement in July 2004. He came from Calvin College in Grand Rapids, Michigan, where he had been a tenured faculty member, teaching modern and contemporary British and American literature. He and his wife, Carey, graduated from Wheaton College in 1985, then Pollard earned a JD at Harvard Law School in 1988, and an MPhil in English literature at Oxford University in 1990. From 1990 to 1993, Pollard worked as a corporate and tax attorney at Latham & Watkins in Chicago. He left the practice of law because he sensed God's strong call to teach and write at the university level, so the family moved from Chicago to Charlottesville, and he completed a PhD in English Literature from the University of Virginia in 1999.

His first teaching job was at Calvin from 1997 to 2004. While there, he also volunteered for three years as the board president for Ada Christian School, during which time the school completed a $12.5 million capital campaign to construct a new building. That project gave Pollard valuable experience in fundraising, board governance, and leadership that helped prepare him to make the transition from Calvin faculty member to president of John Brown University.

Pollard learned of the presidential opening at JBU through a colleague in the Calvin English department, Dr. Edward Ericson Jr., whose son, Dr. Edward Ericson III, was vice president of academic affairs at JBU. Pollard also knew something about JBU because of family relationships: his uncle Don Soderquist had been a chairman of the JBU Board of Trustees and founded the Soderquist Center;

Chip & Carey Pollard

his cousin Wendy Soderquist worked at the center; and his cousin Jeff Soderquist was a 1993 graduate of the school and head women's basketball coach.

Through the search process, Pollard was drawn to JBU because of its interdenominational, Christ-centered identity, which was similar to his experience at Wheaton College, and JBU's combination of excellent liberal arts and professional programs, which mirrored his own career and time at Calvin College. He also deeply appreciated JBU's commitment to Christian formation throughout the educational program, and its kind, dedicated, and excellent faculty and staff. He and Carey came to Siloam Springs with their four children, Chad, Ben, Emma, and James, in July 2004.

***

Pollard's first year as president was a time of listening and learning about the rich history and culture of JBU. It was quickly apparent to him that the Brown family and Lee Balzer had created great momentum at the university. Two building projects—North Hall and the Soderquist Business Center—were in progress as Pollard took office, and three other buildings had been recently completed—the Walker Student Center and Residence Hall, the Bell Science Hall, and the renovation of the first art building in the Cathedral Group, later named Windgate Visual Arts West. In addition, JBU had been enjoying growing student enrollments, expanding academic programs, the founding of two centers, and the generous giving of many to the university.

Pollard was also learning on the job because he had not served in academic administration before becoming JBU president. This led to a humorous exchange with his second-grade son, James, that Pollard retold in his October 8, 2004 inaugural address. As they walked to a soccer game, James asked his father what the JBU president does every day. Not completely confident in his answer, Pollard responded, "What do you think that the president does?" James looked around the beautiful campus and said. "You own all these buildings, so you go around and tell people 'I own this, and I own that.'" Pollard laughed and told his son that not only does he not own any of the buildings, but the university even owned their home. James tried again and said, "Well you go to foreign countries, like Texas, and talk about JBU." Pollard had just returned from an alumni event in Dallas, which of course has its own distinct culture but is not quite a foreign country. Finally, James said resignedly, "You seem to go to a lot of boring meetings where people talk a lot. Do you like being the president of JBU?" Pollard assured him that he did.

Pollard earned admiration from the very beginning of his presidency by being

The Pollard family (from left) James, Chad, Carey, Chip,
Emma, and Ben. (Photo by Luke Davis/Main Street Studios)

willing to gently and publicly acknowledge "that year of which we do not speak," as he wryly put it in his opening staff meeting, referring to the year of presidential turmoil before Balzer's tenure began. Pollard said, "I learned a lot about the strength of JBU's board, leadership, people, and culture that would not let the institution waver from its core mission even during a difficult presidential transition."

In recent years, the lobby leading into the presidential office suite on the second floor of the Chapman Administration Building was renovated, and a row of large portraits depicting each of John Brown University's presidents was prominently displayed. The portraits include, in equal size, not only the three generations of Brown leaders, Balzer, and Pollard, but also Dr. George Ford and Dr. Bill George, the interim president who ably filled the gap after Ford's abrupt departure. The display reflects the full history of JBU even while recognizing that the difficult year is now in the past.

Pollard not only listened to faculty and staff in that first year; he also engaged with students in all sorts of ways. "I was coming from a faculty position in which I enjoyed spending a lot of time with students, both inside and outside the classroom," Pollard remembers. "I was concerned that the formality of the role of president and the demands it would put on my time would take me away from students, which had always been my first love in university education." Accordingly, he made some conscious decisions in that first year to stay connected to students, including teaching one class every year, regularly speaking in chapel, meeting with student leaders, and participating in student activities whenever he could fit it into his schedule, which led to some interesting opportunities.

For instance, at the end of that first fall semester, the men of J. Alvin built a three-story slide in the atrium for its annual Christmas party. When Pollard and his wife, Carey, came into the atrium, the students began chanting "Ride the slide," and he was left with little choice. He did check with the construction management students to assure that it was properly built, but then he took the plunge on a burlap sack. He and Carey also participated frequently in cameo appearances in the annual student Mock Rock and talent shows, including a memorable falsetto rendition of "Bohemian Rhapsody" by Pollard and the penguin dance from *Mary Poppins* with Carey playing the lead and the lyrics slightly revised to "Jolly Holiday with Carey" (instead of Mary). They both also played intramural flag football that first year, but they decided quickly that was not the best long-term strategy to engage students. "I think that students enjoyed a little too much the chance to knock down the president or his wife in a game," Pollard said.

Residents of Walker enjoyed Pollard's story reading during their annual Christmas party for many years. Jake Doerksen '20 Walker resident, said that hearing Pollard read a bedtime story was magical. "Think about it," he said. "Here is the president of your university sitting in your dorm room with a goofy Santa hat on reading 'The Night Before Christmas' or some other classic. It seems almost too good to be true."

The residents appreciated that Pollard took time out of his busy schedule to help students take a break from their academic stresses and shift the focus to the joy that should be associated with the season of Christmas. "It's an incredibly unique experience and one that sticks with many students past their time at JBU," Doerksen said.

Pollard's efforts to stay engaged with students, along with his personable and humble demeanor, have created an almost celebrity-like status among students. He's earned the nickname of Chippy P, he is the subject of frequent student memes, and students often seek out opportunities to take photos with him. The men of J. Alvin ,who routinely paint their bodies blue and gold for athletic events, have been known to write "I love Chip" on their backs.

Pollard also routinely participates in the annual Spy vs. Spy game, a tradition started in the mid 1990s and now organized by the Student Events and Activities office, during which participants are given a water gun and the name of another participant to target with the ultimate goal of being the last one to "survive." Classrooms, the dining hall, and chapel are all established as safe zones, but during the 2015 game Pollard was scheduled to speak in chapel, necessitating a long, unprotected walk from his office to the cathedral. Not about to let their president go down, a dozen J. Alvin residents, dressed in suits and sunglasses and looking very much like secret service agents, arrived in the administration building to surround Pollard and provide protection to and from the cathedral. He made it safely to and from, but his reprieve lasted less than twenty-four hours until junior Belinda Henriquez, '16, took advantage of Pollard's willingness to see students and gained entrance to his office under the guise of a meeting, and took aim with her squirt gun.

Pollard's engagement with students may well have encouraged student leaders to imagine new events, for in the fall of his second year, he received a proposal from the student government president Jennifer Paulson '07 to allow for a greater range of social dances on campus. Students had been involved in a "swing club" at a local church for over a year, but for many decades, JBU's community guidelines prohibited dancing at official events. The students were hoping that they could sponsor a Christmas swing dance for the entire community. Pollard and Vice President Steve Beers brought the proposal to change the dance policy to JBU's board in October 2006, and it passed—although not unanimously. From all accounts the event was a huge success, with over 450 students, staff, and faculty swing dancing to live music from the Jack Mitchell Big Band.

This first Christmas dance also generated interesting press coverage for JBU. Soon after the announcement of the board's decision, JBU received an inquiry from the *New York Times* about sending a reporter and photographer to cover the first dance. The cabinet discussed the possibility, and eventually agreed to the newspaper's request. "We knew that there was some risk of being misrepresented, but we also wanted to be a witness to others that Christians were not just against culture," Pollard said. "We could host a dance that would be fully in keeping with our Christian commitments." The reporter came for a full week, and he was impressed with the students. In the article, he wrote "The students I met at J.B.U. were, for the most part, the kind of thoughtful undergraduates whom top secular colleges would be proud to have." He also said that "the students of John Brown University are unusually polite, and three of them asked me to dance that night."[1] The article ended up as a six-page feature in the Sunday, January 28, 2007, *New York Times Magazine*. It would have cost the university $150,000 to buy the equivalent space in advertising.

Several new student clubs were established during Pollard's presidency, including the addition of women's rugby as a club sport. Interest in a women's rugby club had been growing for some time and was made official when Emily Pearce, '17, convinced Dr. David Brisben, professor of Christian ministries, to be the faculty sponsor. Just before the school year ended in May 2015, men's rugby captain Chris Dye, '15, helped facilitate a practice with approximately a dozen interested female students. Jarrod Heathcote, '08, JBU's coordinator of disability and testing services and a former JBU rugby player, agreed to coach the women's team, and the club team was formed in the fall of 2015. The first women in team leadership were captain Emily Pearce, president Hannah Malone, '18, and match secretary Anna MacLachlan, '18.

Not yet officially recognized by USA Rugby, the first year of play consisted of friendly matches and participation in the Rookie Rumble in Wayne, Nebraska, wearing jerseys borrowed from the men's rugby team.

In summer 2016 the women's team successfully petitioned to join the Mid-America Rugby Football Union in the Women's Division II. JBU played each team in the division twice, ending their season with an 8–2 record, and placed second in the Mid-America Collegiate Women's Division II.[2]

In the 2017–2018 season the women, under the direction of Captain Micah Wood, went 7–0–1, won regionals, and made it to the first round of nationals before losing to Tulane.

In 2014 engineering major Neeya Toleman, '18, was instrumental in bringing a chapter of the Society of Women Engineers (SWE) to JBU to help inspire women to become leaders in the engineering industry. Members of the club attend national and regional conferences each year, take advantage of mentoring opportunities to help them prepare for a career in their field, and use their gifts to love God and serve others. In 2017 SWE held their inaugural "Introduce a Girl to Engineering Day," during which forty-four elementary-aged girls spent the day on campus participating in engineering-related activities focused on science, technology, engineering, and math. In 2018, participation in the day grew to over 110 girls, and the club secured a program development grant from SWE and the ExxonMobil Foundation, as well as sponsorship contributions from local companies Ryan Engineering, Hudson Engineering, EngWit, TC Screen Printing, and McKee Foods.[3]

Dr. Marquita Smith, who joined JBU as associate professor of journalism in 2010, was approached by several African American students in 2011 about the idea of revamping a club for black JBU students that had existed in the mid 2000s, the African Heritage International Fellowship. Working with Steve Beers in student development, the idea expanded to become a more inclusive multicultural group. In 2012 the Multicultural Organization of Students Active in Christ (MOSAIC) debuted with fifteen members offering both social and educational programming. A student-led organization, MOSAIC is intended to create unity among the ethnic-minority American students on the JBU campus.

Over the years the group has organized a Diversity in Literature Symposium to expose the JBU community to literature produced by different ethnic groups, hosted documentary viewings and discussion, and held social gatherings for students that support cultural competency on campus. In 2015 a group from MOSAIC joined over eighty thousand people who participated in the fiftieth-anniversary march in Selma, Alabama, marking the Bloody Sunday/Voting Rights act march. In April 2018, six members attended the MLK 50th Gospel Reflections from the Mountaintop event in Memphis, Tennessee, commemorating the anniversary of Martin Luther King Jr. assassination. After their return the attendees hosted a campus discussion to share what they had learned with other students.[4]

In 2017 MOSAIC was given dedicated space in Soderquist Business Center for its members to meet and fellowship.

The growing visual arts department formed the Communication and Art Students club in 2006 (later renamed the Visual Art Foundry) to develop the talent of its members through conferences, competitions, critique sessions, tutorials, and other projects. After a visit to the art department of George Fox University in Oregon, Todd Goehner, '94, associate professor of visual arts, was inspired to bring their idea of a student award show to JBU. The existing yearly Student Work gallery show was limited to art students, but the Arties would allow JBU to showcase the best students in the communications and music departments as well.

Goehner and his wife, Heather, '95, produced and directed the event the first two years, enlisting the help of the audio, visual, and lighting team to create an "Oscar-style" event complete with black-tie dress, red carpet, paparazzi, and pre-show nominee interviews aired live to the crowd inside the cathedral.

Since moving the event to the Berry Performing Arts Center in 2013 attendance has grown to over four hundred, including community members and students from across all majors. Various JBU faculty and staff, including the Balzers and Steve Snediker, associate professor of visual arts, have served as official show hosts.

The nominees are selected by faculty based on work, character, attitude, and work ethic. Three to four students are chosen in each of about twenty different categories. The nominees then submit portfolios of their work, and professionals in the community judge the work and select the winner.

The winner in each Artie category receives a Manikin statue, the small wooden figure used commonly in art drawing studies.[5]

While lip-synching contests held in the atrium of J. Alvin had been a tradition at JBU since the 1980s, in 2005 the student activities committee reimagined the event and debuted Mock Rock in the Cathedral of the Ozarks. That first year, students competed for first-, second-, and third-place prizes of $100, $75, and $50, respectively, determined by a panel of student judges. In the early years Mock Rock acts featured some props and minimal choreography, but more recent acts have incorporated special lighting effects and more elaborate costumes and

A student favorite — the cafeteria's popcorn chicken bowl — was the centerpiece of the song "Happy Together" at Mock Rock 2018. From left: Lauren Lane, Abby Acker, Allie Welsh, Colton Laptad, Mariana Portillo, KJ Roh, Clancie Sorrell, and Morgan Morris

choreography. Acts frequently find a way to incorporate JBU culture and events into their song, such as using the Miley Cyrus tune "Wrecking Ball" to humorously portray the renovations happening in J. Alvin during the 2014 school year. Faculty and staff have been added to the judging panel in more recent years, and the prize money has increased to $150, $100, and $50.[6]

Of course many students don't need to resort to lip-synching, and some of them found themselves competing in "The Next Big Thing," a competition started in 2011 by Matthias Roberts '13 in which local bands showcase their original songs. After an audition process, several bands or artists are chosen to perform in front of a live audience and a panel of judges from the music and entertainment industry. The winners, chosen by combining audience votes with judges' choice, receive an extended-play record deal.[7]

***

Since the beginning of the Balzer administration, the JBU board had recognized the need for a new president's home, but other campus priorities had taken precedence. Pollard began working with the board to come up with a plan for a new president's home that would meet the needs of his family and the hospitality needs of the university without unduly sidetracking other priorities. He offered to enter into a partnership whereby the university contributed land and he paid for construction of the new house. With that partnership in place, the Pollards engaged Matt Pearson, 1985 alumnus and construction management professor, who began designing a prairie-style home just beyond the soccer fields on a stone bluff overlooking Sager Creek. It was close enough to campus so that faculty and staff could walk to events, but private enough for family living. The Pollards moved into the new house in the fall of 2006, and it has served as a wonderful place to host guests of the university. The Pollards welcome approximately 1,200 people a year to their home for various events, including a picnic for first-year students during orientation, the all-faculty-staff Christmas party, and an annual parents' reception during Family Weekend. In 2014, the JBU board decided to purchase the Pollards' interest in the home.

The former president's home on Holly Street has been used in a variety of capacities since the building of the new residence. For over a decade, it served about three hundred students as the home for JBU's Honors Program and the Leaders Scholars Institute. In 2017, those programs moved to the second floor of the Soderquist Business Center, and JBU renovated the house to make it the Alumni Welcome Center, partly in preparation for JBU's centennial year. JBU moved the alumni and parent-relations office and university archives into the house, and the university provided office space to John Brown III as senior advisor of the Windgate Foundation. President Brown grew up in the house; his new office used to be his older sister's bedroom. Needless to say, there are a lot of memories for him there. With historic photos and artifacts displayed throughout, the home also has a gallery to display some of Windgate founder Dede Hutcheson's art collection, generously donated to JBU in 2018. The new Alumni Welcome Center provides a wonderful venue to greet returning alumni, host events, and tell the story of JBU's history.

***

Something that became readily apparent in Pollard's first year of listening was that there were four major renovation and construction projects that people had been dreaming about for many years, projects that were colloquially described as being on "the List." In his second year, Pollard and his administrative team began to get to work on that list by launching the private phase of the Keeping Faith Capital Campaign with a goal of raising $100 million by 2012, the largest fundraising goal in the university's history.

The first project on the list was a renovation of the Cathedral Group. The Cathedral Group had been completed in 1957, but the university did not have the money at that time to put on the external limestone cladding that was a part of the original architectural drawings. The original cinder block had disintegrated to the point that in several places holes had emerged. Moreover, the Cathedral Group was in general need of renovation and repair after fifty years of heavy use. So JBU launched a project to restore and "finish" those historic buildings on campus. On April 26, 2007, almost fifty years to the day after the original dedication service for the Cathedral Group, JBU held a special chapel service to celebrate completion of the Rock the Cathedral fundraising campaign. In that service, the university invited over twenty JBU alumni who had worked on the original construction of the cathedral as students, some fifty years before, to come back to campus to speak and serve communion to the current students. It was a wonderful moment when different JBU generations celebrated together God's faithfulness. The project included a redesign of the plaza in front of the cathedral, complete with the names of each board, faculty, or staff member who served for twenty-five years or more at JBU.

In 2014, JBU's Board of Trustees funded the addition of a beautiful fountain in that plaza to express their gratitude to the campus community for their service

The Living Water Fountain, a gift from the Board of Trustees in 2014, symbolizes both the Trinity and JBU's threefold mission of Head, Heart, Hand.

to JBU. JBU received $6.1 million to fund the Cathedral Group project, including generous lead gifts from the Kresge Foundation, the Chapman Trusts, and Bill and Donna Berry, as well as gifts from over 87 percent of faculty and staff and 13 percent of the current students. By the fall of 2008, the Cathedral Group was not just as good as new; it was better—with new roofs, windows, and HVAC systems, as well as a striking new limestone exterior.

The JBU community had also eagerly anticipated the enhancement of the sports and performing arts venues on campus to showcase the excellence of JBU students, an excellence reflected in great achievements. For instance, the JBU Golden Eagles men's basketball team, led by Coach John Sheehy, won the NAIA National Championship in 2005, and the team's star guard, Brandon Cole, '06, broke the collegiate record—in both NAIA and NCAA record books—for career three-point shots, with 527 in 2006. Under the leadership of Coach Jeff Soderquist, the JBU women's basketball team made it to the final four of the NAIA tournament in 2014 and the sweet sixteen in 2017. JBU women's soccer also had a string of accomplishments during Coach Kathleen Paulsen's tenure, participating in five consecutive SAC conference tournament finals, three NAIA national tournaments, including going to the final Round of 16 in 2018, and winning two SAC regular-season conference titles.

Serving as the head coach of the women's volleyball team since 1990, Robyn Daugherty, '85, was named director of athletics in 2006 after the retirement of Bob Burns, who had been at JBU since 1975.

Despite the change from being in charge of a couple dozen athletes to now overseeing seventeen coaches and athletic staff as well as 150 athletes, Daugherty has made a concerted effort to keep personal interaction with the athletes. "She knows every athlete's name and she knows their story," said Jeff Soderquist, head women's basketball coach.

Daugherty has modeled JBU's mission of service through her own involvement in caring for people in the community, often getting them involved in the JBU athletic programs, and involving her teams in various service projects. Each athletic team carries out service projects each year, from local youth sports clinics to overseas mission trips.[8]

In 2018 Daugherty was named the 2017–18 NAIA Under Armour Athletics Director of the Year by the National Association of Collegiate Directors of Athletics.[9]

"Robyn is one of the main reasons for the success

Robyn Daugherty

The Bill George Arena opened in Fall 2010 and is home to the Golden Eagle basketball and volleyball teams. Concerts as well as commencement are also hosted in the BGA.

we have had, not only on the field and court, but also in our student-athletes' success in the classroom with athletes recording the highest GPAs in the school history in the last couple of years," Soderquist said. "She has also built up one of the top coaching staffs in all the NAIA, empowering us as coaches to do our job and do it well. Robyn is so well deserving of this award."

Murray Sells Athletic Center was clearly showing its age as a performance gymnasium despite the great performance by the men's and women's basketball teams. Opened in 1965, it held about eight hundred people on older bleachers with hardly any room on the sidelines for the team benches or for concessions. With the generous support of the Soderquist Family Foundation, the Mabee Foundation, and the Chapman Trusts, JBU was able to construct the Bill George Arena in 2010. This modern athletic venue had seating for eighteen hundred for a game, twenty-two hundred for a concert, and almost twenty-six hundred for graduation ceremonies. It also included new locker rooms for men's and women's basketball and women's volleyball teams, as well as coaches' offices, an expanded concession area, and a hospitality suite. The name of the new arena was announced in the spring of 2009 in honor of the recently deceased Dr. Bill George, who had spent nearly his entire adult life in service to JBU, including serving as interim president in 1994 and on the Board of Trustees for fifty-four years until his death in October 2008.

The Bill George Arena provided much-needed seating capacity for JBU's long-standing and well-loved Toilet Paper Game, which increasingly received attention from major sports news outlets such as ESPN and *Sports Illustrated* after *USA Today* named it the "best technical foul in all of sports" in 2010. The arena also enabled JBU to host concerts with nationally recognized artists such as Switchfoot, Toby Mac, and Lecrae as well as national speakers for the larger Siloam community, such as Samaritan's Purse president, Franklin Graham, and Veggie Tales creator Phil Vischer. JBU was also able to enhance Alumni Field with team benches and a press box in 2012 and lights in 2014. This upgraded soccer field created the opportunity to initiate a new athletic tradition, the First Game Under the Lights, complete with a cookout, a bounce house for kids, kettle corn, and over twelve hundred people in attendance. In 2018 the event was renamed to First Friday Fútbol, reflecting in part the international diversity of JBU's student body and soccer teams.

JBU's performing arts students had also waited many years for new space to practice and showcase their God-given gifts in music, theater, and dance. The Jones Recital Hall on the lower level of the cathedral had served the community well since 1992, but it was limited by the size of its stage and backstage, by its lack of formal dressing rooms, and by its seating capacity of only 150. Moreover, JBU's premier performing group, the Cathedral Choir, had no formal space to practice or perform other than the split stage in the cathedral itself. Despite these facility limitations, the performing arts had always flourished at JBU, but it was time to provide a space equal to the performance. Through generous lead gifts from Bill and Donna Berry, the Mabee Foundation, and the Chapman Trusts, JBU was able to complete construction of the Berry Performing Arts Center (BPAC) in the fall of 2010. The auditorium seats five hundred with a full stage, half fly, set construction area, costume storage, full dressing room and makeup area, and practice rooms both for instrumental music and for the Cathedral Choir. The BPAC hosts sold-out student performances three times a year, the "freshman" drama at Homecoming, a musical in November, and an all-school drama during Family Weekend, as well as numerous senior recitals, concerts, lectures, and other events.

The new facility was named for Bill and Donna Berry, who were students at JBU in the 1950s. Bill served as a member of the Board of Trustees from 1997 to 2012 and was generous with his encouragement, wisdom, and resources to further God's work at JBU. He had been the founder and president of Titan Specialties in Pampa, Texas, an explosives company that was involved in the oil exploration

The Berry Performing Arts Center

Kaitlyn Thompson, Elyse Partee, and Chase Poage perform in *Robin Hood* in 2014, produced by The Department of Music and Theatre.

business. The Berry family was instrumental in supporting many of the facility improvements during this time of growth and expansion, and Bill deeply enjoyed being "behind the scenes" in supporting the mission of JBU.

Mrs. Terri Wubbena, JBU professor of music, was grateful that with the Berry Performing Art Center "for the first time ever, whether a choral or an instrumental ensemble, each now has their own rehearsal hall. All aspects of the music and theater programs have facilities to craft their performance media, and all have a beautiful performing area."

Wubbena, who came to JBU in 1976 to teach woodwinds, choral music education methods, and freshman theory and musicianship, served JBU for forty-two years before retiring in 2018. Colleagues credit Wubbena with nearly single-handedly championing the presence and growth of instrumental music on campus and testify that her highest priority was JBU's students.

"For over four decades Terri worked tirelessly to spend money well, hire the right people, pray continuously, listen intentionally, reevaluate, try again, swallow her pride, and defend the unseen, because she believes we are all worth it," said Jen Edwards, '03, assistant professor of worship arts. "Her default in every situation is—'You are good. There might be some not good things in play that are real and we won't ignore those. But you? You are good.' And there is something about that sweet, familiar Texas accent that . . . actually makes you believe it, too."

Terri and her husband, Jan, who met at JBU in 1977, when Jan joined the music faculty, are known for their many unique "isms," which their colleagues and students have learned to interpret.

"I don't mean that unkindly," was Terri's apology for being brutally but appropriately honest. "Oh my . . ." meant "I never would have looked at it that way, but tell me more." And when they said, "I'll be praying like a big dog," they meant that even though they didn't know how something would turn out, they knew God did. One of those "big dog" prayers was answered in the opening of the beautiful new performing arts center.

Mrs. Terri Wubbena

Wubbena also recognized how it benefited the surrounding community by enabling JBU to "bring in performing artists and even orchestras."[10] Mr. Paul Smith, conductor of the Cathedral Choir, was instrumental in the design of the BPAC. He saw the new facility as continuing the tradition of worship in JBU's music program: "The pursuit of excellence in all forms of the performing arts has been a hallmark of the JBU experience for decades. May God give us the continued vision and determination to reflect His creative nature through this most generous gift."[11]

The final project on "the List" was the need for a new facility for the engineering and construction management programs, a need that had been identified as early as the late 1960s, when architectural plans were first drawn up. The engineering and construction management programs had been housed for more than thirty years in the original library building of the Cathedral Group, with overflow into the Hyde Engineering Building. The Hyde Building—the facility that was originally dedicated in 1930 as the Alumni Building—had served JBU in many capacities, including as a heating and electrical plant for the campus, dress factory, laundry, bakery, bank, extension department, science laboratory, and finally for the engineering majors as classrooms, senior student offices, and a fabrication shop. The growth of the engineering and construction management programs had far exceeded the capacity of the existing facilities, and neither building adequately addressed the specialized classroom and project space needed by these technical programs. Again, through generous gifts from the Berry family, the Chapman Trusts, and many others, JBU was able to construct the LeVon and Alice Balzer Technology Center (BTC) in 2011. This new facility had more and larger classrooms, faculty offices, several specially equipped engineering project rooms with the latest technology, intentionally designed group study spaces, and over fifteen thousand square feet of general project space, including a high bay area for the construction management department. Since the building's opening, the Division of Engineering and Construction Management has continued to grow in students, and the students and faculty continue to excel in their work, including securing several EPA innovation grants and placing highly in the annual NASA Robotic Mining Competition. The building was named in honor of President Lee and Alice Balzer for their decade of faithful and outstanding service to JBU.

When Pollard announced funding for the new facility to the faculty, Dr. Leo Setian, who taught engineering at JBU for over forty years, expressed disbelief: "You are kidding, us, right?" Then he teared up as he said, "I have been in so many meetings about the need for this facility, and I thought that it would never happen in my career. Glory be to God." Dr. Larry Bland, chair of the engineering department, also saw the great need. "Teaching and lab spaces were so limited in our old building that it was hurting our recruiting. The new Balzer Technology Center has expanded the possibilities for teaching engineering, improved the perception of our program with new students and parents, and opened doors to new corporate employers for our graduates." Similarly, Mr. Jim Caldwell, chair of construction management, said that "moving into BTC greatly enhanced the holistic training of construction management students. It enabled us to put the planning rooms, computer labs, professors' offices, and high-bay staging area all in close proximity under one roof, which allows professors to work closely with students. It is an ideal place to teach, mentor, and learn."

The Keeping Faith Campaign funded not only the four legacy projects on "the List" but also facility and scholarship endowment needs of a growing student population. From 2003 to 2018, JBU grew at annualized rate of 1.2 percent, with the total student population going from 1,929 to 2,261 and the traditional under-graduate population growing from 1,196 to 1,371. In addition, during this time, JBU recruited stronger traditional undergraduate students who performed better by almost every measure: the average freshman ACT rose from 24.7 to 25.8; the average first- to second-year retention rate from 77 percent to 82 percent; and the six-year graduation rate from 51.3 percent to 65.4 percent. Vice president of enrollment Don Crandall has served JBU for over thirty years, and the growth in number and quality of traditional undergraduates is largely due to the good work of him and his staff. This growth, however, put pressure on JBU to expand the dining and residential facilities. Accordingly, in 2008, JBU renovated the Kresge Dining Hall to expand its capacity and upgrade its features, and also expanded North Residence Hall with a new wing, which added eighty beds to campus.

The final construction project of the Keeping Faith Campaign was the

Balzer Technology Center is home to JBU's engineering
and construction management programs.

renovation of the former library and engineering building for JBU's expanding
art department in 2012. This second art building creatively used the structural
limitation of a building originally built as a library to provide a painting studio
and sound recording studios in the attic; a regular classroom, drawing classroom,
and student gallery space on the second floor; and a printmaking classroom, conference room, and offices on the first floor. It quickly became one of the most
visually interesting interiors on campus.

The Windgate Foundation was a key partner in many of these projects.
Founded by Bill (Hutch) and Dede Hutcheson and led by executive director John
Brown III, the Windgate Foundation had already helped to initiate the Center
for Marriage and Family Studies, led by Dr. Gary Oliver. As part of the Keeping
Faith Campaign, in 2010, the Windgate Foundation established the Dr. Gary
Oliver Endowed Chair in Marriage, Family, and Relationship Studies to sup-
port the work of the center and to honor its long-serving director. The Windgate
Foundation also continued its generous support of advancing the visual arts at
JBU, a passion that stems, in part, because Dede and two of her daughters, Robyn
Horn and Karen O'Neill, are gifted visual artists. The foundation has made gifts
to support the renovations of the two Cathedral Group buildings into JBU's new
art buildings, later named Windgate Visual Arts East and West; it has also made
wonderful endowment contributions to create the Charles Peer Endowed Chair,
and to support student scholarships, faculty development, and international

art tours for JBU's Visual Arts Department. With this support, the Visual Arts Department under the leadership of Charles Peer and David Andrus, '78, has grown to be one of the largest academic departments at JBU, with a national reputation for excellence.

Hutch owned and operated a family shoe sales business in Fort Smith, Arkansas, until 1963, when he was invited by Sam Walton, founder of Walmart, to "sell your shoes in my stores." Hutch was a leading Walmart executive until his retirement in 2000 at the age of seventy-eight, and he was instrumental in the international growth of the company. Hutch served on JBU's Board of Trustees from 1996 through 2008, chairing the student development committee for most of that time. He was a keen advocate for students and would always claim that the student development committee was the best assignment that a board member could have. Hutch was great encourager and was always willing to lend a hand, including the one time that he helped Steve Beers investigate a possible student prank by crawling around the chapel floor searching for alarm clocks taped under pews. They didn't find any that year, but the clocks showed up several years later when President Pollard was speaking during Family Weekend. Hutch died at the age of ninety-four, in February 2017.[12]

The Hutchesons's love for students also helped shape the Windgate Foundation's support of other worthy projects. For instance, the foundation helped to construct both phases of North Residence Hall in 2004 and 2008, which was renamed Hutcheson Hall in their honor in 2012. The foundation also made a challenge grant to renovate Mayfield Residence Hall in 2016, in large part because the Hutchesons enjoyed the idea of providing excellent residential halls so that students could have a "home away from home" during their time at JBU.

The Windgate Foundation was also passionate about making JBU affordable for students and for encouraging other donors to support scholarships at JBU. Pollard and vice president of advancement Dr. Jim Krall presented the foundation with an innovative challenge-grant program that enabled them to achieve both purposes. Windgate made three challenge grants in 2005, 2007, and 2012, in which they agreed, not only to match—dollar for dollar—gifts from other people toward endowing scholarships and programs at JBU, but also to allow those subsequent donors to direct and name the entire amount of the new endowment. These challenge grants have been one of the most successful gift programs in JBU's history, with the university receiving $40 million in new endowment gifts over a decade. Indeed, the program was so successful that JBU continued it with operational surpluses after the Windgate challenges were completed. From 2004 to 2018, this matching program has encouraged people to create 185 new endowed scholarships that are generating over $2.1 million in new scholarship

Windgate Visual Arts East

money every year. JBU has been richly blessed through the example and the generosity of the Windgate Foundation.

JBU sought and received endowment gifts, not only for scholarships, but also for building maintenance and academic excellence. With the construction of so many new facilities, Balzer, Pollard, and the JBU Board of Trustees were concerned about the ability to maintain the financial sustainability of JBU's operations. Beginning with the construction of the Soderquist Center in 2005, JBU has budgeted for and received 20 to 30 percent above the construction cost of a new facility to set up a building maintenance endowment to pay for the increased utilities and staffing for that new building. The JBU board did not want to use student tuition dollars to build or maintain the new buildings; instead tuition is used to pay the faculty and staff, who carry out JBU's educational mission.

Moreover, the JBU facility service group, led by Dr. Steve Beers and Mr. Steve Brankle, implemented a variety of new sustainability programs for the campus that cut JBU's energy costs. In fact, while JBU's square footage grew by 70 percent from 2000 to 2012, through their efforts at conservation its energy costs only grew by 46 percent. In 2018, the university was approaching one million square feet of enclosed facilities on or near the Siloam Springs campus—nearly double the square footage available at the end of the 1990s. In 2012, JBU also became the first "zero-landfill" university in Arkansas. In addition, vice president of finance

Dr. Kim Hadley twice took advantage of favorable debt markets to refinance JBU's long-term debt, in 2009 creating $230,000 of annual savings for a new deferred maintenance account and in 2015 creating a one-time savings of about $500,000, which was used to replace the roof of the Learning Resource Center. This combination of generous giving and wise stewardship of resources helps to keep JBU as affordable as possible for students.[13]

Dr. Kim Hadley

The goal of the Keeping Faith Capital Campaign was to raise $100 million over seven years, but by God's grace and the generosity of over sixteen thousand people, JBU received over $118 million in six years, not only exceeding the goal, but doing so a year early. Krall and his team also did a wonderful job of planning and executing the campaign. The success of any capital campaign is founded on the good work that has gone on before, and in the Keeping Faith Campaign, it was remarkable how many of the lead donors had been giving to JBU for twenty to thirty years. It was truly a legacy of generosity of people and foundations committed to JBU's mission.

JBU was growing not only in facilities, endowment, and students on campus but also in its graduate and adult programming around the state through the leadership of Dr. Richard Ellis. JBU expanded its Fort Smith Center in 2004, moved its NW Arkansas Center from Springdale to Rogers in 2007, moved its Little Rock Center in 2013, and built a new counseling clinic at the Siloam Springs campus in 2013. In the graduate program, JBU has partnered with Kanakuk Kamps, developed fully online business and counseling masters' degrees, started graduate programs in education and visual arts, developed the only play-therapy concentration in counseling in the region, and taken the business and counseling master's degree programs to Little Rock. Enrollment in these graduate programs has grown from just over 200 students in 2004 to about 600 students in 2018.

JBU's degree-completion program has faced stronger competition for students over the last decade, so its enrollment has declined from 500 students to 218 since 2004. Moreover, the degree-completion program underwent a movement away from the face-to-face cohort model to more online programming to better meet the needs of the working adult student. In 2010,

Dr. Richard Ellis

JBU received a $2 million federal grant to expand its online offerings, and it began to develop fully online degree programs in organizational leadership, managerial accounting, liberal arts, and psychology. In April 2017, after graduating more than 4,000 students in its history, the Advance Degree Completion Program was renamed JBU Online to reflect fully the change in teaching of the program. In 2018, because of the shift away from in-person classes, the Fort Smith center was closed, the Little Rock center transitioned to only being used by the counseling program and the Rogers Center lease was adjusted to use less of the space in that commercial building.[14]

Dr. Ed Ericson

In the traditional undergraduate program, even though these first six years under Pollard's leadership were primarily a time of consolidation of programs, JBU did launch a renewable energy concentration in the engineering department in 2009. Dr. Ed Ericson, vice president for academic affairs, led impressively in improving the effectiveness and efficiency of the academic program with innovative new systems of budgeting, strategic planning, faculty evaluation and governance, and hiring. He also supported and encouraged much of the innovation in the graduate and online programs.

JBU experienced some unprecedented weather events during Pollard's early tenure. In January 2009, a severe ice storm swept across Northwest Arkansas, and the university was forced to cancel classes for the first time in many decades. The ice was so heavy on the trees that large branches began breaking, ringing out like fireworks around campus. Only two years later, in February 2011, JBU received 24.5 inches of snow in less than twenty-four hours. Again, the university was forced to close campus for almost a week, which is always a difficult decision because almost two-thirds of the students live on campus. The food service company had pre-positioned some workers to keep the dining room open, and the facilities service crew worked tirelessly to clear sidewalks and streets and keep the primary systems working. Pollard remembers deciding to trudge through the two feet of snow from his house to his office that first morning. "You had about 900 students on campus and about 15–20 adults," Pollard said. "I just wanted to make sure that everything was okay and that any celebration of canceling classes was not getting out of hand." He found students making snow angels, throwing snow balls, and looking for cardboard to create makeshift sleds. He joined in the fun and ate lunch in the cafeteria before making the trek back home.

The Pollards also experienced great sorrow in May 2011, when their son Ben passed away suddenly in his junior year at JBU. He was an English major and cared deeply for the needs of young people, particularly in the developing world. The Pollards found great comfort and support from the JBU community in their grief. The memorial gifts given in Ben's memory established an endowed scholarship for underrepresented students at JBU and also built the first floor of the Rays of Hope School in Guatemala City. Two of the Pollards other children also attended JBU, Emma who graduated with a degree in English education in 2015 and teaches seventh grade, and James, who is expected to graduate in 2019 in engineering and who played for four years on JBU's soccer team. Their oldest son, Chad, went to Calvin College and works as lawyer in Wisconsin.

***

JBU completed the Keeping Faith Campaign in 2011, and within a year, Pollard, senior administrators, and the JBU board began to plan for the celebration of JBU's one-hundredth anniversary on September 29, 2019. As part of that planning, JBU decided to launch a new capital campaign, the Campaign for the Next Century, to run from 2012 to 2019, with the aim of strengthening JBU's capacity to educate the next generation of students to honor God and serve others by setting a goal of receiving $125 million in gifts and pledges over seven years. There were four main initiatives in this new fundraising effort: improve JBU's residential facilities; construct facilities to host and serve JBU's guests and the larger community; launch a new nursing program; and increase JBU's endowment for scholarships and academic programs.

In the modern era, JBU has always been known for its excellent residential programs for students, and part of that success came through providing great housing facilities. As part of this campaign, JBU undertook four major construction or renovation projects. In 2013, JBU finished the Northslope Apartments, which provided ninety-two new beds in three- and four-person apartments for a cost of $3 million. This new apartment complex replaced the beds that were lost when the university demolished most of the married student duplexes of Broadhurst Village for the new construction of the Berry Performing Arts Center and the Balzer Technology Center on the west side of campus. The Northslope project was generously supported again by the Berry family. Pollard recalled a conversation that he had with Bill Berry about the project. In the design process, the student development staff wanted to put two bathrooms in each apartment that held four people. Pollard thought that might be excessive, but they convinced him to ask Berry what he thought. When Pollard asked, Berry smiled and responded, "Chip, I grew up in a family with ten children and one bathroom. I waited my

The Northslope Apartments provide on-campus housing for upperclassmen, married and non-traditional students.

whole childhood for the bathroom. Give the kids two bathrooms." For Pollard, it was just another example of Berry's generous spirit.

In 2013, JBU began the process of renovating the six townhouses that were originally constructed from 1990 to 1994. Plans are in place to finish those renovations by 2019. In 2017, under the leadership of Nate Wertjes, '19, several students constructed a coffee shop, Ground Floor Coffee, in the basement of one townhouse, and it has become a gathering place for study, conversations, and good espresso. The coffee shop is also a student-run business that is a part of the Enactus program, and generated over $25,000 of student wages in the first year. Students now affectionately call the townhouses and Northslope Apartments "the Burbs," and they provide ideal housing for JBU juniors and seniors.

The third residential project was a major renovation of the men's J. Alvin Brown Residence Hall in 2014. J. Alvin has been central to the social life of campus for almost one hundred years, hosting campus-wide Halloween, Christmas, and Super Bowl parties as well as Ping Pong tournaments and impromptu games of whiffle ball. It has also served as a wonderful place for boys to become men of God. The original wing of J. Alvin was built during 1920–1921; it was renovated and a second wing was added by 1963; the atrium connecting the two wings was added in 1985; and new air-conditioning was installed in the early 1990s. The entire structure was in need of renovation and restoration. In 2014, JBU completely gutted the interior and rebuilt the two wings, maintaining the popular suite configuration, putting in new plumbing and HVAC systems, and updating the atrium and exterior. The project cost $5.5 million and again, generous lead gifts from the Berry family, Soderquist Family Foundation, Chapman Trusts, and many gifts from J. Alvin alumni made the project possible. Beers captured the significance of this project when he said, "J. Alvin has been, and will continue to be, a driving factor in shaping the men of JBU to honor God and serve others. The renovation continued the tradition of using this revered space to build a brotherhood that molds our men and influences the future."[15]

The final residential project was a restoration of the women's Mayfield Residence Hall, finished in July 2018 at a cost of $7.4 million. Like its counterpart J. Alvin, Mayfield has served JBU well for many years. The "Old" and "Middle" wings were built in 1964, and the "New" wing was completed in 1979. Over ten thousand women have lived in Mayfield during those fifty-plus years. The renovation project completely rebuilt the rooms, making them more sound-resistant, putting sinks in every room, building in new lounge spaces, and purchasing new modular furniture for every room. The HVAC and plumbing systems were also fully replaced, creating more showers and sink areas in the central bathrooms and installing more efficient and individually controlled heating and cooling systems in each room. These system changes solved two of the long-standing problems in Mayfield. With the new plumbing systems, women no longer have to shout out a warning to those in the shower when they flushed the toilet. With the new heating and cooling system, women will no longer have to open the windows on warm days in the winter or put on extra blankets in the cool days of the spring because they can control the temperature in each room. The renovation also created an expanded lobby in the entrance area, which opens out into a new landscaped patio, complete with a gas firepit. The lobby was renamed in honor of Ida Adolphson, who was the dean of women when Mayfield was originally built and who also served on the Psychology Department faculty and as a part of the graduate counseling administrative staff.

The Next Century Campaign also expanded JBU's capacity to serve and engage the community. In 2013, through generous lead gifts from Simmons Foods, the Simmons family, and the Berry family, JBU received $6.5 million and was able to construct the Simmons Great Hall, a twenty-thousand-square-foot banquet hall that hosts events from fifty to five hundred people. This facility has greatly increased JBU's capacity to welcome guests to campus, whether they come for academic conferences—such as the Giving Voice writer's conference, the Great Plains Honors Conference, or the Diversity Conference—or as part of prospective student events, or the annual scholarship banquet or Grandparents' Day. The Simmons Great Hall has also become a favorite venue for the people of Siloam

Simmons Great Hall, built onto the Chapman Administration Building, provides banquet and conference space.

Springs. As Wayne Mays, chamber of commerce president, said, the Simmons Great Hall filled "a void in meeting space that our community desperately needed. John Brown University is now—more than ever—a wonderful gathering place for school, civic club, Chamber of Commerce, public and private events, and it has clearly become the favorite place to gather."[16] Mark Simmons has served on JBU's Board of Trustees for over thirty years, and three generations of the Simmons family—Mark's dad Bill, Mark, and his son Todd—have led Simmons Foods since 1949. Simmons Foods is one of the top twenty poultry producers in the United States, and it is headquartered in Siloam Springs. The Simmons family is deeply committed to JBU and the quality of life in Siloam Springs, and they saw the Great Hall as a wonderful way to support both of those passions.

With the addition of this space, the cabinet formalized the university Events Office, under the leadership of University Advancement, and set forth goals to strategically steward the university's many facilities and bring in additional revenue by hosting outside guests for weddings, conferences, and banquets, as well as hosting several large youth camps in the summer. During the 2017–2018 fiscal year, among many other events, JBU hosted a record twenty summer camps with over eighteen hundred middle school and high school students on campus, resulting in a net revenue of over $175,000.

JBU also received $5 million to renovate the Walton Lifetime Health Complex.

The Walton Lifetime Health Complex renovation included a new entrance for community members and expansive upgrades to the workout equipment and pool.

The WLHC was originally opened in 1988, and has served as the hub for JBU's intercollegiate and intramural athletic program as well as the only comprehensive wellness and fitness center for Siloam Springs. The renovation project expanded the HVAC system to provide air conditioning throughout the entire facility, created a new entrance for community members on the north side, greatly expanded the fitness and light cardio facilities, renovated the pool mechanicals and decking, and renovated all of the locker rooms and common areas. JBU received lead contributions from the Soderquist Family Foundation, Simmons Foods, the Mabee Foundation, the Chapman Trusts, and the City of Siloam Springs as well as many individuals and local businesses to complete this project.

JBU also initiated a variety of smaller recreational projects that benefited both JBU students and residents of Siloam Springs. For instance, the university partnered with the City of Siloam Springs and the Walton Family Foundation to extend the city trail with almost two additional miles of lighted asphalt trail around the campus in 2009. JBU also partnered with Walton Family Foundation and Simmons Food to construct over seven miles of mountain biking trails on campus in 2016. JBU also worked with the city, the Walmart Foundation, and US Soccer Foundation to build the first Futsal soccer courts in Northwest Arkansas in 2016. Then in 2017, the Davis Outdoor Adventure Center was established in the historic Sager Cabin, allowing students, faculty, staff, and health complex members the opportunity to rent kayaks, paddleboards, mountain bikes, and camping equipment. All of these projects helped to fulfill JBU's commitment to be a good neighbor in Siloam Springs.

The most ambitious new project in the Next Century Campaign was funding the launch of a new nursing program. JBU administrators knew that there was a critical need for BSN-trained nurses, particularly in Northwest Arkansas. Nursing also fit well into JBU's mission of educating head, heart, and hand, but it was an expensive program to begin and the university had been focused on adequately funding existing long-term priorities. Having completed "the List" in the previous campaign, Pollard, Ericson, and Krall proposed to the JBU board in 2011 that the time was right to do a feasibility study to see if JBU could receive the regulatory approval and funding to start a nursing program.

With the encouragement of Ericson, Dr. Brian Greuel, chair of the Natural Sciences Division, initiated JBU's application to the Arkansas State Board of Nursing, and he wisely sought out a consultant, Dr. Ellen Odell, who had already run the Har-Ber School of Nursing in Northwest Arkansas and who was identified as a great future director of the program. JBU's proposal initially met some resistance from other nursing programs in the area because of a concern about the availability of clinical placements in Northwest Arkansas. There was even discussion from some parties about asking the Arkansas legislature to limit the total number of nursing programs in the state. Gratefully, Siloam Springs representative Jonathan Barnett, '77, a JBU alumnus, helped to shepherd JBU's proposal through the regulatory process. JBU received initial state approval for the program in September of 2013, and hired Dr. Odell as the full-time director of the program in December of that same year.

Mrs. Susan Barrett, JBU board member and former president and CEO of Mercy Health Systems in Northwest Arkansas, also played a key role in connecting JBU's nursing program to the various health systems in the region. JBU received financial support for the project or student scholarships from Washington Regional Hospital, Mercy Health Systems of Northwest Arkansas, and the Siloam Springs Hospital; and all of the regional hospitals and clinics have helped JBU's program by providing clinical placements for nursing students.

JBU's second challenge was to determine whether it could raise the $12 million necessary to begin the program with excellence. Pollard and the JBU board agreed on this goal, allocating $6 million to construct the Health Education Building and $6 million in endowment to support the higher operational expenses for nursing: $2 million for building endowment, $2 million in support of faculty salaries, and $2 million for technology and program costs. Once again, JBU received generous and enthusiastic support from the Berrys, the Chapman Trusts, the Mabee Foundation, the Hobby Lobby Foundation, and many others.

In 2015 JBU began construction on a state-of-the-art Health Education Building with over twenty thousand square feet of space, including three classrooms, clinic

The Health Education Building opened in fall of 2016
and houses JBU's nursing program.

teaching space with four exam rooms, four simulation patient rooms, health labs, computer labs, and office space. JBU also purchased several high-fidelity simulation mannequins that faithfully mimic human health conditions so that nursing students can learn some of their clinical technique in the simulation laboratory. JBU even has a mannequin that gives birth to another mannequin, a demonstration that was shown during the grand opening of the new facility in the fall of 2016. As Pollard walked down the hall that morning, he heard one of the nursing faculty ask the visitors to "clear the room because we need to reload the mother," a phrase likely never said before at JBU.

The program has been a great success, and in the fall of 2017 it was the year's largest undergraduate enrollment program. The first class of pre-nursing students began in the fall of 2014, officially entering the nursing program as juniors in 2016. In May 2018, the first graduating class of the program held twenty-eight students. The excellence of JBU's nursing program was demonstrated when 96 percent of those taking the NCLEX licensure exam that June passed on their first try, compared to the national average of 90 percent.[17] In June 2018, JBU announced that the nursing program had received full accreditation from the Commission on Collegiate Nursing Education, and full approval from Arkansas State Board of Nursing.

The final facility project of the Next Century Campaign was the Peer-Andrus Studio and Project Barn, an almost seventeen-thousand-square-foot pre-engineered metal building for JBU's visual arts and engineering programs. Both programs needed "dirty space" in which students could create art or design and work on engineering projects. The visual arts' side of the building consists of a commercial photography studio, woodworking shop, senior studio space, painting classroom, and regular classroom. The engineering side is completely open with fifteen to twenty flexible work stations to accommodate all of the junior and senior engineering design teams. The building was named in honor of Charles Peer and Dave Andrus, who led the visual arts program for over thirty years and grew it from a handful of students to over two hundred. The project cost $3.25 million, and JBU received generous support from the Windgate Foundation, the Sunderland Foundation, and the Chapman Trusts.

JBU has been deeply blessed by God and his people in being able to undertake this expansion of the campus facilities. Since the Walker Center in 2002, JBU has undertaken twenty-one major building or renovation projects (six during Balzer's time and fifteen under Pollard's) and over 90 percent of its almost one million square feet are new or completely renovated. All but one of the projects were built exclusively on gifts, and all but one of the new academic buildings have generous building endowments to help pay for increased operating expenses. Wonderful generosity and wise stewardship have been a hallmark of JBU throughout its history.

Pollard and the JBU board also set goals for endowment gifts and, for the first time, estate gift commitments as part of the Next Century Campaign. In particular, JBU received $10 million in new scholarship endowment gifts and over $7

The Peer-Andrus Studio and Project Barn features over 16,000 square feet of project space for art and engineering students.

million in endowment gifts to encourage academic excellence, including a gift from the Windgate Foundation, to establish the Charles Peer Endowed Chair in Visual Arts, a gift from an anonymous donor to fund the Abila Archaeological Dig under the leadership of Dr. David Vila, professor of religion and philosophy, and a gift from the Soderquist Family Foundation to support the Soderquist College of Business.

Estate gifts have always been an important part of JBU's support throughout its history, but Krall and his advancement team decided to make requesting estate gifts a priority for the Next Century Campaign. By July 2018, over fifty families had consulted with PhilanthroCorp, an independent Christian estate planning firm that partnered with JBU, and over thirty families had completed the process. Through these efforts and other contacts by JBU's advancement team, JBU had received over forty-nine estate commitments with estimated future gift value of over $14.5 million. Almost all of these future gifts will go to support scholarship endowments to keep JBU affordable for families.

JBU had again experienced the overwhelming grace of God and the generosity of his people through this Next Century Campaign. In September 2018, with just under a year to go, JBU had already received gifts and commitments to meet its overall goal of $125 million. Pollard, Krall, and the advancement team remained focused on finishing the funding for a couple of specific projects, including the Peer-Andrus Studio and Project Barn, endowed student scholarships, the endowment for academic excellence, and estate commitments, but they were deeply grateful for the results to date.

The two capital campaigns over the last fourteen years have been an unprecedented time of reaping at JBU, with gifts received of over $235 million, a result that reflects God's wonderful blessings and the faithful sowing under the presidencies of all three Browns and of Balzer. JBU's endowment also grew from $50 million to over $125 million during these years, mostly through new gifts, but also through wise investments and sound endowment policies. In particular, Pollard, Hadley, and the JBU board endowment committee led by Keith Holmberg '77 worked diligently to reduce the endowment spending rate from 5.75 percent in 2003 to 4.45 percent in 2018 to ensure that the endowment would grow to cover future spending needs of the university. The generosity of JBU's donors and the wise stewardship of its board—led, since 2016, by Susan Barrett, the first woman to chair JBU's board—have been instrumental in JBU's financial health.

***

JBU reaped God's blessings, not only in fundraising, but also in its programs and people, which extended JBU's mission. One notable example of those blessings was the Northwest Arkansas Healthy Marriages programs sponsored by JBU's Center for Relationship Enrichment. CRE received two federal grants in excess of $5 million to provide marriage and relationship programs for over 35,000 people locally and nationwide from 2006 to 2015.[18] Under the continuing leadership of Dr. Gary Oliver, the newly renamed Center for Healthy Relationships (CHR) has also continued to receive a grant to provide a weekend marriage enrichment program (Growing Healthy Relationships) to students at CCCU schools. In 2017, this program affected around seven hundred students at twenty-four different Christian colleges and universities, with over eight thousand participants since its inception.[19] Finally, in a reflection of its growing impact beyond marriage preparation and enrichment services, CHR developed its ChurchStrong initiative in 2016 to increase its reach to pastors, churches, and church leaders. It also developed the RelationshipsMatter program to help men and women—from backgrounds ranging from generational poverty to corporate leadership—develop the emotional and relational intelligence skills necessary to be effective in their personal and professional lives.[20]

Similarly, Soderquist Leadership—renamed Milestone Leadership after the passing of Don Soderquist in 2016—has served nearly thirty-five thousand customers at its events since it was founded in 1999. It has served leaders in some of the largest companies in the world, including Walmart, Tyson Foods, Del Monte Foods, and Proctor & Gamble, as well as influential regional nonprofits such as Circle of Life Hospice, Hope Cancer Resources, the United Methodist Church, and Baptist Health. Milestone Leadership has also had a lasting impact on JBU students through the Soderquist Fellows and Graduate Milestone program for JBU graduate business students, their teaching and mentoring of undergraduate students in Enactus, and their bringing national and international leaders to campus through Leadership Week. Throughout the last twenty years, the people of Milestone Leadership have remained committed to developing others to become leaders worth following, and those people and their organizations have grown stronger as a result. JBU's mission has been greatly extended to new audiences through the work of the Center for Healthy Relationships and Milestone Leadership.

JBU's radio station, KLRC, also realized phenomenal growth and progress during this time under the direction of general manager Sean Sawatzky, '96, and his team. In 2011, KLRC moved its broadcast center from campus to a building in downtown Siloam Springs, doubling its footprint and adding new studio and technical equipment. The new site also allowed people to watch and listen to the KLRC broadcast through the storefront window on Broadway Street. In

The Cathedral of the Ozarks receives a limestone exterior in 2007; the incoming 2006 class at Big Games; 2007 Day of Caring service project; President Pollard gets ready for the annual toilet paper game; JBU orchestra practices in the Berry Performing Arts Center

Enactus JBU captures the national championship title in 2017; visual arts students at the 2012 Addy Awards; undergrad and graduate business students compete at the 2011 Governors Cup

JBU's first graduating class of nursing students in 2018; the Cathedral Choir Ireland tour in 2017; 2012 Eaglenauts team at the NASA Robotic Mining competition

Clockwise from top: 2017 aerial view of campus;
Walton students at the dedication of the Angel of
Vision sculpture; 20th anniversary of the Walton
International Scholarship Program in 2005; students
at the Abila Dig in Northern Jordan in 2018

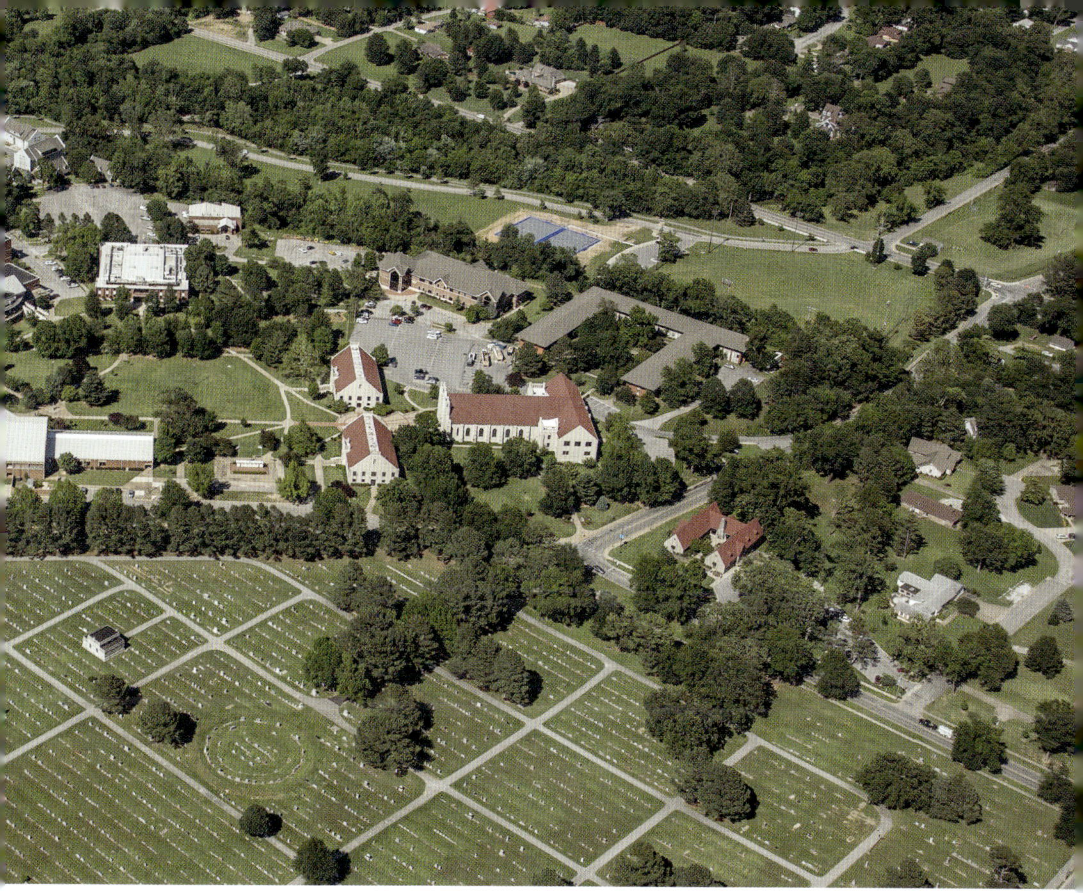

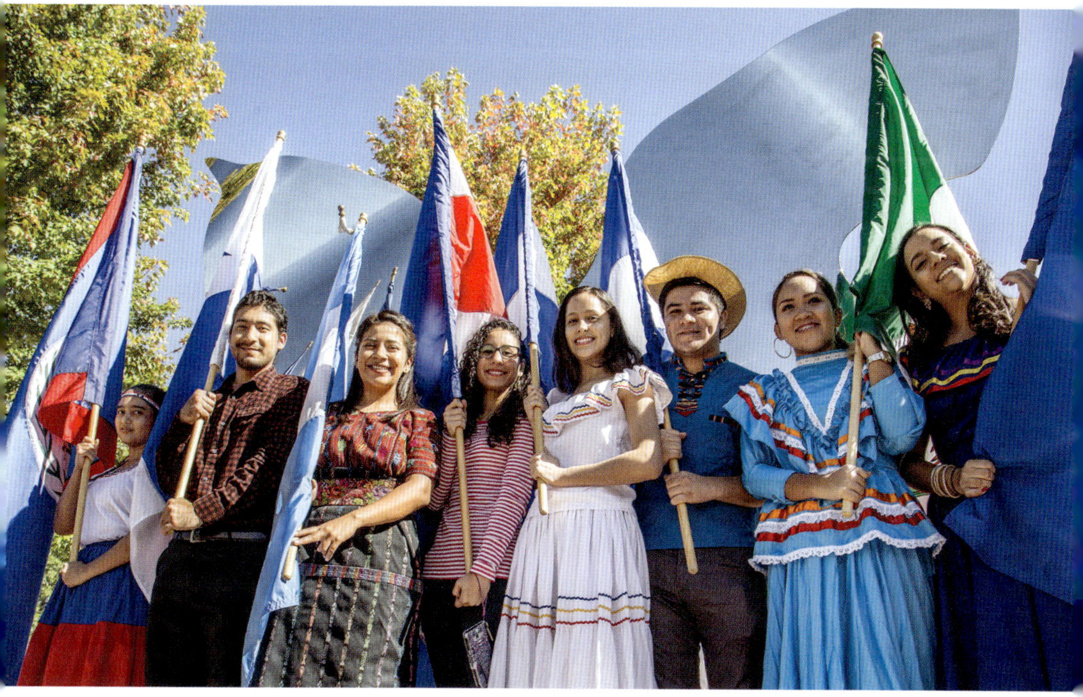

Clockwise from top left: Women's soccer captures the Sooner Athletic Conference championship in 2016; women's rugby; late skate; student-run coffee shop, Ground Floor Coffee; KLRC staff celebrates the 2013 launch of 90.9 with a new 100,000 watt signal that expands their coverage area; Golden Eagle fans ramp up the crowd during First Friday Fútbol

The Mayfield Hall renovation is completed in 2018; the Peer-Andrus Studio and Project Barn (SPB) opens in 2018; the new lobby of Mayfield Hall is named after former dean of women Dr. Ida Adolphson, pictured here with the Mayfield Hall residence life staff; art class space in the SPB; engineering students work in the new project space in SPB

The KLRC broadcast center in downtown Siloam Springs
(Photo by Main Street Studios/Luke Davis)

2012, KLRC received FCC approval to expand its signal from 6,000 to 100,000 watts by moving to 90.9 FM and building a new tower, which greatly increased its coverage in Oklahoma and Missouri while improving its signal in Northwest Arkansas. KLRC is regularly recognized for its excellence, including in 2013 as the Religious Station of the Year by the National Broadcasters' Marconi Radio Awards and in 2016 as the most listened to station in Northwest Arkansas. KLRC is also known for its capacity to move its listeners to acts of service, including its annual campaign to fill students' backpacks, "pay it forward" weeks, or diaper drives for Loving Choices Pregnancy Center.

JBU has clearly contributed to the success of the region, including Siloam Springs' being named by *Smithsonian* magazine as one of the twenty best small towns in America in 2012. Downtown Siloam Springs has, since the turn of the millennium, once again become a vibrant hub of commerce, dining, and community, thanks in large part to the many JBU alumni who have established successful businesses there. Siloam was voted one of the four Best Main Streets in America in a survey by *Parade* magazine in 2014, and in 2017 was named a Volunteer Community of the Year, due in part to the approximately fifteen thousand hours of volunteer service performed by JBU students each year. Whether it be through "Serve Siloam" during freshman orientation or hosting the Symphony of Northwest Arkansas, JBU continues to seek to be a good neighbor in our community and to benefit from the growth and development of our town.

JBU's influence has been realized not only locally but also globally. JBU international programs have grown tremendously in the last fourteen years. In 2009, Bill Stevenson and Hadden Wilson, a JBU Irish Studies faculty member, helped JBU acquire a lease to use Lakeside Manor, a residential facility two miles outside of Belfast, Northern Ireland, that can sleep over forty people. This new facility enabled JBU Northern Ireland to expand its program to include multiple academic and mission trips in the summer, a fall semester program, and regular visits by JBU's Cathedral Choir and athletic teams. In 2017, JBU partnered with the Council for Christian Colleges and Universities to run a spring semester program at Lakeside Manor. Similarly, JBU has developed ongoing international programs in Guatemala through the leadership of Dr. Joe Walenciak, who regularly runs mission trips and graduate studies programs there.

Walenciak has been recognized twice by the Guatemalan government for his work, being named an Ambassador of the Peace in Guatemala and participating in the daily rose ceremony that symbolizes the need to work for peace every day.

Through the leadership of Dr. David Vila, JBU took over operations of the Abila Archaeological Project in northern Jordan. Abila's rich history dates from the Chalcolithic period all the way into the later Islamic period, but it is most well known as one of the cities of the Hellenistic league called the Decapolis, and then as the home of five prominent churches during the Byzantine period. Vila helped to secure over $2.5 million in endowment gifts as part of the New Century Campaign to support both the archaeological site and the Jordan Summer Studies program, through which JBU students and others travel with him every other summer to work for five to six weeks at the site. In 2015, Vila also added a biblical studies trip to the Middle East in the off years when they were not going to Abila to dig.

JBU students also regularly visit France, England, the Netherlands, and Italy as part of the Visual Arts Department's international study tours. In the last decade, faculty have also led trips to Germany to study the Reformation; to China, Costa Rica and Panama, Brazil, and South Africa to study business; to New Zealand to study graphic design; and to Spain, Switzerland, and France to study spiritual formation. Students also participate regularly in international mission trips to Guatemala, Northern Ireland, Ecuador, and Lithuania. Typically over 15 percent of JBU students were overseas in one program or another every year.

Not only do JBU students engage the world through international study and mission programs, but also students from around the world continued to come to

JBU to study. Around 15 to 20 percent of JBU's under-graduate students grow up overseas either as children of missionaries or as international students.

The Walton International Scholar Program (WISP) has thrived during the Pollard presidency. When he first met the WISP scholars, they asked him two questions: "Do you speak Spanish? Have you ever been to Central America?" He answered no to both questions, but assured them that he would have a better answer on the second question soon. Pollard and Carey have made frequent trips to visit the JBU WISP alumni in Central America, including two trips in which President John Brown and his wife, Stephania, and

John McCullough

President Lee Balzer and his wife, Alice, joined them to connect with students from every generation of the program. The WISP students also continue to make wonderful contributions to campus, including organizing and teaching salsa dancing to the rest of campus under JBU's new dance policy.

Under the direction of Ruby Bowles, administrative assistant for the international programs office, the Friendship Family program, which started in 1991, has flourished and been able to match 100 percent of the WISP and international students with families in the community. Friendship Families welcome those JBU students into their home for meals and family outings and serve as an integral part of their support system while at JBU. Over 85 percent of the Friendship Families are JBU faculty and staff, and many have been doing it for years.

John, '71, and Judy, '72, McCullough are one such shining example. John, who started working for JBU in 1974 in the development office, joined the business faculty in 1981 and helped the Soderquist College of Business gain accreditation. John and Judy have served as a Friendship Family for over twenty years and have opened their home to the collective WISP and international students each year, both at the freshman welcoming party and at the end-of-the-year bash, even after John's retirement in 2015.

Often their open-door policy extended to the family of JBU students. Irina Barnett, '08, remembers the McCullough's hosting her mother and sister when they came to JBU for her graduation. During that visit Irina's mom asked about John and Judy's beautiful marriage. John answered, "When it comes to finding a partner, you need to find someone who will not rush you nor drag you. You need to find a partner who will walk with you, as you cherish your journey together you will grow together and love together."

"To this day I give this same advice to all those who ask me about my marriage," said Barnett. "God works in mysterious ways and provides us angels like John McCullough and his sweet wife Judy so that in them we find the true meaning of love."

John came out of retirement to serve as interim director of the WISP after the passing of longtime leader of the Walton Scholar program, Ron Johnson. In the spring of 2018 JBU announced that Gabriel Williams, a JBU construction management alumnus from 2004, would be taking over leadership of the program. Williams grew up in Costa Rica as the son of missionaries, and he spent much of his time after graduation serving as a missionary in Uganda. He and his wife, Andrea, were JBU's missionaries in residence during the 2014–2015 school year.

JBU faculty and students are also increasingly receiving international recognition. Since 2004, five JBU faculty members have been selected to participate in the prestigious international Fulbright Scholars Program: Dr. Rick Ostrander in Germany in 2004; Dr. Randall Waldron in China in 2006–2007, while he was teaching at University of South Dakota; Dr. Jessica Wilson in Czech Republic in 2014; Dr. Marquita Smith in Ghana in 2016–2017; and Dr. Kevin Simpson '89 in Slovakia in 2019. In addition, Sarah Hubbard, an English education graduate in 2014, was JBU's first student to be elected to the Fulbright English Teaching Assistantship. She served in Turkey in the 2014–2015 academic year. JBU's global impact continues to grow.

JBU's national reputation and influence also continue to grow. For instance, from 2008 to 2015, JBU was ranked in first or second place by *US News and World Report* in its Southern colleges category. In the fall 2016 rankings, due to JBU's rapid growth in its graduate programs, it was promoted to the magazine's regional university category, where it has remained in the top twenty among Southern universities as well as the best-ranked university in its category in Arkansas.[21] The *Chronicle of Higher Education* also named JBU as one of its "Honor Roll" institutions in its annual "Great Colleges to Work For" survey for four consecutive years from 2015 to 2018.[22] The *Wall Street Journal* ranked JBU in the top third of the 968 institutions it chose to review for its 2019 College Rankings, placing the university only below Hendrix College of all the Arkansas institutions and number nine of all the CCCU schools ranked.[23] *Money* magazine named JBU the best college or university in Arkansas in 2018,[24] and Zippia found that JBU had the highest earning graduates in Arkansas.[25]

One of the ways JBU has sought to meet the needs of its employees is to partner with a local day-care provider to meet some of the child-care needs of the JBU community. Vice president for finance and administration Kim Hadley worked with a team of faculty and staff to come up with a plan. JBU renovated an older house on the edge of JBU's campus to create a day-care space and then leased that space to Sunshine Montessori School, a favorite provider of faculty and staff. The location of the school near campus and the fact that Sunshine offered priority registration to JBU faculty and staff were great benefits to campus. JBU also worked to secure additional space reservations for JBU children at two other preschool facilities in town.

From 2010 to 2012, JBU undertook a major project to implement a new enterprise resource planning system, the computer platform for JBU's entire operating systems. Hadley and chief information officer Paul Nast led the effort, and the entire JBU community embraced the change even when it meant learning new procedures, systems, and programs. The implementation was so successful that JBU's vendor, Ellucian, sent a team of senior executives to visit JBU to find out why it went so well on campus. They thought that it might be in JBU's training program or documentation, but they found these to be very similar to other clients. They eventually concluded that it was JBU's shared sense of mission and culture that was the key to success. Ellucian has since asked JBU to participate in national marketing campaigns, beta test several new applications and services, and serve as a reference for many schools going through the daunting software selection and implementation process. JBU has benefited in return with free national exposure, early access to new products, and the opportunity to give witness to its unique mission and culture.

Technology advances and cost decreases also began to change the landscape of the computer labs on campus. By 2010 over 85 percent of undergraduate students nationwide were bringing their own laptop to college.[26] JBU's technology infrastructure needed to adapt to keep up with the growing demand for internet access. The university was able to greatly reduce the number of general-use computer labs while investing in enhanced labs in academic-specific areas like engineering, visual arts, nursing, and natural sciences that required more expensive software that students could not be expected to purchase.

The rise of streaming options for television and movie programming led to a decline in the student use of cable television offered in the residence halls and other areas of campus. Faced with imminent price increases, the university chose to discontinue cable, a yearly cost savings of over $35,000. The students barely seemed to notice.

Technology also continued to influence the way the admissions team recruited and interacted with prospective students. What was previously a very linear process shifted. The team saw in an increase in "stealth applications" from students they had no previous contact with until they filled out an application online or registered for a visit. Social media became a much greater part of the prospective student communication and engagement strategy. JBU developed a mobile-optimized website and online forms, and admissions adopted a customer-relationship-management tool to track the various channels of communication—calls, emails, texts, events, personal contacts, and social posts. The recession of the early 2000s also forced JBU and other schools to escalate financial-aid leveraging strategies. President Pollard helped create a campus-wide recruitment culture in which admissions was tasked with getting students and their parents to campus and faculty were tasked to sell their programs. The integration of predictive modeling also allows admissions counselors to

Don Crandall

better target inquiries for various levels of follow-up, reducing the number of printed brochures and viewbooks. In 2017 admissions piloted an early commit process for fully engaged applicants ready to decide early in their senior year. Their commitment to JBU allows them to receive early financial aid offers, secure a dorm room, and register for classes early. This is a great benefit to a growing number of our applicants.

Under the leadership of Don Crandall, JBU also established relationships with over one hundred Christian high schools around the region by hosting an annual conference for guidance counselors and a retreat for headmasters.

Social media platforms also became an avenue for marketing and communication not just to prospective students and their parents but also with alumni and donors. JBU's Facebook page debuted in February 2008 and by the end of 2018 had over sixteen thousand followers. The university also maintains a Twitter account for news and information and created an Instagram profile in 2013 geared toward current and prospective students.

Staff in other areas of the university also shone during these years. Under the leadership of Krall, Lucas Roebuck, '97, and Julie Gumm, '95, JBU's communications department excelled in marketing JBU in the new digital age. In 2009, university communications had a new logo created as part of a rebranding campaign that adapted traditional iconic images such as the cathedral tower and symbolized JBU's mottos of Christ Over All through the central cross, and Head, Heart, and Hand through the colors in the remaining quadrants. The communications team also refreshes JBU's website every two to three years, increasing the amount of visual and video content, easing the navigation through the site, updating with the latest technology, and capturing important digital data on those who view the site. They also created innovative social media campaigns, including "Chip on a Trip" in 2015. They handed out over six hundred cutout images of Pollard's face, mounted on a popsicle stick, and asked JBU students to take pictures with "Chip" on their spring break trips. Over three hundred photos were taken in twenty states and six countries. JBU's creative marketing campaigns have been routinely recognized by the Council for Advancement of Support in Education.

JBU students also continue to impress in national academic conferences and competitions. For example, JBU engineering students compete annually in the invite-only NASA Robotics Mining competition, which challenges students to design and build a robot that "can traverse the challenging simulated chaotic off-world terrain, . . . excavate the ice simulant [gravel], and return the excavated mass for deposit into the collector bin."[27] Teams from the top engineering schools in the country, including University of Michigan, Texas A&M, Vanderbilt, and Purdue, regularly participate in this competition. JBU has always done well, placing fourth in 2012 but in 2015 the JBU Eaglenauts were the only school to design and build multiple autonomous robots, and all thirty judges came to their demonstration. JBU won the Judges' Innovation Award by unanimous vote that year, and their work was featured in Robotics magazine.

JBU's construction management program has annually hosted a Disaster Shelter Competition since 2012, an event that has been sponsored both by World Vision and Samaritan's Purse. In this event, teams of students design and build a rapidly deployable transitional shelter that could be erected following a natural disaster such as a tornado, earthquake, or hurricane. The judges then test each prototype on a "shake" table to mimic an earthquake, for heat retention, and with a large, architectural fan that simulates winds up to one hundred miles an hour. JBU construction management students have done well both in hosting and presenting in this competition. They also participate annually in the TEXO design competition in Dallas and the national ethics competition put on by the American Institute of Constructors, often placing first or second in each event.

Similarly, JBU's business students have had a period of sustained excellence over the last two decades. Since 2003, JBU has had teams of entrepreneurial students participate in the Donald G. Reynolds Cup Business Plan Competition. Those teams have won over $500,000 during that time, and several businesses have been launched. JBU business students have also participated in the SIFE (Students in Free Enterprise)/Enactus program almost from the beginning, in 1975. Enactus believes that "investing in students who take entrepreneurial actions for others creates a better world for all of us."[28] Over 72,000 students from 1,730 universities in 36 countries participated in Enactus in 2018. Again, JBU has regularly done very well in the US national competition, routinely placing in the top 16 in the country out of 300–400 schools. In 2016, JBU placed second, and then in 2017, JBU won the US competition and had the honor of representing the United States in the Enactus World Cup in London in September 2017. JBU projects included establishing a paper shredding business in partnership with Siloam Springs Adult Development Center, creating an app called Yellow Crate that connects grocery store customers with the needs of their local food pantry, and several water purification projects in rural communities in Guatemala.

The student newspaper, The *Threefold Advocate*, took first place in general excellence in the 2008 Arkansas College Media Association and has continued to win awards in the years following, including Newspaper of the Year, Editor of the Year, Reporter of the Year, and Photographer of the Year in 2015.

JBU's Honors Program has continued to flourish under the direction of Dr. Brad Gambill, Dr. Trisha Posey and Dr. Jessica Wilson. Honors students regularly present their research at the Great Plains Honors Council Conference or the National Council on Undergraduate Research, and they have won a Dennis Boe Award for Outstanding Undergraduate Research, a Joseph E. Pryor Fellowship, and an Edwin W. Gaston Jr. Scholarship. Many of JBU honors students also coteach with JBU faculty, and a few each semester participate in the CCCU's Scholarship and Christianity in Oxford (SCIO) program. Graduates of the Honors Program have been accepted to some of the leading graduate programs in the world, including Oxford, Cambridge, Cal Tech, University of Chicago, University of Virginia, Carnegie Mellon University, and Yale Law School.

Another cross-disciplinary group of students received national acclamation in 2017. The American Enterprise Institute (AEI) ranked John Brown University's Executive Council, a bipartisan group of student leaders who promote meaningful discussions about today's issues within JBU's community, the best in the nation. The University of Pennsylvania, Columbia University, Baylor University, and Azusa Pacific University rounded out AEI's top five listing.

JBU faculty have also received national recognition for their outstanding work. Mr. Charles Peer retired from JBU in 2018 after a distinguished career as professor of visual arts. His work has been not just accepted but often received best in show or honorable designation in some of the most competitive art exhibitions around the country, including the Richeson75 Art Competitions, the Pastel Society of America juried exhibits, the Northwest Pastel Society Annual International Open Exhibit, and the International Association of Pastel Societies. Peer has also received personal recognition for his work, including as a Full Signature Member of the Pastel Society of America since 2003, the Summer Artist-in-Residence at the Buffalo National River Park in 2010, and being inducted into the Master Circle of the International Association of Pastel Societies in 2018. The work of Peer's colleagues in the Visual Arts Department has also received distinction. For example, Mr. Bobby Martin's work was featured in a cover article in the Gilchrist

Museum magazine, and his work was a part of a national touring exhibit, called *Return from Exile*. Mr. Peter Pohle was named Master Artist by Expose 10, an annual of the best digital illustrations worldwide. Dave Andrus had two paintings accepted into the nationally juried show at the Rice Gallery of Fine Art in Overland Park, Kansas. Enjoying works of beauty has been a regular part of JBU's communal life because of the gifts of the visual art faculty and students.

Not only did Peer and Andrus found and grow JBU's Visual Arts Department, but the two also "became BFFs [best friends forever] before BFF was even a thing," said Jeannie Abbot, administrative assistant for the department since 2000. Until Peer's retirement in 2018 the two would share lunch around an office table nearly every day.

One of the favorite days in the art department was Plaid Day, held each semester when students and faculty would wear as much plaid as possible. Peer could complete an entire outfit in plaid—socks, pants, shirt, tie, and jacket.

"I remember one year he wore his plaid pajama pants to class," said Kyle Agee, '05 and '18, instructor of visual arts. "I don't think Cecelia [his wife] was particularly thrilled about that."

Peer was also known to tell wild stories around the lunch table, like the time when he was living in Stuttgart, Arkansas, and it was so cold that the ducks froze in midair and fell from the sky, said Agee.

Those lunchtime meals in the department often carried a particular odor due to Andrus's routine lunch—one can of sardines, an apple, and some crackers.

Andrus, who loves the North Woods and nearly every summer takes his canoe to the lakes in northern Minnesota, is known to dress like North woodsman, according to Abbott.

Both Peer and Andrus have led regular art tours with JBU students, and their contagious enthusiasm and passion for art and design has inspired many students to continue to travel and appreciate the world's art.

Since the early 2000s, there has truly been a period of remarkable growth in the recognition of JBU faculty and their scholarship. In 2014, Dr. Jessica Wilson and Dr. Robert Moore were both selected to participate in the National Endowment for the Humanities Summer Institute on Dante in Florence, Italy. Wilson was named the 2017 Emerging Public Intellectual by the Center for Christian Scholarship at Redeemer University College, and Moore was selected in 2017 as one of only nine fellows to study at Islamic Research Center in Bonn, Germany, on his sabbatical. SIFE/Enactus selected Pollard as the Most Supportive President of the Year in 2006, Dr. Joe Walenciak as the Sam Walton Fellow of the Year in 2010, and Mr. Clayton Anderson '09 for the same recognition in 2017. The Evangelical Press Association named Dr. Marquita Smith to their board in 2015.

JBU faculty also were more active in funded research during this time. In 2005, Dr. Brian Greuel was part of a statewide team of Arkansas scientists to receive an IDeA Networks of Biomedical Research Excellence grant. Greuel's project focused on gene research related to myelin sheath. A decade later, in 2015, biology professor Dr. Joel Funk was awarded a $265,000 grant by the Arkansas Network of Biomedical Research to research the rare Q fever disease. Both Greuel and Funk included students as part of their research team, invaluable primary research experiences for JBU students. Engineering professor Dr. Ted Song and chemistry professor Dr. Susan Newton also collaborated with students on several projects that were funded by the Environmental Protection Agency, and chemistry professor Dr. Jill Ellenbarger was awarded a grant to develop color-changing compounds that can detect contaminants in drinking water—a project that allowed her to hire undergraduate research students to assist in the work.[29]

Early in his presidency, Pollard sought to recognize and support faculty scholarship, both symbolically and financially. He requested a copy of each book published by faculty and staff and placed them prominently on a table outside his office. He also requested that an anonymous donor establish Summer Faculty Fellowships to support faculty who were working on longer-term research projects. Each year, two faculty are awarded these three-year fellowships, and they receive financial support both for their research needs and as an extra salary stipend. The scholarship written by JBU faculty and staff during this time was impressive, with some of the more prolific writers including Patty Kirk, Preston Jones, Jessica Wilson, Gary Oliver, and Robbie Castleman. In fact, Castleman reached a milestone in 2016 when her books exceeded 500,000 copies sold.

Castleman, who joined the Biblical Studies faculty in 2001, was known for the creative ways in which she shared her delight and love for the Scripture with her students. When her New Testament book study class reached the section on Titus they would dress in flowered shirts for "Island Day" and take a couple laps around the classroom in a Conga line. Dr. Maxie Burch, chair of the Division of Biblical Studies, recalls Robbie's unique sense of humor, illustrated by her coming to class on Halloween wearing a necklace with five fishing hanging from it.

"Who am I?" she asked.

"You're a dead theologian."

"Yes, but which one? I'm a Poly-carp, get it?"[30]

Castleman had started a college Dead Theologians Society (Delta Theta Sigma) while at Florida State

Dr. Robbie Castleman

University in 1990 after the popular film *Dead Poets Society* had been released. She and the members would read the work of a dead theologian and get together to discuss it from week to week. It was a big hit and spread to several campuses both in the United States and the United Kingdom. Naturally, a chapter was started at JBU to disciple students through the classic works that have proven themselves substantial over time. Meetings are a very interactive time, but there is one big rule. No living person can be quoted or even mentioned.

"It's lots of fun to catch each other quoting a Bible faculty person or a pastor or some contemporary favorite—everyone erupts with loud sounds and we cross our arms above our heads to indicate the 'foul'!" Castleman said.[31]

Pollard has benefited from an unusually stable and capable senior administrative team. Kory Dale has served as the executive associate to the Pollards during their first fourteen years, running the office and presidential events with grace, efficiency, professionalism, and creativity. In his first fourteen years, there has been only one change among his vice presidents, when Hadley became vice president of finance upon Ms. Pat Gustavson's retirement in 2009. Pollard also invited Rod Reed, JBU's university chaplain, to join the cabinet in 2017. Moreover, JBU's senior administrators have filled key leadership roles in national higher education organizations: Crandall served twice as president of the North American Coalition for Christian Admissions Professionals; Beers served as president of the Association of Christians in Student Development; Hadley served on several National Association of College and University Business Officers national committees; Reed has conducted spiritual formation audits for over twenty-five different Christian institutions; and all six of them, including Krall and Ericson, served on, and in many cases chaired, their respective peer commissions for the CCCU.

Pollard himself was asked to serve in a variety of leadership positions outside of JBU, the most significant of which was with the CCCU. The CCCU represents about 180 institutions around the world, 142 of which are in the United States. CCCU serves its members by providing public advocacy, primarily at the federal level in Washington; by providing professional development opportunities through conferences and institutes; and by providing experiential educational opportunities in key cultural centers in the United States and around the world. JBU was a charter member of the CCCU in 1976, and both John Brown III and Balzer served on the CCCU board, so there is a long history of JBU's participation. Pollard was elected to the board in 2009, served as chair of the board from 2013 to 2018, and will conclude his service in 2020. As chair, he helped to lead the organization through a difficult CCCU presidential transition, in hosting two international forums, in clarifying its membership criteria and expanding its membership, and in sharpening its advocacy strategy to be more proactive in legislation. Pollard was grateful for the opportunity. "The CCCU is the most important national organization in preserving JBU's ability to carry out its Christian mission," he said. "I was a student in one CCCU institution, a faculty member in another one, and now a president in a third, so it was wonderful to have the chance to give back to an organization that helped to shape my life." Pollard also served as the chair of the Sooner Athletic Conference's Council of Presidents and on the NAIA Council of Presidents from 2012 to 2019 as well as on the boards of Gordon-Conwell Theological Seminary and Arvest Bank–Siloam Springs, and on the community board of Mercy Northwest Arkansas.

With all of the growth in facilities, enrollment, and excellence, JBU has not lost sight of its mission to educate students to honor God and serve others. That "student first" approach orients budget conversations, curriculum revisions, and daily life at JBU. Everyone at JBU has a role to play in educating students, whether that be as a faculty member in the classroom, as a resident director in late-night conversations, or as a grounds supervisor with a work-study student. Even the president and his wife seek out opportunities to be actively involved in educating students. Every spring, the Pollards teach a course called "Eating, Reading, and Thinking," in which eighteen students come to their house on a biweekly basis, cook and eat dinner together, and then discuss great literature. The class is a highlight of the Pollards' academic year because they spend concentrated time with a small group of students learning together about each other, about God, and about his world.

Pollard has also chosen to emphasize worship as central to JBU's mission. When he first came to JBU, he initiated a worship service as the starting event for the faculty-staff opening workshop in mid-August. He also requested that a baccalaureate worship service be added to the May graduation weekend, so the graduating students and their families can worship together one last time. He also frequently creates space in the board agenda so that the board can attend a chapel service during their two days of meetings. Chip and Carey themselves regularly attend chapel services throughout the school year, even when Pollard himself is not speaking. "Worshiping Christ with students in chapel helps to remind me who really is in control of what is happening at JBU," said Pollard. "Chapel is the place where we should wrestle with the difficult questions of life because it is only in the context of communal worship that we can help one another find good answers to those questions." Pollard even initiated a Q&A chapel where students could ask him whatever they wanted about school policy, spiritual challenges, or political or cultural issues as a gesture toward transparency in the context of worship. "We should stand ready to give faithful answers to hard questions from the next generation, answers that reflect both the truth and the grace of our faith," Pollard explained.

Stan McKinnon and Rod Reed served as university chaplains during this time in JBU's history, and they have led well the formal chapel program and the Christian formation activities on campus. These activities span the campus, helping students grow in their faith through their studies and cocurricular activities. In addition to exploring faith in the classroom, hundreds of JBU students regularly participate in the fall Breakaway retreat, small group Bible studies, CAUSE ministries, and short-term mission trips both domestically and overseas each year. Reed stated, "One of the ways that students and faculty know that spiritual formation is central to a JBU education is by hearing how Dr. Pollard speaks of his faith, and the ways that God works in various ways throughout campus. He embodies our motto, Christ Over All."

Pollard speaks in chapel six or seven times a year, and his talks often include illustrations such as a digital felt board version of the Scripture reading, or a falling tower of wooden blocks to exemplify doubt, or a favorite movie clip from *Lord of the Rings*. He is also known to choke up at some point in his chapel talks. "I most often get emotional in chapel when I recognize my or others' brokenness, the immensity of God's grace, or the gift of Christ's redemption," Pollard said. "In preparing or delivering a chapel talk, I am regularly reminded of my fundamental convictions and hopes and those truths can trigger deep emotions. Worship is at the heart of the Christian life, and I am grateful that it is at the center of JBU." In 2011, he published a collection of his chapel addresses called *May It Always Be True*.

As JBU looks forward to celebrating its one hundredth anniversary and to what God may do through JBU in the future, we also look back grateful to God, for the people who have given of their lives to create, sustain, advance, and protect JBU's unique mission. Throughout its history, JBU has adapted to its changing economic, educational, and cultural context, but it has never lost sight of its core mission to educate students to put Christ over all and to serve others with their heads, hearts, and hands. As Pollard says at the end of every one of his chapel talks, "may it always be true of us at JBU."

President Pollard speaks in chapel six or seven times each year.

The Cathedral Plaza in 2017

AFTERWORD

LOOKING TO THE NEXT CENTURY

by Charles W. Pollard

It is humbling to read the pages of this book and recognize how God has preserved the mission of JBU through the commitment and sacrifice of so many people. Carey and I also hold it to be a great privilege to be a part of the work that God is doing here. As I look back on almost one hundred years of history, it is hard not to look forward to imagine the opportunities and challenges that JBU may face in the future. Predicting far into the future is always a risky proposition, but I can imagine four trends that will likely have a great influence on JBU in the coming years: the cost of higher education, the place of Christian higher education in a growingly pluralistic culture, the benefits of being located on the border of Northwest Arkansas/Northeast Oklahoma, and increasing diversity at JBU.

COST OF HIGHER EDUCATION

Higher education in the U.S. is the envy of the world, yet it is also under significant economic stress. The market has more than recovered from the Great Recession of 2008–2009, yet incomes for middle-class families have remained relatively stagnant, making access to college more difficult for many. Students are increasingly taking out more loans to pay for college, and the default rate on those loans is increasing. The federal and state governments are increasingly concerned about these trends, so they are initiating new oversight and reporting requirements for higher education. Many colleges and universities are under significant financial stress, and they have had to cut positions and programs to try and balance their budgets.

JBU has performed better than many colleges and universities during this time of economic stress. JBU has also limited its increases in tuition and fees (the 2.75 percent increase for 2018–2019 was the lowest in over thirty years) and increased its endowed and institutional scholarships for students. Unlike many schools, JBU has also continued to grow its enrollment and its net revenue, which has led to regular operating surpluses and relative financial health.

JBU also still offers a good value to students with a stated tuition in the bottom third among member schools of the CCCU and with endowment support per student that is among the top 5 percent in the CCCU. Families with financial need are still coming to JBU in significant numbers, with about 30 percent of JBU families being Pell-eligible every year. The average JBU student's loans have gone up from $15,900 over four years in 2004 to $26,651 in 2016, but that amount is still below the state average of $29,390 and the national average of $30,281. Moreover, JBU's loan default rates are 3.1 percent, which are well below the state average of 12.2 percent and the national average of 11.5 percent and are the second lowest in Arkansas among four-year schools (2014 cohort). Those low default rates suggest the strong character of JBU alumni, the responsible decisions that they are making after graduation, and that their debt load is not unreasonable.

Even though JBU has performed well and offered good value to students in the past, the trend lines on the cost of higher education are still concerning. JBU is not immune to these trends, and there are no easy answers. The things that make a JBU education so valuable—the residential experience with robust academic, musical and theatrical, athletic, student, and spiritual life programs led by full-time people—come at a cost. Higher education is a people-intensive business. Over 65 percent of JBU's costs are related to people, so most cost-saving proposals come at the expense of people. However, certain strategies could help to mitigate the rising costs. JBU should continue to grow its endowment to help subsidize student scholarships and academic programs. The strongest colleges and universities in the future will have healthy endowments. JBU should also continue to offer students increased flexibility in completing their degrees to maximize value without compromising quality, whether that be through online courses, accelerated degree programs, or 3/2 programs that combine undergraduate and graduate degrees. JBU should continue to evaluate rigorously its programs, invest in those that are growing, and eliminate the ones that are no longer meeting the needs of students. JBU should continue to advocate at the state and federal level for the public value of private Christian higher education in order to ensure that JBU families can receive government assistance to help pay for college. Over 40 percent of JBU's revenue comes from state or federal grants or loans that are received by students to help pay for JBU. It is difficult to imagine JBU's future if its families no longer have access to that government assistance, and that is why it is so important that JBU and other Christian colleges and universities remain active in advocating for Christian higher education at both the federal and state level.

CHRISTIAN HIGHER EDUCATION IN A PLURALIST SOCIETY

Christian higher education is a small but significant segment of higher education in the United States. Approximately 3–4 percent of all colleges and universities are similar to JBU in their distinctly Christian mission, and 142 of them are members of the CCCU. These schools collectively educate 445,000 students, employ 72,000 faculty and staff, and serve 3.5 million alumni around the world. The CCCU hired an outside economic firm to conduct a study in 2017, and they found that CCCU member schools generate more than $60 billion in economic impact each year. For every dollar that a CCCU student receives in federal grants, the CCCU institutions provide $5 in grants and scholarships to that student, and the CCCU institutions generate more than $20 in federal tax revenue through operations, capital investments, and additional alumni earning power. CCCU institutions are a good investment, and they make valuable contributions to the public good in their communities, their states, and the nation. JBU and other CCCU schools will need to tell that story more broadly and effectively.

The most significant legal challenge to Christian higher education may be how the changing cultural, legal, and regulatory treatment of lesbian, gay, bisexual, and transgender (LGBT) people will affect the operations of Christian colleges and universities. Almost all of the CCCU institutions, including JBU, have employment and student life policies that reserve sexual intimacy for a man and woman in a covenantal relationship of marriage before God, as well as policies for single-sex residences, locker rooms, and bathrooms. The Supreme Court's decision in *Obergefell v. Hodges* (2014) established the civil right to same-sex marriage across the United States, and a variety of cases and regulatory actions have called into question legal understandings of sex and gender identity. While it remains unclear at this time how these decisions may affect CCCU schools such as JBU, it is likely that some CCCU employment or student-development policies could be challenged through the courts, legislation, regulation, or accreditation standards. These challenges could affect whether an institution qualifies for federal funding for its students, which would be a significant financial hardship for JBU students and the university.

At the same time, many Christian colleges and universities, including JBU, are also seeking to offer support, love, and encouragement to LGBT students and employees on their campuses within the context of their Christian commitments about sexuality and gender. Communicating on these issues with wisdom, clarity, truth, love, and grace both to internal and external constituents will continue to be an increasingly important and difficult task for JBU's leadership.

This particular challenge may represent a larger trend in which JBU's Christian commitments are increasingly seen as a minority position within the cultural and moral norms of the United States. At a minimum, the United States seems to becoming a more pluralistic and secular society, and any former Christian consensus in civic or cultural life seems on the wane. Such trends may well challenge JBU, but the United States also has a rich legal tradition of protecting religious liberty, particularly of religious minorities, and that tradition should provide some protection for JBU to live out its Christian commitments.

Moreover, these cultural changes may also provide opportunities for clearer witness to Christ and service to others. Exile is a common biblical theme for the people of God, and there is much in Scripture that offers us instruction in how to live as "resident aliens" in a culture that is not completely our home. In particular, Scripture teaches that we should live in obedience to God's teaching and that we should serve our neighbor. Daniel doesn't compromise his prayer life, but he also brings all of his administrative skills to benefit Nebuchadnezzar's kingdom. Jeremiah tells God's people to "seek the peace and prosperity of the city to which I have carried you into exile. Pray to the Lord for it, because if it prospers, you too will prosper" (Jeremiah 29:7 NIV). Peter urges us, "as foreigners and exiles, to abstain from sinful desires," but he also calls us to submit "for the Lord's sake to every human authority" (1 Peter 2:11, 13 NIV). JBU's historic mission to educate students to honor God and serve others may be a more relevant witness than ever in this changing cultural context.

NORTHWEST ARKANSAS/NORTHEAST OKLAHOMA

JBU has greatly benefited from being located in Siloam Springs, right on the border of Northwest Arkansas and Northeast Oklahoma. Northwest Arkansas has grown to over 500,000 people and has one of the fastest-growing economies in the country. Its unemployment rate historically runs 2–2.5 percent below the national average, and the projected job-growth rate over the next five years will be third best in the country behind only Austin, Texas, and Charlotte, North Carolina. This economic vitality has historically been driven by the three global companies located in the region—Walmart, Tyson Foods, and J. B. Hunt—but there is an increasing diversification of the economy in the region.

We have also seen great investments in the quality of life in the region, including Crystal Bridges Museum of American Art, Siloam Springs Kayak Park, the Greenway Bike Trails, Arvest Ballpark, the Walmart Arkansas Music Pavilion, and Arkansas Children's Hospital Northwest. There are also extensive natural recreational areas, including Beaver Lake, Devil's Den State Park, and the Buffalo National River. We also have approximately 75,000 neighbors to the west of campus in Northeast Oklahoma, many of whom face significant financial challenges, with about 15–20 percent of the families below the poverty line. As Christians, we should learn from, and serve with, people from all walks of life, and JBU's location is a great opportunity for that to happen.

Siloam Springs has also grown in ways that have been good for JBU. Main Street Siloam Springs has done a wonderful job of encouraging revitalization in the downtown, with new restaurants, coffee shops, and boutique stores added in the last decade. A new hospital, high school, public library, splash park, and outdoor amphitheater have also greatly enhanced the quality of life in this community. There is a dynamic and cooperative "town and gown" relationship between the City of Siloam Springs and JBU, which benefits everyone. Moreover, JBU benefits from a denominationally diverse, strong, and supportive church community in Siloam Springs and from the economic strength and partnerships with thriving local corporations, including Simmons Food, McKee Foods, Dayspring, and La-Z-Boy.

Most people from outside our region do not realize the advantage that comes with living and studying in our city and region, so JBU will need to communicate better the value of the region in recruiting faculty, students, and staff. Moreover, JBU will need to deepen its partnerships with regional corporations, hospital systems, and nonprofits to enable JBU students to benefit from the economic growth in the region. JBU's future will increasingly be intertwined with the success of Siloam Springs and the larger region.

DIVERSITY

JBU should also continue its focus on increasing the diversity of its faculty, staff, and students to honor the fact that all humans are created in the image of God, to reflect better the diversity of the kingdom of God, to further our Christian commitment to justice, and to increase the quality of a JBU education. Historically, JBU was somewhat unique for its time in admitting women from its inception in 1919, and the university has long had good success in recruiting international students and economically diverse students. However, JBU has had less success in recruiting faculty, staff, and students from different ethnic and racial backgrounds even though the university has made attempts, including a federally funded outreach to Native Americans in Oklahoma in the 1970s.

Some of that difficulty is, in part, related to the homogeneity of the region. Northwest Arkansas has become more ethnically diverse in recent years, but it is still significantly white (74 percent white in 2013 as compared to 81 percent in 2005). The Latino population has grown from 12 to 16 percent, but less than 50 percent of Latinos in Northwest Arkansas have earned a high school diploma. The rest of the region is 3 percent Asian, 3 percent black, 1 percent Native American, and 3 percent other. The Northwest Arkansas Regional Council recognizes the need for a diverse and engaged population in the region, and has made it a priority of their latest strategic plan. Siloam Springs' demographics are similar to Northwest Arkansas, with a slightly more white and Latino population. Northeast Oklahoma has a significant Native American population, but the area does not have the same regional identity as Northwest Arkansas, so there are fewer readily available statistics for Northeast Oklahoma as a region.

Through the excellent leadership of Dr. Marquita Smith and members of JBU's diversity committee, JBU has made some progress in recruiting a more diverse faculty, staff, and student body. For instance, in the last twelve years, JBU has increased its racial and gender diversity in its teaching faculty, from 5 percent to 12.5 percent nonwhite faculty and from 24 percent to 34 percent women faculty. Moreover, JBU's traditional undergraduate students increasingly reflect the ethnic and racial profile of the region: in 2017–2018, 73 percent of JBU students were white, 7.3 percent international, 6.4 percent Latino, 2.1 percent Native American, 1.7 percent black, 1.5 percent Asian, 3.8 percent two or more races, and 3.9 percent other or unknown. Smith and the diversity committee have also made good progress in educating the JBU community to be more culturally competent and humble in engaging people from different ethnic or racial backgrounds through monthly faculty and staff conversations, book studies, chapel speakers, residential hall forums, an annual diversity symposium, faculty workshops, and a revised cultural engagement requirement as part of the core.

In addition, Dr. Ted Song and Vice President Beers have led a recruitment effort with Korean and Korean American communities in major cities near JBU, particularly in Dallas. As part of those efforts, in 2016, JBU signed a memorandum of understanding with Handong Global University in Pohang, Republic of Korea, that created the opportunity for student and faculty exchanges between the two institutions. Dr. Aminta Arrington and others have been leading a First Generation Latino Task Force to help Latino students in their transition to JBU.

I am grateful for all of the efforts by these faculty and administrators in leading the JBU community to better understand and reflect the diversity of God's kingdom. This work is essential, not just because the United States is increasingly becoming a diverse society from whom JBU will need to recruit students and into which JBU graduates will need to work, but also because the splendor, complexity, and depth of God is reflected in the diversity of human beings created in his image. This work is not easy. There are historical patterns of mistrust, injustice, and oppression that reflect the deep brokenness of human beings, and make some conversations difficult and painful. However, JBU should continue in these conversations because they reflect the hope to which we are committed, a hope that someday we will all be counted among the "great multitude that no one could number, from every nation, from all tribes and peoples and languages, standing before the throne and before the Lamb" (Revelation 7:9 ESV).

When I imagine the future, I sometimes get overwhelmed by the size of the task of leading JBU. I am also certain that there will be challenges and opportunities for JBU that no one has yet even imagined. However, as I read this book, I am reminded again and again that JBU has survived and thrived over the last one hundred years only because of God's grace and blessing, and that gives me comfort that the same will be true for its future. We are called to be faithful and diligent. As the founder would say, "Trust God and get to work." May his admonition always be true of us at JBU.

Lee Balzer, Chip Pollard and John Brown III in 2018

AUTHOR'S ACKNOWLEDGMENTS

by Paul Semones

The musty aroma of decades-old paper enveloped us in the JBU Archives room, one day in the fall of 2017. Over the previous months, I had already become familiar with the delicate, crumbling copies of JBU's alumni bulletins of the 1940s, and with the much sturdier copies of the school's early yearbooks, while I was researching a feature article in the *Brown Bulletin* about our alumni who died in World War II. Now I sat with John Brown III, talking over an early draft of this centennial history book.

While discussing the fascinating early years of the university his grandfather founded, and my passion for adding as much personal detail to the story of those early decades as I could, the archivist, Marikit Schwartz Fain, '05, brought out something she thought might be an interesting source for me to consult. It turned out to be, in my mind at least, a holy grail.

In her hands were two green metal-bound volumes of typed pages. In hand-written script, the covers bore the titles "The Magnetic Power of Dreams" and "History of the John Brown Schools—The First Fifteen Years." Both were by a woman named May Boudinot—a name I had never heard, despite my more than twenty years of association with JBU as a student, teacher, copy editor, and alumnus. The books were, to all appearances, Miss Boudinot's original typed pages, more than half a century old, complete with strikethroughs and pencil edits. Here was a detailed treasure trove of incidental, human moments—glimpses into the lives of John Brown Sr. and the staff and students associated with him in those early years—captured by a woman who was there almost from the beginning, and who served the institution almost until the founder's death.

As it turns out, I was not the first to discover Miss Boudinot's foundational texts while attempting to capture a history of John Brown University and its people in print. Over the decades, others have written lengthy works about JBU and its founder, although perhaps with less of the anecdotal, student-centric perspective that I have strived for in this book. Dr. Irvin Wills of the JBU faculty wrote a sketch of JBU's history in 1958; Ralph C. Kennedy and Thomas Rothrock wrote the book *John Brown of Arkansas* in 1966; Earl Williams wrote his 1971 doctoral dissertation on Brown Sr. and the school he founded; Brown III and Dr. Ed Nichols contributed to the historical record of the school by chronicling the lives of several important faculty members in their 1984 book *By These Stones*; Dr. Niswonger wrote an addendum to Kennedy and Rothrock's book in 1999 to cover the intervening three decades since the book's original publication; and Rick Ostrander wrote *Head, Heart and Hand* in 2003.

To some degree all of these prior works evidently relied on Miss Boudinot's unpublished manuscripts for essential details of the early years of the founder and the university.

You will hear Miss Boudinot's voice in many of the stories told throughout the early chapters of this book, and if she has been perhaps neglected as an unsung hero of JBU's founding era, I am determined that she at least be credited as a vital contributor here.

Indeed, the writing of this book has been a thoroughly collaborative effort, with John Brown III assembling a history of the three Brown family presidents' eras, and with presidents Lee Balzer and Chip Pollard contributing accounts of the university's history during each of their own times. I must thank my original editor, Lucas Roebuck, for giving me the opportunity, a year and a half ago, to harmonize these stories. Many of the stories from more recent years were compiled by my editor Julie Gumm and her staff in University Communications, and they deserve a large portion of the credit for the latter chapters. Marikit Schwartz Fain, archives coordinator, was invaluable in gathering photos to accompany the text and help it come to life. Still other long-serving staff members gave of their time as the publishing deadline neared, offering timely correspondence and written recollections of certain key events that helped greatly in adding color and interest to many stories of recent years.

I must thank John Brown III for offering his guidance and time in the preparation of this book, and for placing so much trust in me as I rewrote and reorganized much of the Brown family presidents' eras, while also adding many new and previously untold tales.

At its core, this is a book about God's people, and his work through them across the years to build a special community that has changed untold numbers of lives.

I spent the most important five years of my life living on the campus of John Brown University as I pursued my bachelor's degrees—but it was not the university in some disembodied sense that changed my life; it was the people of JBU. It was the professors who exemplified to me patience and professional ethics in the engineering program; the Bible scholars who urged me to make my faith my own, reconcile science and Scripture, and who demonstrated selfless love in their own lives; the students who challenged me and provided examples of leadership and fervent Christian belief through their fellowship and ministry initiatives; the administrators who embodied the fruits of the Spirit with every smile and greeting; the fellow alumni who, in the years since our graduation, have become lifelong, stalwart friends.

A few months ago, as I was gathering additional research material for this book, I took my little girl Taylin with me to visit my alma mater for the first time. At eight years old, she had plenty of energy to climb up and down the One Hundred Steps and ride the J. Alvin elevator multiple times, but she also got tuckered out fast enough that I spent much of the time walking across the campus with her on my shoulders. It was a Saturday night, and there was understandably little activity on campus, but when we visited the California Café in the Walker Student Center for a snack, there were a few women students chatting in the common area. Taylin wanted to see a college dorm room, and when I approached the students to ask if they would mind taking her up to see their room in Walker, the women were as kind, caring, and enthusiastic about giving my little girl a tour as I could have hoped. Now Taylin wants to be a member of the JBU class of 2032.

The history of JBU is filled with the selfless acts and devoted lives of many heroes of the faith. May their testimonies, so few of which could be adequately recounted in the pages that follow, inspire future generations of JBU leaders, faculty, staff, and students—including, I hope, my own daughter—to preserve this historic institution as a unique place where students are instilled with a complete education for life under the enduring banner of Christ Over All.

ENDNOTES

Chapter 1: The Early Years of Founder John Elward Brown Sr.

1. "Pennsylvania in the Civil War," PA-Roots, https://www.pa-roots.com/pacw/cavalry/cavalrynew.html; "11th Cavalry Pennsylvania Volunteers, Company A," PA-Roots, https://www.pa-roots.com/pacw/cavalry/11thcav/11thcavcoa.html.

2. May F. Boudinot, "The Magnetic Power of Dreams," unpublished manuscript, ca. 1950, John Brown University Archives, 3–6; Earl Williams, "John Brown University: Its Founder and Founding, 1919–1957" (EdD diss., University of Arkansas, 1971), 34.

3. Ralph C. Kennedy and Thomas Rothrock, *John Brown of Arkansas* (Siloam Springs, AR: John Brown University, 1999 [originally written 1966]), 3, 5, 7; Boudinot, "Dreams," 5; Williams, "John Brown University," 35.

4. Williams, "John Brown University," 36–37.

5. Boudinot, "Dreams," 15; for more on carousels, see Arthur Levine, "Merry-Go-Rounds: 10 of the Oldest Carousels in the USA," *USA Today*, February 2, 2016, https://www.usatoday.com/story/travel/experience/america/2016/02/02/10-oldest-carousels-operating-usa/79662506/.

6. Williams, "John Brown University," 36.

7. Boudinot, "Dreams," 7; Williams, "John Brown University," 37; "Rogers (Benton County)," *Encyclopedia of Arkansas History and Culture*, http://www.encyclopediaofarkansas.net/encyclopedia/entry-detail.aspx?entryID=837#.

8. Kennedy and Rothrock, *John Brown of Arkansas*, 7.

9. Kennedy and Rothrock, *John Brown of Arkansas*, 8.

10. Kennedy and Rothrock, *John Brown of Arkansas*, 8.

11. Kennedy and Rothrock, *John Brown of Arkansas*, 9.

12. Boudinot, "Dreams," 10.

Chapter 2: The Founder as Evangelist

1. Earl Williams, "John Brown University: Its Founder and Founding, 1919–1957" (EdD diss., University of Arkansas, 1971), 45.

2. Williams, "John Brown University," 44; "Siloam Springs (Benton County)," *Encyclopedia of Arkansas History and Culture*, http://www.encyclopediaofarkansas.net/encyclopedia/entry-detail.aspx?entryID=838.

3. May F. Boudinot, "The Magnetic Power of Dreams," unpublished manuscript, ca. 1950, John Brown University Archives, 11–12.

4. Ralph C. Kennedy and Thomas Rothrock, *John Brown of Arkansas* (Siloam Springs, AR: John Brown University, 1999 [originally written 1966]), 17;

5. Williams, "John Brown University," 46; Boudinot, "Dreams" 12–13.

6. Williams, "John Brown University," 48.

7. Williams, "John Brown University," 55;

8. Williams, "John Brown University," 48.

9. Boudinot, "Dreams," 33.

10. Williams, "John Brown University," 71.

11. Williams, "John Brown University," 71.

12. Williams, "John Brown University," ref. 105.

13. Williams, "John Brown University," ref. 104.

14. Williams, "John Brown University," ref. 103.

15. Boudinot, "Dreams," 32, 44.

16. Williams, "John Brown University," 66.

17. Images of America: Siloam Springs, Siloam Springs Museum, Siloam Springs.

Chapter 3: A College in a Cornfield

1. Earl Williams, "John Brown University: Its Founder and Founding, 1919–1957" (EdD diss., University of Arkansas, 1971), 129.

2. Ralph C. Kennedy and Thomas Rothrock, *John Brown of Arkansas* (Siloam Springs, AR: John Brown University, 1999 [originally written 1966]), 25.

3. *American Evangelist*, September 1919, 8.

4. May F. Boudinot, "History of the John Brown Schools: The First Fifteen Years," unpublished manuscript by May F. Boudinot, ca. 1940, John Brown University Archives, 1.

5. Kennedy and Rothrock, *John Brown of Arkansas*, 37.

6. "Brother, Can You Spare a Billion? The Story of Jesse H. Jones," PBS, http://www.pbs.org/jessejones/jesse_bio1.htm; May F. Boudinot, "The Magnetic Power of Dreams," unpublished manuscript, ca. 1950, John Brown University Archives, 42.

7. Ancestry.com. 1940 United States Federal Census [database on-line]. Provo, UT, USA: Ancestry.com Operations, Inc., 2012.

8. Kennedy and Rothrock, *John Brown of Arkansas*, 39; Boudinot, "First Fifteen Years," 2.

9. Boudinot, "First Fifteen Years," 20–21.

10. Boudinot, "First Fifteen Years," 64.

11. Boudinot, "First Fifteen Years," 2; Boudinot, "Dreams," 63.

12. Kennedy and Rothrock, *John Brown of Arkansas*, 38; ancestry.com. 1940 United States Federal Census [database on-line]. Provo, UT, USA: ancestry.com Operations, Inc., 2012.

13. Boudinot, "First Fifteen Years," 1–2.

14. Boudinot, "First Fifteen Years," 4.

15. Boudinot, "First Fifteen Years," 7.

16. Boudinot, "First Fifteen Years," 3.

17. *Brown Bulletin*, summer 2013. "In the beginning . . . ," 14.

18. Boudinot, "First Fifteen Years," 11.

19. Kennedy and Rothrock, *John Brown of Arkansas*, 69–70.

20. Boudinot, "Dreams," 159.

21. Boudinot, "Dreams," 44.

22. Edward L. Nichols and John E. Brown III, eds., *By These Stones: Biographies and Writings of Former Faculty at John Brown University* (Siloam Springs, AR: John Brown University, 1984), 9–10.

23. Original document in John Brown University Archives.

24. Boudinot, "Dreams," 59.

25. Submitted by family member James Van Sickle.

Chapter 4: The Era of Two Schools

1. Earl Williams, "John Brown University: Its Founder and Founding, 1919–1957" (EdD diss., University of Arkansas, 1971), 111.

2. Ralph C. Kennedy and Thomas Rothrock, *John Brown of Arkansas* (Siloam Springs, AR: John Brown University, 1999 [originally written 1966]), 108.

3. May F. Boudinot, "The Magnetic Power of Dreams," unpublished manuscript, ca. 1950, John Brown University Archives, 69.

4. May F. Boudinot, "The Magnetic Power of Dreams," unpublished manuscript, ca. 1950, John Brown University Archives, 69.

5. Kennedy and Rothrock, *John Brown of Arkansas*, 27.

6. Kennedy and Rothrock, *John Brown of Arkansas*, 72.

7. Kennedy and Rothrock, *John Brown of Arkansas*, 74-78.

8. 1928 Yearbook, Ministerial Club; May F. Boudinot, "History of the John Brown Schools: The First Fifteen Years," unpublished manuscript by May F. Boudinot, ca. 1940, John Brown University Archives, 48.

Chapter 5: A University and a Radio Tower

1. Earl Williams, "John Brown University: Its Founder and Founding, 1919–1957" (EdD diss., University of Arkansas, 1971), 119.

2. Ralph C. Kennedy and Thomas Rothrock, *John Brown of Arkansas* (Siloam Springs, AR: John Brown University, 1999 [originally written 1966]), chap. 11.

3. May F. Boudinot, "History of the John Brown Schools: The First Fifteen Years," unpublished manuscript by May F. Boudinot, ca. 1940, John Brown University Archives, 80.

4. Boudinot, "First Fifteen Years," 136.

5. Kennedy and Rothrock, *John Brown of Arkansas*, 54–55.

6. Edward L. Nichols and John E. Brown III, eds., *By These Stones: Biographies and Writings of Former Faculty at John Brown University* (Siloam Springs, AR: John Brown University, 1984), 17.

7. Boudinot, "First Fifteen Years," 120–21; May F. Boudinot, "The Magnetic Power of Dreams," unpublished manuscript, ca. 1950, John Brown University Archives, 160; Nichols and Brown, *By These Stones*, 7–8.

8. Boudinot, "First Fifteen Years," 145; John E. Brown *The Why of Suffering.* (Siloam Springs, AR: University Press, 1937), 6.

9. Kennedy and Rothrock, *John Brown of Arkansas*, 99.

10. Boudinot "Dreams," 96, pdf 165.

11. Boudinot "Dreams," 88, 97, 169.

12. *John Brown University Bulletin*, February 1940, 3.

13. Boudinot "Dreams," 160.

Chapter 6: The Crucible of World War II

1. *John Brown University Bulletin*, September 1940 1.

2. *John Brown University Bulletin*, July 1940, 2.

3. *John Brown University Bulletin*, September 1940, 3.

4. *John Brown University Bulletin*, October 1941, 2.

5. *John Brown University Bulletin*, October 1941, 3.

6. *John Brown University Bulletin*, May 1941, 2–3.

7. *John Brown University Bulletin*, June 1941, 1.

8. *John Brown University Bulletin*, July 1940, 2.

9. *John Brown University Bulletin*, September 1940, 3.

10. Earl Williams, "John Brown University: Its Founder and Founding, 1919–1957" (EdD diss., University of Arkansas, 1971), 153, ref to John Brown University Bulletin, February1942.

11. *John Brown University Bulletin*, September 1942, 1.

12. *John Brown University Bulletin*, October 1941, 2.

13. Gary L. McIntosh, War Diary: USS Stevens: 1941–1946 (Victoria BC: Trafford, 2004), 203.

Chapter 7: A New President, and the Founder's Final Years

1. Marquita Smith, "John E. Brown Jr.'s Lasting Impact on JBU," *Brown Bulletin*, winter 2012, 18.

2. May F. Boudinot, "The Magnetic Power of Dreams," unpublished manuscript, ca. 1950, John Brown University Archives, 119.

3. Master Builders of the World, March 1957.

4. Edward L. Nichols and John E. Brown III, eds., *By These Stones: Biographies and Writings of Former Faculty at John Brown University* (Siloam Springs, AR: John Brown University, 1984), 65.

5. Ralph C. Kennedy and Thomas Rothrock, *John Brown of Arkansas* (Siloam Springs, AR· John Brown University, 1999 [originally written 1966]), 99, 101.

6. Nichols and Brown, *By These Stones*, 65.

7. Earl Williams, "John Brown University: Its Founder and Founding, 1919–1957" (EdD diss., University of Arkansas, 1971), 158.

8. "R. G. LeTourneau," LeTourneau University Museum and Archives," http://www.letu.edu/opencms/opencms/_Academics/library/museum/Machines/index.html.

9. Kennedy and Rothrock,*John Brown of Arkansas*, 63.

10. Kennedy and Rothrock, *John Brown of Arkansas*, 104.

11. Nichols and Brown, *By These Stones*, 53.

12. Kennedy and Rothrock,*John Brown of Arkansas*, 114.

13. Kennedy and Rothrock, *John Brown of Arkansas*, 115.

14. Patenaude, and Lionel V. "Jones, Jesse Holman." The Handbook of Texas Online, Texas State Historical Association (TSHA), 15 June 2010, tshaonline.org/handbook/online/articles/fjo53.

15. Williams, "John Brown University," 176.

16. Kennedy and Rothrock, *John Brown of Arkansas*, 120.

Chapter 8: The Legacy of the Founder's Character

1. John Brown, *Let There Be Light*, 1933, talk no. 26, 187, John Brown University Archives.

2. Newspapers, November 3, 1924.

3. May F. Boudinot, "The Magnetic Power of Dreams," unpublished manuscript, ca. 1950, John Brown University Archives, 30; Ralph C. Kennedy and Thomas Rothrock, *John Brown of Arkansas* (Siloam Springs, AR: John Brown University, 1999 [originally written 1966]), 72.

4. John E. Brown *Upon This Rock*. (Sulphur Springs, AR, Siloam Springs, AR: International Federation Publishing Co., 1923), Talk No. 2, 32.

5. Brown, *Upon This Rock*, Talk No. 4, 53, 55.

6. Brown, *Upon This Rock*, "Introductory," n.p.

7. Brown, *Upon This Rock*, Talk No. 3, 37.

Chapter 9: Growth of the University under John E. Brown Jr.

1. John E. Brown III, "A Brief History of the JBU Board," *Brown Bulletin*, summer 2013, 6.

2. Brown, "Brief History," 6.

3. Brown, "Brief History," 6.

4. JBU Trustee Handbook.

5. Brown, "Brief History," 2013, 6; JBU Trustee Handbook.

6. *Master Builders of the World*, October 1957; *Master Builders of the World*, March/April 1959.

7. Brown, "Brief History," 2013, 7; Trustee Handbook.

8. JBU Trustee Handbook.

9. *Master Builders of the World*, June 1957.

10. *John Brown University Bulletin*, October 1959.

11. *John Brown University Bulletin*, October 1959.

12. Correspondence with John Coates.

13. Edward L. Nichols and John E. Brown III, eds., *By These Stones: Biographies and Writings of Former Faculty at John Brown University* (Siloam Springs, AR: John Brown University, 1984), 25–26.

14. *Master Builders of the World*, March/April 1959.

15. *Lantern*, November 2010.

16. *Lantern*, March 2013; *John Brown University Bulletin*, March 1972.

17. Correspondence with Earl Larkins and Gary Elliott.

18. *Lantern*, February 2012.

19. Nichols and Brown, *By These Stones*, 47.

20. Ralph C. Kennedy and Thomas Rothrock, *John Brown of Arkansas* (Siloam Springs, AR: John Brown University, 1999 [originally written 1966]), 124.

21. Marquita Smith, "John E. Brown Jr.'s Lasting Impact on JBU," *Brown Bulletin*, winter 2012, 18.

22. Smith, "Lasting Impact," 18.

23. Smith, "Lasting Impact," 20.

Chapter 10: The Third President Brown

1. Edward L. Nichols and John E. Brown III, eds., *By These Stones: Biographies and Writings of Former Faculty at John Brown University* (Siloam Springs, AR: John Brown University, 1984), 3.

2. "ECFA History," Evangelical Council for Financial Accountability, http://www.ecfa.org/Content/GeneralBackground.

3. *By These Stones: Biographies and Writings of Former Faculty at John Brown University Vol. 2* (Siloam Springs, AR: John Brown University, 2018), 117.

4. "Our History," KLRC, http://www.klrc.com/about-us/our-history/.

5. Johnson, Ronald. *Our Story: The JBU Walton International Scholarship Program.* 2012, 63; Walton International Scholars Program, http://www.wispweb.org/.

6. *Our Story*, 87–88.

7. *Our Story*, 20.

8. *Our Story*, 76.

9. John E. Brown III, "Harold and Mildred Ward—"The Old Apple Tree," *Brown Bulletin*, summer 2013, 20.

Chapter 11: The Board of Trustees' Leadership in a Year of Transition

Much of the material in this chapter is taken from "History of the Board of Trustees" in the 2018 JBU Trustee Handbook.

1. Ralph C. Kennedy and Thomas Rothrock, *John Brown of Arkansas* (Siloam Springs, AR: John Brown University, 1999 [originally written 1966]), 130.

2. Kennedy and Rothrock, *John Brown of Arkansas*, 131.

3. John E. Brown III, "Reflections on Dad," *Brown Bulletin*, winter 2012, 15.

4. Jim Krall, "Now Is the Time to Keep Faith," *Brown Bulletin*, winter 2009, 24.

Chapter 12: The Balzer Era

1. Wikipedia, s.v. "Foundation for New Era Philanthropy," https://en.wikipedia.org/wiki/Foundation_for_New_Era_Philanthropy.

2. *JBU Course Catalog*, 1999/2001, 12.

3. Correspondence with Lucas Roebuck.

4. Johnson, Ronald. *Our Story: The JBU Walton International Scholarship Program.* 2012, 232.

5. *Our Story*, 236.

6. *Our Story*, 239.

7. *Our Story*, 239.

8. "JBU Names U Of A Dean Mel Fratzke To Provost Post," John Brown University press release, March 28, 1997, https://www.jbu.edu/news/press-releases/?id=211.

9. Find A Grave, Nov. 2009, www.findagrave.com/memorial/44807762/james-hume-barnes.

10. Correspondence with Gary Oliver.

11. Correspondence with Gary Oliver.

12. Conversation with Gary Oliver.

13. Julie Gumm, "Business Visionary," *Brown Bulletin*, spring 2016, 25.

14. Correspondence with Steve Beers.

15. Correspondence with Frank Huebert.

16. Correspondence with Steve Beers.

17. *Threefold Advocate*, April 5, 2001; April 19, 2001.

18. "JBU Campus Responds to Tragedy," John Brown University press release, September 11, 2001, https://www.jbu.edu/news/press-releases/?id=171; "President Balzer's Response to Our Nation's Tragedy," John Brown University press release, September 21, 2001, https://www.jbu.edu/news/press-releases/?id=167.

19. "JBU Cathedral Choir Tours Ireland," John Brown University press release, June 23, 2003, https://www.jbu.edu/news/press_releases/?id=441.

20. Correspondence with Steve Brankle.

21. "Construction Begins at JBU on New 37,000 Sq. Ft. Science Hall," John Brown University press release, September 5,

2001, https://www.jbu.edu/news/press_releases/?id=173.

Chapter 13: The Pollard Era

1. Mark Oppenheimer, "The First Dance," *New York Times Magazine*, January 28, 2007, https://www.nytimes.com/2007/01/28/magazine/28dancing.t.html.

2. Correspondence with Jarrod Heathcote.

3. Interview with Dr. Ted Song.

4. Correspondence with Dr. Marquita Smith.

5. Correspondence with Todd Goehner.

6. "Mock Rock Keeps Rockin' after a Decade," *Threefold Advocate*, November 19, 2014, http://advocate.jbu.edu/2014/11/19/mock-rock-keeps-rockin-after-a-decade/.

7. Gute, Melissa. "JBU Talent Vie to Be 'Next Big Thing'." Siloam Springs Herald Leader, March 14, 2012. https://www.pressreader.com/usa/siloam-springs-herald-leader/20120314/281492158262550.

8. Correspondence with Jeff Soderquist.

9. "JBU Athletic Director Robyn Daugherty Named 2017-28 NAIA Under Armour Athletic Director of the Year," John Brown University press release, March 6, 2018, https://www.jbu.edu/news/press-releases/?id=24496.

10. Pollard correspondence with Terri Wubbena.

11. "JBU Announces $5 Million Lead Gift to Performing Arts Center," John Brown University press release, August 18, 2008, https://www.jbu.edu/news/press-releases/?id=2969.

12. William Loyd 'Hutch' Hutcheson, Jr.," Obituary, Dignity Memorial, https://www.dignitymemorial.com/obituaries/fort-smith-ar/william-hutcheson-7298758.

13. Correspondence with Steve Brankle.

14. "JBU's Degree Completion Announces Name Change to JBU Online," John Brown University press release, April 3, 2017, https://www.jbu.edu/news/press_releases/?id=23466.

15. https://www.jbu.edu/giving/next-century/

16. https://www.jbu.edu/giving/next-century/

17. Correspondence with Ellen Odell.

18. "The Center for Relationship Enrichment Changing Name to Center for Healthy Relationships," John Brown University press release, June 6, 2014, https://www.jbu.edu/news/press_releases/?id=12030; Correspondence with Gary Oliver.

19. Correspondence with Gary Oliver.

20. Correspondence with Gary Oliver.

21. "JBU Named '2018 Great College to Work For'," John Brown University press release, July 17, 2018, https://www.jbu.edu/news/press-releases/?id=24959.

22. "JBU Ranks Top 20 in Upgraded U.S. News Regional University Category," John Brown University press release, September 13, 2016, https://www.jbu.edu/news/press_releases/?id=22477; https://www.jbu.edu/news/press_releases/?id=23925.

23. "Explore the Full WSJ/THE College Rankings," *Wall Street Journal*, September 5, 2018, https://www.wsj.com/articles/explore-the-full-wsj-the-college-rankings-1536187754.

24. "This Is the Best College in Every State," *Money*, September 28, 2018, http://time.com/money/5401092/best-college-in-every-state-2018/.

25. David Luther, "These Are the Colleges with the Highest Earning Graduates in Each State," Zippia, https://www.zippia.com/advice/best-colleges-for-high-salaries/.

26. Aaron Smith, Lee Rainie, and Kathryn Zickuhr, College Students and Technology," Pew Research Center, Internet and Technology, July 19, 2011, http://www.pewinternet.org/2011/07/19/college-students-and-technology/.

27. "NASA Robotic Mining Competition." NASA, NASA, 16 Apr. 2015, www.nasa.gov/offices/education/centers/kennedy/technology/nasarmc.html.

28. Enactus, enactus.org/.

29. "JBU Professor Receives 2017 Christian Scholars Foundation Grant," John Brown University press release, August 21, 2017, https://www.jbu.edu/news/press_releases/?id=23870.

30. Correspondence with Dr. Maxie Burch.

31. Correspondence with Dr. Robbie Castleman.